T0030042

Note on the title:

This book is titled N*gga Theory *because I do not want to encourage non-black people to say the word "nigga" out loud, and because I recognize that some black folk also feel uncomfortable publicly uttering the troublesome epithet. I address these concerns within. Nevertheless,* **this book is really titled Nigga Theory,** *which is what I've called my brand of Critical Race Theory for years in law review articles, lectures, documentaries, and on social media.*

—Jody Armour

Praise for *N*gga Theory*:

This book is revolutionary. Prof. Armour challenges us all to reject the vast systems of oppression and dehumanization that seek to sow—and capitalize on—fear and division among us. **With compassion and rigor, Prof. Armour renders a new political, moral, legal, and philosophical framework for a more equitable world**—one centered around our shared humanity, our shared vulnerability, and the dignity that we all deserve.

> —*Matt Ferner, Editor-in-Chief at* The Appeal

In *N*gga Theory*, **Jody Armour takes the most reviled word in the English language and uses it as performative art and a battle cry to unite African Americans** divided by class because they share a vital common interest in eradicating the racism rooted deeply within the criminal justice system. Armour demonstrates—through lived experience, empirical data, and storytelling—that the historical and deeply racist view of black people as inherently more blameworthy, punishment-deserving, and disposable transcends class and implicates us all.

> —*Lara Bazelon, Professor of Law and Director of the Criminal Juvenile Justice Clinic and The Racial Justice Clinic*

Jody Armour's *N*gga Theory* **is a powerful exploration of race, class, and justice, particularly criminal justice, in today's America.** Whether you agree or disagree with one or more of Armour's approaches, this book will again and again make you stop and think. And thinking, deep thinking, in those areas is something all of us—citizens, policy makers, academics, stakeholders all—sorely need to consciously confront and then address the injustices and inequalities we all know are there.

> —*James F. McHugh, Former Associate Justice of the Massachusetts Appeals Court*

N*gga Theory **is a provocation, a poem, a lyric urging racial solidarity with every body caged in the American penal state, even or especially those classified as "violent offenders."** Through riveting personal narrative and rigorous interdisciplinary research, Jody Armour gives us the transgressive penal theory necessary in this racially troubled era.

> —*Professor Aya Gruber, author of* The Feminist War on Crime: The Unexpected Role of Women's Liberation in Mass Incarceration

N*gga Theory **is a masterpiece.**

This book is a confirmation and a revelation. My copy is marked with underlines and exclamations, circles, and folded-down corners of pages. It confirms what anyone who has worked for and with a Black person caught in the American criminal legal system knows in our bones and in our hearts, but for which we have had no theory to explain. This entire system—from the police officers roaming our impoverished streets, looking for Black adults and children, to the ordered and crushing restrictions on the evidence that may be presented in the courtroom, to the words of the jury instructions a judge gives to the jury, to the bars of the actual cage—is one that is indeed rigged, its scales always weighted in favor of Black "guilt."

The revelation in this book comes in what we could not see before: how all the pieces of this system, a system infused with white America's individual and collective racism have been fitted together to create a class of "criminals," deserving of our condemnation. Professor Armour shows us a way forward and out. However, turning away from mass incarceration and extreme retribution will require much more of us, individually and collectively, than the cheap grace of current criminal justice "re-form."

> —*Kate Chatfield, Senior Advisor for Legislation and Policy at The Justice Collaborative*

Part memoir, part hard-core critique, its in-your-face title lets you in on what's ahead in the radically progressive moral, legal, political and linguistic, scholarly takedown of our legal system, particularly criminal (in)justice.

Law professor Jody Armour, from a decidedly lofty academic chair, applies the charged title of his book to himself as well as to 'otherized' brothers in San Quentin, Attica, Angola, or death row anywhere. Demanding an alliance of Ivy League diplomas and messy rap sheets, solidarity between the 'socialized' and the 'wicked,' emphasizing the dichotomy created by not only conservatives, but also liberals and progressives regardless of race, this is not beach reading.

After three decades of judging, I'm ready to go back to law school and take Professor Armour's classes.

> —*Justice Emily Jane Goodman, New York State Supreme Court (Ret.)*

Jody Armour's new book is **a timely and forceful contribution to the criminal justice reform movement** combining legal research and reasoning with critical race theory into a radical and urgent demand for reevaluating this country's commitment to draconian punishment.

Armour makes a frontal assault on false moral equivalencies, mass incarceration, and calls into question virtually every aspect of the criminal justice system. Provocative prose and rigorous research, radical race theory and rethinking blame and punishment, this book is **a must read for anyone interested in understanding and dismantling mass incarceration.**

—Chesa Boudin, District Attorney of San Francisco

I applaud Jody's heroism and bravery for illuminating the entrenched failures of the criminal justice system and its disproportionate impact on Black and Brown communities. His keen insight in this book unpacks the dreadful stain of mass incarceration on this country and helps show how this unfortunate reality has led to overcrowding, severe racial disparities, and the criminalization derived from a systemic "lock them up and throw away the key" mentality. The painful lessons of failed public safety policies from the past 25 years are still evident in cities across this country through the decimation of poor and under-served communities.

Jody pushes prosecutors to accept that the time has come to repair the broken criminal justice system that has destroyed communities. Prosecutors can be a force for good, for reform, for dismantling this system of racial injustice and mass incarceration and help right the wrongs of the past to create a justice system that we all believe in.

Jody's narrative reminds us all that when we invest in people—as mothers, daughters, husbands, brothers, and fathers—we can help them thrive and create safer and healthier communities for everyone.

—Marilyn J. Mosby, Baltimore City State's Attorney

Prof. Armour has radically re-purposed "The N-word" to describe a new theory of race, law and justice, and he uses unflinching language to reveal uncomfortable truths about racial bias in the justice system. He unpacks the moral judgments underpinning criminal law and procedure that serve to "otherize" certain criminal defendants to their detriment, and he offers a new lens through which we should view justice reform.

As an advocate for both the most despised wrongdoers and socially marginalized victims, Jody Armour has articulated a critical race theory that is ultimately a call to uplift the human dignity of the individual.

In this challenging book, Professor Armour also calls upon prosecutors like me to be more than merely "progressive." Real change like he calls for in *N*gga Theory* will happen only when we all get a lot more uncomfortable with the true state of our legal and carceral systems.

—Dan Satterberg, King County Prosecuting Attorney

For too long we have justified and normalized the demonization and excessive punishment of those who commit crimes—rather than aiming to understand and address the struggle that led to this conduct—and in the process destroyed the lives of millions who are incarcerated, along with their families, loved ones, and communities. In this new book, Jody Armour dispels the notion that any person is unworthy of compassion by underscoring that often all that separates people from perceived evil or good is luck, unfortunate and dehumanizing labeling, and the circumstance of their birth.

He also appropriately points out the profound impact prosecutors historically have had in perpetuating the narrative that some people are irredeemable and the role a new generation of reform-minded prosecutors is playing in bringing about a dramatic shift in the justice system. **This critical and timely work, and the important personal and professional experience Professor Armour brings to it, is invaluable as we look to build a new paradigm that recognizes the humanity of every individual, regardless of wrongdoing.** It is this starting point that will promote a truly just system that heals people and communities.

> —*Miriam Aroni Krinsky, Founder and Executive Director of Fair and Just Prosecution*

In its most moral moments, the Black Lives Matter movement called for a repudiation of respectability politics and challenged Black Americans throughout the country to reject sorting ourselves into "Good Negroes" and "Bad Negroes," and to resist being seen as either "worthy" or "unworthy" of civil rights. *N*gga Theory* answers that call, in an explosive analysis of language and law.

Combining critical race theory, rap, legal scholarship, a wholly fresh theoretical approach, and his signature, poetic prose from Twitter, Jody Armour maps out a new form of solidarity—a solidarity which can both undo mass incarceration and grant our nation new frames for healing that aren't predicated on a "regressive moral framework." **Sparring with figures as diverse as Tommie Shelby, Bill Cosby, Emile Durkheim, Michelle Alexander, and Chris Rock, Armour parses major questions about race, worthiness, and criminality in American society.**

His answer, time and again, is to "Call me a Nigga"—to form a cross-class alliance from the academy to the prison. I can't wait to teach this book to students.

> —*Dr. Steven W. Thrasher, Daniel H. Renberg Chair of Social Justice in Reporting and Assistant Professor of Journalism, Northwestern University*

N*gga Theory **demands moral consistency that has been lacking in popular and academic narratives of mass incarceration.** Armour rejects absolute moral categories—violent vs. nonviolent, innocent vs. guilty—that have driven reform discussion. The book forces readers to confront a simple truth: ending mass incarceration is impossible without viewing people who have done bad and violent things as individuals worthy of freedom. To decarcerate, America needs a new theory, one that recognizes the racial goals of the criminal justice system, shapes language and law, and places individuals—not categories of offenders—at its center.

—Abraham Gutman, **The Philadelphia Inquirer**

Jody's masterpiece should be a mandatory read for every police leader. The issue of race in society, and how race and labeling impact the criminal justice system need to be understood by those who oversee the men and women who police in today's world. His views on mass incarceration and the need to take a deeper dive into how we look at sentencing and diversion are revolutionary and have certainly made me rethink my own stance on these complex societal issues.

—Chief (Ret.) Brendan Cox, Director of Policing Strategies at LEAD Bureau

Jody Armour's wonderful new book, *N*gga Theory*, is **a powerful call for solidarity** with the most socially marginalized members of our society: violent African American criminals. His devastating critique rebukes the current orthodoxy of respectability politics, which separates the world into "good" non-violent African Americans, and "bad" violent ones. He shows how social hierarchies based on race produce structures of oppression characterized by violence. He identifies the ways in which sympathy drives our moral judgment of wrongdoers, and examines why people of all races find it so hard to empathize with the African Americans who are singled out for disproportionately harsh treatment by our criminal justice system, even as they sympathize with the police who shoot, beat, and taze them. **He draws on examples taken from rap, literature, and life to provide profound yet instantly accessible insights into the complex structure of oppression, social marginalization, and the criminal law.** One moment, the reader will be humming along as Professor Armour discusses a favorite song; the next, bowled over when he exposes the hidden racial impact of criminal law doctrine. Through it all, *N*gga Theory* explores and applies the transformative practice of radical empathy with the most demonized members of society to guide us out of the current morass of mass imprisonment and racial oppression, and forward into a more just society.

—Eric J. Miller, Professor of Law and Leo J. O'Brien Fellow at Loyola Law School, Los Angeles

This is a LARB Books publication
Published by The Los Angeles Review of Books
6671 Sunset Blvd., Suite 1521, Los Angeles, CA 90028
www.larbbooks.org

ISBN: 9781940660684
Library of Congress Control Number: 2019956993

N*GGA THEORY

THEORY

Race, Language, Unequal Justice,
and the Law

JODY ARMOUR

Foreword by Larry Krassner
Introduction by Melina Abdullah

LARB
BOOKS

TABLE OF CONTENTS

FOREWORD
by Larry Krasner

When I heard that Kobe Bryant died in January, 2020, I immediately thought of USC Law Professor Jody Armour. A little-known fact about Professor Armour is that he held Lower Merion High School basketball records for more than a decade before Kobe broke them during his own high school years. That high school is public, affluent, and located in the suburbs of Philadelphia, where Kobe was born, spent part of his childhood, and is still a favorite son. Jody Armour's enrollment in that high school, so far from where he was born and spent his younger years, was unexpected. Professor Armour's years at Lower Merion High may seem like a small detail, but it's a detail that matters in his challenging and successful life, like all details in a life we care to see.

It would be easy for Armour to trumpet the many achievements in his remarkable career as a critical legal theorist and law professor, easy for anyone to suggest his exceptionalism. Others claim their own superiority often—in writing, from the bench, in politics. They suggest their success was inevitable and certain, in their nature and deserved. They erase the true story of their mentors and their luck. Armour, though, tells the truth. He admits that his outcome was uncertain—no more certain than anyone else's and no more deserved. In this book, intermingled with his theory, Armour gives us a few of his life's details.

At its beginning and end, the book is an homage to Armour's father, who jailhouse-lawyered his way out of a prison cell, past the dirty prosecutor who unjustly convicted him. His father's "other-ization" was at the hands of an unscrupulous prosecutor who lied to win a conviction rather than tell the truth and risk losing. As Professor Armour explains, his father overcame this "other-ization" (a 22- to 55-year sentence in jail on charges of selling marijuana) by sitting on the floor of his cell banging away on a manual typewriter for years. This jailhouse lawyer, perhaps inadvertently, mentored his son, encouraging him to become a lawyer and law professor. The jailhouse writer used the written word to free himself, and his son wrote a book affirming the power of words to free other people.

Armour tells us a few details of his youth in Akron, Ohio. His family slid into poverty during his father's incarceration; his city simultaneously collapsed economically as the tire industry disappeared; his talented friend suffered a downfall after being convicted of a crime in his youth (Armour himself just missed the same outcome); and he then had the unexpected good fortune to attend an excellent high school far from home, thanks to a government program.

He lets us see how within his beloved black community the politics of division do sweeping harm that no amount of success can shake. He uses the details of his family's life, again, to explain the duality of civil rights achievement and harmful division, a duality that created the relatively privileged black neighborhood where he lives in LA. He explains his own and his children's complex connection to the neighborhood, to policing, and to the city that is still defined by division, division by and within race.

These occasional details taken from his and other people's lives bind together so many of the important themes of his theory, attaching them to the reader's memory and simultaneously explaining the deep humility and compassion in Armour's thinking. Armour rejects the divisive tactics of our current, racist, carceral criminal justice system. He rejects the "other-ization" of anyone by anyone for any reason. No one gets a free pass to divide and scapegoat and over-incarcerate, not even radicals and progressives opining on powerful people who have committed crimes.

For me, as a criminal defense and civil rights attorney whose life's work has been in criminal justice and who now tries to be fair as a progressive prosecutor, this book directly and indirectly illuminates so much of what needs reform in our criminal justice system. Armour's father's life was truly individual and unexpected, much like Armour's has been, and much like yours has been and mine, and much like anyone else's life we actually try to see.

And there, for me, is an essential point. We need to try to see individuals in order to do any kind of justice. The idea of a binary world of monsters and saints whose unchanging goodness or badness is evident from one or a few actions, from their poverty, or from their race, is false. Stereotypes and assumptions based on the idea of a static and unchanging criminality either in individuals or in groups are false. And we have codified these falsehoods into laws and procedures that deliberately refuse to see individuals' lives, and especially refuse to see details that are unexpected. Our broken criminal justice system has rejected individual justice and the discretion it requires, and instead insists on robotic and inflexible mandatory sentencing, sentencing guidelines, death sentences, life without possibility of parole, the actual or de facto elimination of sentence modifications, pardons, commutations, expungement, and record sealing.

Real change in the broken criminal justice system we have built requires real change in its foundation, which requires us to care enough to see people's lives within our own community and within all communities, and requires us to operate under a new theory, one that allows us to reject division and reject turning our brothers and sisters into "the other." With much greater theoretical nuance and sophistication than this foreword can provide, this hopeful and aspirational book reminds us to see individuals and their lives, including the details, however unexpected.

INTRODUCTION
by Melina Abdullah

I was born in East Oakland ... a city defined by the kind of lumpen radicalism that gave birth to the Black Panther Party, neighborhoods teeming with Texas- and Louisiana-born grandparents on front porches, teenagers on corners, dirty-faced kids hopping backyard fences to steal neighbors' plums. Every Friday night, my Beaumont-born-elementary-school-teacher-community-other-mother-brilliant-single-mama would load my brother and me into her faded Volvo station wagon to head to Flint's Barbeque on San Pablo Ave., one of the most formidable "ho-strolls" on the planet. In the 1970s, "ladies of the night" dressed in shiny magenta pants, tube tops, rhinestone-studded heels, and extra-long painted nails, with matching lip-gloss ... the epitome of glamour. My face pressed against the car glass, I longed to be like them. Beautiful and free. Through the cracked window, I heard the accompanying sounds: loud-talking, cussing, and laughter. The "n-word" abounded—dripping from the lips of men dressed in flashy suits, snakeskin shoes, and matching hats ... an extended "aaahhhhh" at the end, n**** danced to the rhythm of the pounding bass that poured out the open doors of double-parked Cadillacs. A piece of those Friday night rituals lived throughout the week, following us back to our homes and schools. N**** was a forbidden claiming of space and each other. It was familial and community. Parents would add "Lil" to the front of it when they were disciplining their children. As adolescents, we did what children do ... turned it into a rhyme ... "Honey Boom! Chedda Cheese ... N**** Please!" But there was also a heaviness to it. My mom never used the word, and somehow I knew I was never to use it in front of her.

By the time I was in ninth grade the world changed for me. East Oakland was under siege. The crack cocaine that flooded our communities turned our schools into battlefields. My mother made the decision to use her godmother's sister, Granddear's, address to get me into Berkeley High School. Each morning, I would wake up at 5 a.m and take the public bus more than an hour to hippie-town, where I met Mr. Richard Navies—a man to whom I owe my life. Berkeley High was the only public school in the nation with a Black Studies Department and Mr. Navies was the larger-than-life figure who served as its chair. Ninth graders were immediately reprogrammed to love who we were as Black people, to understand Black culture and history as something worthy of study, and to replace the "n-word" with "Brother" and "Sister." You see, the "n-word" was not some reclamation of Black community; it was part of a process of dehumanization required by chattel slavery. We weren't human beings; we were n*****. I have not used the word since walking into Mr. Navies' class. I was 13 years old.

Jody Armour has been a good friend, a colleague, and a comrade for almost 20 years. Still, it has been challenging for me to even follow his Twitter handle, which bears the name of this book @N****Theory. When he invited me to write the foreword, his brilliance, commitment, and deep love for our people took precedent over my own discomfort with the word. His work has challenged me to be deeply introspective, to grapple with my identity, my beliefs, and my outward praxis. It has forced me to question and to grow.

This volume is not about the word, but about the imposed dichotomy between "Black people" and "n*****s." It is about the strategic and ethical decision to align with n****s, especially when we have the option to be seen as "good Negroes."

On February 26, 2012, 17-year-old Trayvon Martin was murdered by aspiring white supremacist George Zimmerman. Zimmerman was arrested only after a massive public outcry and deep community organizing among Black Floridians and across the nation. Trayvon was not the first Black boy to be murdered by a vigilante who was protected by the state. In the years leading up, social media and video recordings had raised awareness and sparked outrage in Black communities. In writing about Oscar Grant, journalist Thandisizwe Chimurenga called these state-sanctioned killings "double murders": the theft of the body and the assassination of the character. I would actually make it a "triple murder," adding the killing of the entire community's standing. As media elicited sympathy for George Zimmerman, the white-passing child killer, Trayvon was somehow transformed from a fun-loving high-schooler into a vicious-truant-gold-tooth-wearing-weed-smoking thug. Trayvon was cast as a n****, sub-human, property. As Trayvon's parents and community were fighting to bring some semblance of justice in the actual killing of Trayvon's body, they simultaneously had to defend his character. Online campaigns of celebrities wearing hoodies and people with Trayvon's favorite snacks—Skittles and Arizona Iced Tea—

were meant to reclaim Trayvon's innocence. As it became apparent that the "justice" system had no intention of providing justice for Trayvon, the reclamation of his character became paramount. There was a community struggle for Trayvon to be seen as a child, a good person, not a n**** ... and for the Black community at large to also be seen through a humanizing lens. This struggle for the humanity of our children following the theft of their bodies by police and white supremacists repeated itself with each state-sanctioned murder. Each was heartbreaking.

At the two-year memorial for #AndrewJosephIII in Tampa in 2016, Deanna Hardy-Joseph, the 14-year-old's mother (who is also my cousin), recounted how Andrew was perfectly-mannered, a scholar-athlete, never in trouble, a joy. The Josephs were Huxtable-level perfect; the parents, Andrew (the elder) and Deanna, had been high school sweethearts, were college-educated, professionals, lived in a gated community, invested in charity work, and had two smart, charismatic, beautiful children—Andrew and Deja. They survived intact despite being ravaged by Hurricane Katrina and having to resettle from New Orleans to Tampa. It was outrageous that 14-year-old Andrew—a kind boy, who was simply trying to help his friend who was being harassed by police at "Student Day" at the County Fair—would be targeted, detained, strip-searched, labeled a gangster, removed from the fair, dumped on the side of the freeway (along with five others ... of 99 total "ejected" that night ... all of them Black boys), and marked for death by police. As Deanna's shiny round face, perfectly-shaped mouth, motherly softness, with hauntingly sad eyes, tells the story to the crowd circled-up outside the fairgrounds, we are all outraged that they could treat her son like less than a dog. Our chests fill with rage and pain. There is stillness in the circle. Then #CaryBall's mother steps forward. She had come to support Deanna from St. Louis, where Cary had been an honor roll student, with a 3.86 GPA, high ambitions, promise ... .stolen by the gun of a police officer who didn't see who he was; they saw him as a thug, a n***** . Mike Brown, Sr. then moves in. He spoke of how his son #MikeBrown planned to become an aircraft mechanic, of how he loved his grandmother, of his warmth, of who he was as an 18-year-old young man and how Ferguson police portrayed him as an animal, a brute.

As we stood in that circle, the warmth of the Florida sun baking in the tears that flowed freely, I thought about my own three children. None of them had a 3.86 GPA. My middle daughter was a "free spirit" who could often be found under her desk at school, carried slime in her pocket, spoke out of turn in class, found humor in everything, and laughed loudly, defi-antly, in a manner that filled entire campuses, and frustrated teachers, administrators, school police…and her mother to no end. My oldest is a born revolutionary, who regularly challenged authority, and organized others to do the same, especially in the face of white power-holders and "good Negroes" who propped up racist institutions. I couldn't say of them what these parents were saying of Andrew, Cary, and Mike, but weren't they worth their lives, too?

Why must our children be perfect to live? Why do they have to pull up their pants, or get good grades, or be respectful, and have ambitions, to live? Why can't they be children who hop fences, cuss when they're out of their parents' earshot, smoke a little weed, hate math, have dangerous-joy-ful lives, make mistakes, and recover from them? What if Yuvette shoplift-ed at Home Depot? What if Ezell jaywalked? What if Mike stole cigars? What if Redel robbed the pharmacy? Or if Devin went for a joyride in his dad's girlfriend's car? What if Jesse were tagging? What if Wakiesha cussed out the prison guard? What if Kisha and Marquintan were high in the car? What if Richard spent his childhood in Youth Authority? Or if Carnell had a gun in his waistband? What if AJ were in a gang? I'm not saying that any of these things are true, but what if? If the folks on whose behalf we struggle weren't perfect, if they were n*****, are they not worth their lives?

White-supremacist-patriarchal-heteronormative-capitalism socializes us to aspire to "good Negro" status. It convinces little Black girls from East Oakland to graduate from Howard—summa cum laude and Phi Beta Kap-pa, to pledge the oldest Black sorority, to earn PhDs, to be in the "right" rooms … with other "good Negroes," to learn to taste wine, to only laugh intentionally, to favor jazz over hip-hop, to submit to a political and social grooming process that sets us up for "firsts," titles, and the illusion of power. It convinces us to revel in exceptionalism, that there is a such thing as in-dividual advancement, and that those who are denied pats on the head by benevolent elites are somehow inferior. We are told that to buy in is not the same as selling out, that we can be a "credit to our race" without being of the people. "Good Negroes" are not n****s. We are trained to have disdain for them, to despise them, to deny the n**** within our own selves, to redeem ourselves from it, to kill it. But our position as "good Negroes" is tenuous. It's bestowed by a power structure that preys upon us, but requires us few to veil its existence.

Killed just two days after #MikeBrown in Ferguson, #EzellFord became the touchpoint for Black Lives Matter organizing in Los Angeles. The 25-year-old, intellectually-disabled Ezell was well-known and beloved in his neighborhood, 65th and Broadway, a space where young Black men were especially targeted by police. LAPD officers Antonio Villegas and Sharlton Wampler were harassing Ezell on August 11, 2014. They escalated, got him face down in the street, and shot him point-blank in the back. The official autopsy showed a muzzle imprint burned into Ezell's skin, likely the fatal shot. The neighborhood and Ezell's family were retaliated against for speaking out; police berated his family, ran up in their house, and arrested one of Ezell's most outspoken cousins on an "unrelated" charge. Community outrage sparked Occupy LAPD, an 18-day, 24-hour encampment in front of LAPD headquarters that ran from December 2014 to January 2015. LAPD Chief Charlie Beck justified police actions. As the Civilian Police Commission prepared to rule on whether or not Ezell's murder was in-policy, we knew it was important to pressure the mayor, who appointed the commissioners.

On Sunday, June 7, 2015, two days before the scheduled ruling, about a dozen of us, dressed in white, prayed together and sang spirituals as we filed down Irving Ave., gathering in front of the wrought iron and brick fencing that encircled the mayor's mansion. I had been to the mansion before, gathered in its lush gardens, eating decadent hors d'oeuvres, blending in with women of means decked out in flowery dresses and floppy hats. I knew Eric Garcetti. We shared mutual friends. He'd given me his personal phone number just months before. I was being considered for commission appointments and had been contracted by the city as a researcher. I was on most "good Negro" lists, and the Black elite often saw me as next up in the line of Black political succession.

It was still dawn when we knelt at the front gate and poured libation in Ezell's name. As the sun rose higher in the sky, we took to social media, pledging to occupy, challenging the mayor to come out, and finally catching him trying to leave out the back door the next morning. We blocked his blacked-out SUV with our bodies. As I approached his open window, I could feel my fledgling good-Negro status slip away.

I've been arrested six times as a part of movement work (after a few times as a juvenile ... for less noble reasons). I have been threatened with trumped-up charges that could have gotten me some serious time. I've been threatened, surveilled, intimidated, and physically roughed-up by police. I've been doxed by white supremacists. My children have been targeted and placed on lists. My name no longer appears on lists for official gatherings. I'm no longer the "good Negro" at the dinner table. The husband of a public official pointed a loaded .45 at my chest and said, "I will shoot you." I have plummeted from the "good Negro" pedestal upon which I was once positioned.

The truth is, such status is always illusory. It is never assured. The pedestal is always wobbly. The truth is, we are all n****s ... even when we pretend to be "good Negroes." We must not reach for a status that is only bestowed by a white supremacist system that really despises us. We must resist. To claim not only our alignment with n****s, but our identity as N****s ourselves is the greatest act of defiance; it is our sacred duty as descendants of enslaved people, freedom fighters, street corner hustlers, and our own grandparents. Ultimately N**** theory—and praxis—is what will get us free.

N*GGA THEORY

Race, Language, Unequal Justice and the Law

JODY ARMOUR

PROLOGUE

NIGGA THEORY: A SONG OF SOLIDARITY

*C*all me a Nigga.

Call ME a Nigga: I utter these words as a political battle cry for the Black, damned, and forsaken—that is, for the staggeringly high percentage of poor black boys and men languishing in jail cells, for those selling drugs, gangbanging, or otherwise scrambling for survival and self-respect.

I say it because we have a fundamental divide that needs bridging. This divide is cultural fact as well as a social fact. It is an economic divide crossed by moral judgment. It is the divide between the haves and the have-nots, but it is also, for many, seen as a divide between the morally upstanding and the morally corrupt. This book will dismantle that distinction.

And it will dismantle it with Nigga Theory. So call me a Nigga With Theory. NWT.

◆

Call me a Nigga is what language philosopher J.L. Austin would call a "performative"—a form of symbolic communication that *performs* a social action, a "speech act" that doesn't simply *say* something—it *does* something.[1]

Phrases like "I pledge allegiance" and "with this ring, I thee wed," and "I promise" epitomize *linguistic* bonding performatives. *Nonlinguistic* ones include flags (like Old Glory), personifications (like Uncle Sam), and melodies (like instrumental versions of the *Star-Spangled Banner* and *America the Beautiful*). In political communication bonding performatives like these unify and rally individuals; they create collective social actors and forge social identities. And re-appropriating ugly racial epithets like "nigga" and "niggas" can turn them into forceful bonding performatives. Reviled and revered rapper Tupac Shakur bonded with black criminals by expressly linking "brothas," "Niggas," and "criminal gangstas," or "G's" in the following hook, from his solidarity dirge, "Life Goes On"[2]:

> How many brothas fell victim to the street
> Rest in peace, young Nigga, there's a heaven for a G
> Be a lie if told you that I never thought of death
> My Niggas, we the last ones left.

Despite having no criminal record myself, I say *call me a Nigga* to perform my solidarity with and rally political support for black criminals and convicts: those in my family, those in the poverty-stricken neighborhoods down the hill from my own economically gated community, and those in cynically de-industrialized rustbelt cities like my hometown of Akron, Ohio, where crime goes hand-in-hand with concentrated disadvantage. I also say *call me a Nigga* to promote unity and assert solidarity among blacks across moral lines of good and bad, right and wrong, wicked and worthy. And because a grossly disproportionate number of the black criminals we judge to be bad, wrong, and wicked are poor, I utter this profane performative to promote a necessary political alliance: an alliance between the statistically less "crime prone" black bourgeoisie and the more "crime prone" black underclass.

◆

The vilification of a "crime prone" underclass figures centrally in what I call "Good Negro Theory": the values, beliefs, and assumptions that underlie efforts to morally and politically distinguish between law-abiding "good Negroes" and law-breaking "niggas." In its place I offer "Nigga Theory."

Earlier generations of civil rights advocates found that they were most successful—their rhetoric most effective—when they distinguished and distanced themselves from the most stigmatized elements of the black (for present purposes, disproportionately poor, law-breaking black) community and drew the attention of the public and policymakers to *certain* black people, namely, those understood by mainstream whites as "good," "sympathetic," and "respectable" (for present purposes, disproportionately better off, law-abiding black people). This political strategy—commonly called the "politics of respectability"—was practiced by civil rights era activists and rested on the belief that racial oppression can only be ended if black people prove to whites that they are worthy of respect and sympathy. Even if the basic social order is unjust and racist, this theory goes, blacks must show they look at the world through conventional moral lenses and aspire to the same moral codes as the white middle class.

Nigga Theory is a repudiation of Good Negro Theory and the politics of respectability on which it rests.

But first a quick word to those who might object. As part of my political practice, I have made my performative declaration, *call me a Nigga*, in many venues, under many different conditions. I have said it, or performed it, in prisons and intervention programs for juvenile and adult offenders; in black churches and before formal gatherings of black judges and justices; and in the company of scholars at conferences, in performing arts halls, university auditoriums, downtown law firms, alumni magazines, and on social media. In other words, I've vetted this invitation to bond with black criminals with three key audiences: 1) the objects of our criminal condemnations themselves, namely, the truly disadvantaged blacks who are doing time or still doing street crime; 2) the weightiest authorities on morality and justice in the black community, namely, the black church and judiciary; and 3) those who must morally assess black wrongdoers on juries, in legislative chambers, and at the ballot box, namely, ordinary Americans of all races and walks of life.

Some vehemently reject my use of the emotionally charged catchphrase, and they do so on one of two grounds. First, some contend that any sentence that wholeheartedly embraces the word "nigga" cannot be a progressive performative utterance and cannot unify Blacks or produce positive social change; I respond to their concerns in a chapter devoted to ordinary language philosophy and the N-word. Others object not to the word "nigga" itself but to my self-referential use of it—that is, they see the statement *call me a Nigga* as a claim that cannot be authentically uttered by a respectable law professor in reference to his own privileged black self. The following blog criticizing my exhortation succinctly captures this viewpoint and the righteous invective that often accompanies it:

> Prof. Armour, I've met niggas. I know niggas. I have nigga clients. You, sir, are no nigga. First, you graduated high school, then you graduated college, then you became a professor. You've probably never even fired a gun, let alone killed anyone. Your son will never visit you in prison. You've probably never sold a single gram of cocaine, and I'll bet a thorough inspecting would reveal no gang tats anywhere on your body. You drive a German sedan with GPS but not 22" chrome wheels. You don't receive public assistance, daydream about starting a record album, or have half-dozen illegitimate children you don't support. You probably have a six-figure salary from legitimate sources. You are about as far away from a "nigga" as a black man can be. Hell, I may be more nigga than you.

So I say *call me a Nigga* despite not fitting this popular stereotype—despite my lack of a criminal record, my light-skin privilege (I've been called a yellow nigga, a sand nigga, and a Spic), my Ivy League diplomas, my respectable salary befitting the occupant of the Roy P. Crocker Chair at the University of Southern California Law School, my residence in the Black Beverly Hills, my three sons who attended exclusive private high schools and colleges, my respectable rims, my fluency in "talking White," and my red-headed Irish Catholic mom. Thanks to my lighter shade, academic pedigree, chaired professorship, tax bracket, ZIP code, speech patterns, and mixed ancestry, I am not what cognitive science would call a "prototypical" nigga.[3]

If the sentence *call me a Nigga* were a statement of fact, or if the blood-soaked epithet on which it turns had a fixed meaning, which it does not, then perhaps I could not authentically utter it and perhaps its use could not produce "real" social change. But the boundaries of "nigga" (lower-case "n") and "Nigga" (upper-case "N"), like most linguistic boundaries, are malleable and always up for grabs, and I, like many others, am repurposing the words as *terms of art* in an oppositional discourse that uses words as tools, tools that can accomplish two tasks, one critical, the other political: 1) I use "nigga" (lower-case "n") critically, conceptually, and analytically to highlight and isolate and ultimately refute illegitimate and unreliable moral condemnations of disproportionately poor black wrongdoers whom many outside and inside the black community "nigger-" and "nigga-rize" and, 2) I use "Nigga" (upper-case "N") politically to stand in solidarity with wrongly vilified black criminals and rally resistance to a common foe, namely, "tough on crime" "eye-for-an-eye" "lock 'em up and throw away the key" retributionists responsible for the disproportional incarceration of black criminals, especially violent ones. I say *call me a Nigga* to contest what that condemnatory word and concept mean, and through that contestation to unite law-abiding and law-breaking blacks and more generally to undermine the moral distinction between criminals and non-criminals of all races. This book rests on the basic premise that struggles over the meaning of troublesome and transgressive words and symbols can drive radical social change.

◆

But I say *call me a Nigga*, first and foremost, to assert solidarity with and express love for a criminally condemned man whose conviction relegated him to the status of a nigga in the eyes of many and whose legacy lives in every word I speak or scribble about blame and punishment: I look at our criminal justice system through lenses ground and polished by *his* experience. I cannot think about legal writing without seeing a black man desperately click-clacking on a Royal manual typewriter on his cell floor, deep into the night, in search of his own salvation. That man, doing 22 to 55 in the Ohio State Penitentiary for possession and sale of marijuana: he was my dad. All that stood between him and a lifetime of iron bars and cell blocks and prison yards was word work—nothing but the Queen's English he and that Royal keyboard could crank out. After teaching himself to talk and think like a lawyer from the warden's own law books, he drafted his own writs and represented himself *pro se* through the state and federal court system, delivering his own oral arguments to appellate tribunals along the way, and ultimately vindicating himself in *Armour v. Salisbury* (492 F.2d 1032), a Sixth Circuit Court of Appeals case I now teach to my first-year criminal law students. #PoeticJustice.

My love for and sympathetic identification with this particular black convict makes me, according to the logic of those who seek to niggerize black criminals, a Nigger Lover. That logic makes my mom, grandmom, eight brothers and sisters, and everyone else who sympathetically identified with him, Nigger Lovers. Indeed, given the millions of moms, dads, sons, daughters, relatives, and friends who sympathetically identify with black criminals, including violent and serious ones, Nigger Lovers in this poignant and supremely ironic sense number in the millions. Indeed, it will be useful to make Nigger Lover a term of art, properly applicable to anyone who empathizes or sympathetically identifies with a black criminal, including those who are violent. The substantive criminal law requires that jurors convict only morally blameworthy wrongdoers, under the ancient legal maxim *actus non facit reum, nisi mens sit rea*—in Blackstone's translation, "an unwarrantable act without a vicious will is no crime at all." Under this *mens rea* principle, as it has come to be known, it is unjust to punish someone who commits an "unwarrantable act"—the *actus rea*—unless he acted with a "vicious" or wicked will. This requirement invites jurors to fully or partially excuse wrongdoers with whom they sympathize, and so a black defendant's freedom in a criminal trial often rides on the ability of his lawyer to transform often racially resentful jurors into Nigger Lovers. Ironically, as a child I often heard other whites refer to my mom as a "Nigger Lover" for her participation in what many around her viewed as morally condemnable conduct: the dreaded commingling of gene pools called miscegenation. Of course, the commingling of black and white gene pools has been going on in America since its inception. White male slave owners violently injected their genes into the black population through the rape of black female chattel for hundreds of years under slavery. Nevertheless, the sight rankled many in the late 1950s and early 1960s: my Irish American mom, with her head full of flaming red hair, and my 6'8" barrel-chested black dad, the two of them looking like Lucille Ball and LeBron James, kicking along main street in stride—one, two—arms locked, unmistakably matched. The obscene thought of this big black man skinny-dipping in their European gene pool provoked racially resentful cops and prosecutors to railroad him.

I also say *call me a Nigga* to forcefully assert my solidarity with and love for the black boys I grew up with in Akron, Ohio, once home to all four major American tire makers (Goodyear, Goodrich, Firestone, and General Tire) and known as "Rubber Capital of the World." Until, that is, tire makers took their unionized, good paying, low-skilled jobs to cheaper labor markets down South and overseas, leaving behind neighborhoods mired in joblessness, alienation, and crime. If the Midwest is America's heartland, this nation suffered a myocardial infarction and gross necrosis in the 1960s, 1970s, and 1980s due to interruption of the job supply to this area. The destructive consequences of rustbelt necrosis never reached our family while my dad was a free man, but when he essentially got "25 with an L" (a sentence of 25 years to life) a week after my eighth birthday, his eight kids and wife went from a comfortable Cliff Huxtable and the "Cosby kids" standard of living to crumbs and roaches and rats. Most of the poor black boys I suddenly began running those cynically de-industrialized streets with have been convicted of criminal wrongdoing—especially the ones with ambition, backbone, and grit. That makes them, by the Black Criminal Litmus Test of a nigga—by our shared history, and by our bonds of mutual love and respect—"my Niggas." In calling them *my Niggas*, I am saying that even though they meet the litmus test of criminal condemnation and I do not, and even though they are morally responsible for criminal acts that I have never committed, there is no real moral difference between them and me. All that distinguishes us is luck.

In my years writing these reflections on the power of *linguistic* bonding performatives like *call me a Nigga* to promote unity and political action, I inadvertently grew a vociferous *nonlinguistic* political performative on the top of my head: a lengthy, kinky, loud-and-proud Afro. Unabashedly nappy and self-affirming, big Afros in my youth represented the gravity-defying antithesis of the wind-flapping-in-your-hair white standard of beauty by which many black people's full lips, broad noses, kinky hair, and dark skin were deemed inherently ugly. Many world cultures shared this negative view of natural black features and many black Americans internalized Eurocentric beauty standards, frequently referring to straight hair as "good" and their own naturally nappy variety as "bad"—fit only for lye and presses and weaves and relaxers. Thus, those who donned big "naturals" took so-called "bad hair" and contested its negative social meaning, inverting and transvaluing nappiness into a sensuous nonlinguistic bonding performative, the exact equivalent of linguistic ones like "Black is Beautiful" and "Say it loud, I'm black and I'm proud." Both the Afros and the slogans promoted social and political solidarity among black people in the mid-to-late 1960s, creating alliances of loyal individuals capable of producing change through unified social action. This is why Black Power proponents of that era—including members of the Black Panther Party and iconic political activist Angela Davis—routinely "uttered" big Afros as part of their oppositional political discourse.

Black Power proponents who donned Afros and used follicle fashion to protest undemocratic subordination were far from the first "radical" Americans to use the symbolic power of fashion to fight illegitimate assertions of power. This honor and distinction goes to the early revolutionist Philadelphia militiamen, who in the mid-1770s resisted putting on conventional uniforms, preferring instead hunting shirts, which they said would "level all distinctions" within the militia. In so doing, they were both struggling over the meaning of symbolic communication and using the symbolic force of fashion to bond together.[4] This American political tradition of using the bonding force of fashion to rally resistance in the face of illegitimate assertions of power resulted in suffragette bloomers in the mid-19th century[5] and, more recently, produced another forceful nonlinguistic performative: the hoodie. This article of clothing was worn by black 17-year-old Trayvon Martin on the occasion of his fatal shooting by neighborhood watchman George Zimmerman, who claimed to reasonably believe that Martin posed an immediate threat of death, serious bodily injury, or "forcible felony." After the killing, students, pundits, and politicians donned hoodies to stand in solidarity with victims of racial profiling and to bond with others who saw a miscarriage of justice in the failure of police to properly investigate the shooting or charge Zimmerman. Like "nigga" as a word and "bad hair" as a physical characteristic, a hoodie as an article of clothing carries a negative social meaning. Especially when pulled over the head of an unidentified black man, the hoodie is strongly associated with wicked criminality in the minds of many Americans: one often sees them in grainy black and white photos of armed assailants on local newscasts, prompting Geraldo Rivera to assert on *Fox and Friends* on March 23, 2012, that the hoodie was as responsible for Trayvon's death as Zimmerman, which in turn inspired a "Million Hoodie March" in New York that attracted hundreds of protesters, many of them wearing hoodies.[6] Whatever the merits of that assertion, it is hard to deny the association in the popular American imagination between hoodies, young black males, and crime.

Nevertheless, I had no intention of shouting a nappy political statement from the top of my head. Instead, my prodigious performative grew out of my preoccupation with researching and writing this book, which caused me to miss months of trips to my neighborhood barbershop, Hair Architects. As my thesis expanded and grew more radical, so did my nappy hair. Over time, my thesis and hair became increasingly intertwined, like serpentine vines of ivy climbing a redbrick wall. I did not realize how intertwined they had become until I overheard lawyers from LA's oldest "city" clubs, the California Club and the Jonathan Club, describe my waxing nappiness as "impertinent" and "unprofessional." These clubs are bastions of corporate and civic power where restraint in bearing, manner, and style are de rigueur and where, following strict dress codes, soberly attired movers and shakers dine and hang out and cut deals. Both clubs barred blacks, Jews, and women from membership until the mid-1980s, when privilege holders were dragged kicking and screaming into the 20th century by lawsuits, threats of lawsuits, a city ordinance, regulatory agencies, and the harsh glare of publicity. What's more, some of my law students referred to my escalating Afro as "ironic," in that it made me "look like a criminal" at the same time I teach criminal law. Over time and quite by accident, my hair has grown into a nappy illustration of nonlinguistic political discourse: once dormant, it has been stirred to life by my reflections on the revolutionary power of words and symbols—even ugly epithets and "bad hair"—to pinpoint injustice and bond people together. In this spirit, each morning I activate the performative power in my kinky coils by grabbing a wide-toothed pick by its clenched black fist and sinking its teeth into densely woven mats of hair, followed by choppy outward thrusts in rapid succession that propel spiral shafts vertically into a big, rounded Bat-Signal of solidarity with Black Lives Matter.

◆

My father litigated his way out of prison by proving that the District Attorney who prosecuted him deliberately lied to the jury. The DA repeatedly assured them that he had not promised the state's principal witness (then serving a long sentence) leniency in return for testifying against my dad, when in truth they had struck that very bargain. My professional observations of DAs over the last 25 years have only deepened my distrust. As Professor John Pfaff shows in *Locked In: The True Causes of Mass Incarceration and How to Achieve Real Reform,* first among those true causes of racialized mass incarceration is the nearly unchecked power of DAs: more than stiff drug laws, punitive judges, overzealous cops, or private prisons, prosecutors have been the main drivers of the prison boom over the last 30 years. Pfaff found that although crime was steadily declining in the 1990s and 2000s, which one would expect to be accompanied by decreasing incarceration rates, these rates instead soared, for a simple mathematical reason: the probability that a DA would file a felony charge against an arrestee roughly doubled from about one in three to nearly two in three. More than any other single class of elected officials, prosecutors are responsible for quadrupling the number of people incarcerated since the mid-1980s. Excessive blame and punishment has been the stock in trade of prosecutors for many years, at least in part because many DAs have attempted to bolster political careers by racking up convictions.

Therefore, any criminal justice reform, any way out of the carceral state, any way out of the New Jim Crow, any way forward from our current gulag culture, lies in reform at the prosecutorial level. And that will require a new way of thinking. A new theory of justice. It will require Nigga Theory, and it will require progressive prosecutors.

◆

Until very recently, I would have scoffed at the notion of a "progressive," let alone a "radically progressive" or "revolutionary" prosecutor. It would have seemed a ridiculous oxymoron.

But since 2013, voters have elected roughly 30 reform-minded prosecutors, some of them fundamentally reinventing the role of the modern District Attorney. For instance, Larry Krasner, who campaigned on eliminating cash bail, reining in police and prosecutorial misconduct, and ending racialized mass incarceration, won the race for District Attorney of Philadelphia, with 75% of the vote in the general election. In a packed lecture hall in 2018, DA Krasner told my USC law students that ending racialized mass incarceration is "the most important civil rights issue of our time" and, moreover, that the difference between a "traditional" and "progressive" prosecutor is that the latter is a "prosecutor with compassion" and "a public defender with power." This growing crop of "prosecutors with compassion" and "public defenders with power" has upended my pat, binary way of thinking about the role of the DA. I now recognize the potential of radically progressive DAs to promote deep cuts in racialized mass incarceration. Such prosecutors adopt a fundamentally different moral compass and conception of justice than do traditional "law and order" DAs, the ones whose moral, legal, and political compass sharply distinguishes between victims and perpetrators. They recognize that "hurt people hurt people" and refuse to subordinate the values of restoration, rehabilitation, and redemption to those of retribution, retaliation, and revenge.

I will refer to a truly transformational DA committed to rolling back racialized mass incarceration as a "radically progressive prosecutor" because the simpler "progressive prosecutor" is already becoming a hollow buzzword, fashionable in political circles, but too often used to paper over unprogressive prosecutorial pasts. For instance, in her new book, *The Truths*

We Hold, erstwhile 2020 Democratic presidential candidate Sen. Kamala Harris (D–Calif.) touts her record as a "progressive prosecutor," from the start of her career as a line prosecutor in San Francisco, up through her tenure as California Attorney General. But does a "progressive prosecutor" defend cheating DAs who have been thrown off cases for withholding evidence (Orange County), falsifying evidence (Kern County) or lying under oath, as happened in a Riverside case, *Baca v. Adams*, involving a corrupt prosecutor chillingly similar to my dad's DA?[7] In *Baca*, Harris' office opposed an appeal by a defendant who was convicted after the prosecutor in his case, just like my dad's DA, lied to the jury about whether an informant received compensation (in the form of leniency) for his testimony. Harris' office only withdrew its opposition to the defendant's appeal after a panel of Ninth Circuit judges asked embarrassing questions about why none of the lying DAs were being charged with perjury and threatened to release an opinion that named names if Harris' office kept up its misguided opposition to the appeal. And does a "progressive prosecutor" fight the release of a wrongfully convicted man, incarcerated based on the testimony of lying cops, as in the case of Daniel Larsen?[8] Does a "progressive prosecutor" advocate for and then enforce an anti-truancy policy that arrests and jails mothers of kids who are chronically truant?[9] Does a "progressive prosecutor" in 2014 simply laugh in the face of a reporter when asked about her position on marijuana legalization? Does a "progressive prosecutor" refuse to join other states attempting to remove marijuana from the DEA's list of most dangerous substances? Does she refuse to resist the federal crackdown on weed?[10] Of course not! But in every case Kamala Harris did, making her a "progressive prosecutor" only in a Pickwickian sense. To distinguish such so-called progressive prosecutors from truly transformative ones, I will refer to the latter as "radically progressive" or even "revolutionary" prosecutors, labels that incrementalists, centrists, and shape-shifting traditionalists may find harder to misappropriate in furtherance of their political ambitions.

And true criminal-justice reform requires not only radically progressive prosecutors, but equally radical lawmakers, ones with totally different moral compasses than those guiding centrist Democrats like Joe Biden, who, in an address on live television in 1989 excoriated then-president George H.W. Bush for proposing a billion-dollar investment in the War on Drugs that, in Biden's view, did "not include enough police officers to catch the violent thugs, enough prosecutors to convict them, enough judges to sentence them, or enough prison cells to put them away for a long time." As recently as April 2016, Biden insisted that he was "not at all" ashamed of his central role in passing the draconian 1994 Violent Crime Control and Law Enforcement Act, an accelerant for mass incarceration better known as the "Clinton crime bill." Biden, Bill Clinton, and Kamala Harris are vivid reminders that many leading liberals and "progressives" rose to prominence by pushing carceral policies that treated punishing black people as political currency, in the process separating families, destroying communities, and hobbling whole generations.

Radical criminal justice reform will also require the involvement of activists, advocates, journalists, commentators, clergy, public defenders, grassroots political organizations, and radically progressive voters, since they, ultimately, decide the political fate of radically progressive elected officials. Radical reform will require all these agents of change to take on the monumental task of redefining this nation's values and moral norms in matters of blame and punishment. And the urgent question confronting any and all truly progressive reformers is this: Through what moral, legal, and political lenses do radically progressive people committed to making deep and lasting cuts in racialized mass incarceration look at blame and punishment?

Nigga Theory expounds a radically progressive moral, legal, and political framework for DAs, Public Defenders, lawmakers, activists, and voters to help transform how we think and feel about the disproportionately Black minds, bodies, and souls we currently cage in the name of justice. At the heart of this framework is someone whom liberal critics of mass incarceration too often discount or deny: the violent offender. The widely accepted liberal narrative about racialized mass incarceration, as popularized by Michelle Alexander's important and influential book, *The New Jim Crow: Mass Incarceration in the Age of Colorblindness* (2010), argues that racist lawmakers responded to the civil rights era triumphs of Blacks over state-sanctioned racialized segregation—Old Jim Crow—by shifting to another institutional mechanism of racial oppression: the criminal justice system. According to Alexander, the federal government launched the War on Drugs, with "low-level nonviolent drug offenses" driving the explosion in US incarceration rates. "The impact of the drug war has been astounding," Alexander writes. "In less than 30 years, the US penal population exploded from around 300,000 to more than 2 million, with drug convictions accounting for the majority of the increase." Recognizing that "violent crime tends to provoke the most visceral and punitive response," Alexander spells out the most forceful argument of "defenders of mass incarceration" who claim that it is not a form of racial oppression:

> They point to violent crime in the African American community as a justification for the staggering number of black men who find themselves behind bars. Black men, they say, have much higher rates of violent crime; that's why so many of them are locked up.

Her go-to response to those who defend racialized mass incarceration as centered on violent offenders, reiterated in no uncertain terms throughout the book, is that "violent crime is *not* responsible for mass incarceration." Warning readers not to be "misled by those who insist that violent crime has driven the rise of this unprecedented system of racial and social control," Alexander proclaims: "the uncomfortable reality is that arrests and convictions for drug offenses—not violent crime—have propelled mass incarceration." [11]

The clear implication, of course, is that the "uncomfortable reality" of racialized mass incarceration might not be so uncomfortable if it afflicted mostly violent offenders rather than nonviolent drug offenders; a core premise of this book is that it should be an intolerably "uncomfortable reality" in relation to both violent *and* nonviolent offenders. This deep conventional moral distinction between violent and nonviolent offenders drives the liberal New Jim Crow narrative, centering it on the latter and repeatedly making their draconian treatment the touchstone of injustice. As recently as 2015, President Obama publicly propagated this factual cornerstone of the narrative: "Over the last few decades, we've also locked up more and more nonviolent drug offenders than ever before, for longer than ever before, and that is the real reason our prison population is so high." It's infinitely easier to carry a brief for nonviolent than violent offenders in the court of public opinion. Accordingly, Alexander places great rhetorical weight on the distinction, declaring in one passage that "[w]e ought never excuse violence," while urging in another that we ought to excuse low-level nonviolent wrongdoing because "all people make mistakes," "all of us are sinners," "all of us are criminals," "all of us violate the law at some point in our lives," and "most of us break the law not once but repeatedly throughout our lives." For instance, "most Americans violate drug laws in their lifetime," she observes, and "[y]et there are people in the United States serving life sentences for first-time drug offenses," she laments—lost generations of Blacks "rounded up for crimes that go ignored on the other side of town." [12]

The rhetorical force of this language rests entirely on the factual assumption that we are talking about low-level, nonviolent offenses, for from the standpoint of prevailing values and moral norms it sounds preposterous to say *all of us are violent criminals* or *all of us violate laws against robbery, rape, homicide, and assault at some point in our lives.* And of course violent crimes are not ignored in privileged predominantly white communities, so it's hard to say that violent offenders in black neighborhoods are being rounded up for, say, murders that go ignored on the other side of town. If anything, far too few murders and other violent crimes in the black community are solved, prompting a community organization like Baltimore's Mothers of Murdered Sons and Daughters to sponsor billboards calling on the mayor to "STOP POT ARRESTS. SOLVE MURDERS INSTEAD." But this rhetoric invites a political distinction in criminal matters between an "us" of low-level, nonviolent, eminently excusable wrongdoers and a "them" of violent ones, the ones who "jeopardize the safety and security of others" and whose violence "we ought never excuse."[13] It invites a politics of compassion for ordinary human frailty, as long as that frailty does not express itself in violence. And most importantly, it promises that deep cuts in racialized mass incarceration can be accomplished on the cheap, without radically challenging our "comfortable" moral frameworks or political identities; all that it asks for is sympathy and leniency for low-level nonviolent offenders who deep down are morally indistinguishable from the rest of us.

This is why facts matter: different factual realities demand different moral lenses and different us-them politics. Factually, the liberal New Jim Crow narrative could hardly be more wrong and misguided, rendering its underlying moral compass and politics profoundly regressive and counterproductive for anyone seeking deep and lasting cuts in racialized mass incarceration. As Pfaff points out in *Locked In,* "only about 16% of state prisoners are serving time on drug charges—and very few of them, perhaps only around five or six percent of that group, are both low level and nonviolent." "At the same time," he continues, "more than half of all people in state prisons have been convicted of a violent crime." Because the vast majority (87%) of US inmates are held in state prisons, most people in US prisons simply are not there for low-level nonviolent drug offenses.[14] The problem with telling the public that racialized mass incarceration boils down to low-level, nonviolent drug offenders (perhaps who simply need to be diverted into non-carceral programs) is that this false factual account lulls lawmakers and concerned citizens into the comfortable but counterproductive fantasy that deep cuts in the prison population can be achieved by targeting a lot of relatively sympathetic prisoners. Nevertheless, this false narrative has become an ingrained article of faith for many progressives.

The New Jim Crow deserves great credit for helping many Americans—especially but not exclusively white liberals—begin to think about racialized mass incarceration as a civil rights crisis rather than simply a "law and order" problem resulting from the bad choices of bad people. When *The New Jim Crow* was published in 2010, the debate over issues like affirmative action in higher education was consuming much of the time, attention, and other resources of the civil rights community, and Alexander's book, more than any other, helped establish racialized mass incarceration as the main battlefront in US race relations, which is why the book became, in the words of one commentator, "the bible of a social movement"—truly a monumental achievement. But because of fatal flaws in its factual account, moral compass, and politics, the liberal New Jim Crow narrative now actually hurts more people locked in American prisons than it helps.

For instance, in a 2016 *Vox* poll, more than 2,000 registered voters overestimated how many people are in prison for nonviolent drug offenses. A total of 61% of respondents said that half of all prisoners in the US are incarcerated for drug offenses. In fact, most of the growth in state prison populations was driven by sentences for violent crimes like murder, assault, robbery, and rape.[15] Such misconceptions about the makeup of prison populations may lead voters and policymakers who want deep cuts in mass incarceration to think they can make a real difference simply by reducing prison time for nonviolent offenders: 78% of respondents said that "people who committed a nonviolent crime and have a low risk of committing another crime" should be let out of prison earlier, but only 29% (including only 42% of liberals) said they supported reducing prison time for "people who committed a violent crime and have a low risk of committing another crime." No majority of any race, religion, ideology, political party, or any other category evaluated by pollsters supported reducing prison sentences for violent criminals with "a low risk of committing another crime." Further, about 55% of voters said that one acceptable reason to reduce sentences for nonviolent drug offenders is "to keep room for violent offenders in prisons." In other words, many viewed making cuts in the incarceration of nonviolent drug offenders as desirable, in part, because such cuts make it possible for the state to *lock up more violent offenders*. The much-heralded bipartisan First Step Act of December 2018 (FSA) reinforced this logic by providing programming and early release measures targeting the "non, non, nons"—those convicted of nonviolent, nonserious, and nonsexual crimes. FSA critics worried that by sharply distinguishing nons from other criminals, the legislation might actually bolster the carceral state by improving the conditions of confinement for the few—and thus defusing criticisms of prison conditions—at the expense of the many.

By distinguishing and distancing nonviolent from violent criminals and focusing on low-level nonviolent drug offenders, the liberal New Jim Crow narrative promotes sentence reductions for that relatively small subdivision of the prison population while doing little to reduce numbers or improve the fate of the many more violent offenders left behind. Ironically, Alexander criticizes traditional proponents of respectability politics for failing to prioritize the needs of the most disadvantaged blacks and for aggressively pursuing policy reforms that would harm them, yet her own rhetoric fails to prioritize the needs of the most maligned and marginalized criminals, the violent ones. It affords inclusion and acceptance for a few but guarantees exclusion for most. Justice, leniency, and compassion for the majority of people behind bars cannot be purchased on the cheap—it will require deep and uncomfortable changes in our collective moral compass and us-them politics. Traditional respectability politics distinguished itself from *all* black lawbreakers, whereas the liberal New Jim Crow narrative's refined brand of respectability politics distances itself only from the violent ones. Under the old, crude respectability politics, *all* black criminals were "damaged goods" as representative victims around whom to rally in the name of racial injustice, but under the liberal New Jim Crow narrative's more refined version, only violent black criminals are "damaged goods," and the representative victims of racialized mass incarceration are the non-nonnons. In crude respectability politics, no blacks with criminal records are "seen as attractive plaintiffs for civil rights litigation or good 'poster boys' for media advocacy"[16]; in refined New Jim Crow respectability politics, none with violent criminal records are.

The New Jim Crow analogy must reckon with a wide moral gulf—a yawning moral chasm in politics and everyday morality—between the innocent victims of state-sanctioned segregation and the more blameworthy, violent victims of racialized mass incarceration. Through respectability-tinted moral lenses, victims of traditional Jim Crow were the morally innocent Negroes—exemplified by iconic leaders like Medgar Evers, Martin Luther King, Jr., and Rosa Parks—subjected to state-sanctioned social oppression for being black. Even if some of these civil rights era victims of social oppression ended up in mug shots or jail cells for protesting their subjugation, typically it was for civil disobedience in the name of morally praiseworthy resistance. By stark contrast, most blacks who are subjected to state-sanctioned racialized mass incarceration are not morally innocent. Most are violent or serious offenders who made criminal choices to commit crimes of moral turpitude, often preying on the most vulnerable members of their own already marginalized communities. The state blames and punishes such offenders on the basis of what they did, not *simply* for who they are, making them problematic as "attractive plaintiffs for civil rights litigation." Viewed through respectability-politics-tinted moral lenses, the Old Jim Crow oppressed morally innocent Negroes, making them true victims of racial oppression, while the so-called New Jim Crow oppresses mostly serious black wrongdoers, making them authors of their own plights, not true victims.

Nigga Theory says, let's see things clearly.

Good Negro lenses reinforce the common but regressive distinction between social oppression and self-destruction, that is, between the kind of racial injustice at the heart of the Old Jim Crow (innocent Blacks suffering racial oppression for which America clearly can be held collectively accountable) and the kind of racial injustice really at the heart of the New Jim Crow (culpable Blacks, disproportionately trapped in criminogenic social conditions, who consequently disproportionately make bad choices). These bad choices might be seen to *break the causal chain* between racial oppression in America and racialized mass incarceration, thus absolving America of accountability for the foreseeable and violent criminal consequences of its unjust basic structure. Through such distorting lenses, there is no moral equivalence between social oppression and self-destruction—that is, between Medgar, Martin, Rosa and a murderer or an armed robber serving a life sentence. Nigga Theory begs to differ.

Death penalty cases provide another illustration of how the lenses of Nigga Theory differ from approaches to blame and punishment that seek to garner greater support and leniency for wrongdoers solely by focusing attention on those who are more appealing when looked at through conventional moral lenses. The great rhetorical force of DNA exonerations—the possibility of executing the innocent—has played a big role in the decline in public support for the death penalty over the last 20 years. For instance, Republican Governor George Ryan of Illinois, once a supporter of capital punishment, declared a moratorium on executions in the state, then granted clemency to all 171 inmates on death row, after 13 Illinois inmates who had been convicted and condemned to death were exonerated, some just hours before their scheduled lethal injections. "Until I can be sure that everyone sentenced to death in Illinois is truly guilty," said Ryan, "no man or woman [facing execution] will meet that fate."

But Nigga Theory rests on the premise that the greatest driver of mass incarceration and threat to racial justice in criminal matters is not false convictions of factually innocent people or excessive sentences for low-level nonviolent offenders, but rather the disproportionate blame and punishment of guilty black people who have committed serious or violent offenses. Just as deep cuts in racialized mass incarceration cannot come simply from diversion programs for low-level nonviolent drug offenders, deep racial injustices in capital punishment cannot be remedied simply through the protection of innocent people from wrongful convictions and executions. In fact, just as focusing decarceration efforts on low-level nonviolent drug offenders perversely deepens the plight of most American prisoners, focusing anti-death penalty efforts on avoiding the execution of innocent people can deepen the plight of most death row inmates because the factual guilt of most may not be in any real doubt. My dad was given a life sentence despite his factual innocence, but he'd be the first to tell you that the factually guilty far outnumber the factually innocent behind bars. Certainly Stanley "Tookie" Williams, whose execution by the state of California I fought and then wrote a play about—called *Race, Rap, and Redemption*— was factually guilty of committing multiple premeditated murders. Innocent black people disproportionately condemned to death can be readily recognized as victims of social oppression, whereas guilty wrongdoers are routinely viewed as authors of their own demise, echoing the "social oppression of innocent Negroes" vs. "self-destruction of guilty niggas" dichotomy embraced by proponents of respectability politics and refuted throughout this book.

By keeping attention trained on serious, violent, and guilty wrongdoers, Nigga Theory makes clear its rejection of even an error-free death penalty. Even if we achieve practical certainty about a person's factual guilt, and thus save all the falsely accused innocent lives that can be saved by wringing that kind of error out of the criminal justice system, the determination that a factually guilty person is deathworthy is profoundly and directly a moral judgment about their subjective culpability and just deserts, and this moral judgment can be just as rife with error, bias, and arbitrariness as factual, killer-identification "whodunit" judgments. The excessive blame and punishment of guilty black offenders, especially the violent and serious ones who most inflame the urge for retaliation and revenge, is a much more pervasive and pernicious problem, running throughout every phase of the criminal justice system, than the problem of wrongful convictions or executions of innocent blacks (which is not meant, at all, to minimize the grave seriousness of the latter).

In order to break out of the trap of mass incarceration, we, as a society, need to rethink the basic processes of our criminal justice system through the moral and legal lenses of Nigga Theory, lenses that expose a system corrupted by racism of an absolutely mundane, everyday kind, and corrupted at every level:

At the level of arrest.
At the level of charging.
At the level of factfinding.
At the level of trial.
At the level of sentencing.

It is the project of Nigga Theory to interrogate the system at every one of these levels in order to expose where racial bias lives in the criminal law and adjudication of just deserts.

◆

Harvard University law professor Randall Kennedy, in *Race, Crime, and the Law*, urged morally innocent and law-abiding "good Negroes" to distinguish and distance themselves from morally culpable and criminal "bad Negroes"—a classic instance of the politics of respectability. This same wicked-worthy moral dichotomy runs through popular culture, figuring centrally in a famous standup routine by iconic black comedian Chris Rock (*Bring the Pain*, 1996), in which he paces the stage and declares that "it's like there's a civil war going on in black America" between respectable, law-abiding, lovable "black people" and disreputable, criminal, blameworthy "niggas." He liberally sprinkles his long and sneering rant against morally condemnable black wrongdoers with the trenchant punchline: "I love Black People, but I hate niggas." As James Boyd White points out, jokes, like all texts, are invitations to share the speaker's response to the world, an invitation which we accept through our laughter,[17] and implicit in Rock's joke is a *political* invitation to sharply distinguish between a law-abiding and morally upright "us" and a criminally blameworthy "them." It's an invitation to niggerize black wrongdoers, which black audiences in packed auditoriums merrily accepted through peals of laughter and a chorus of "amens," "uh-huhs," and "preach!" No utterance in the English language more forcefully distinguishes and distances a respectable "us" from a contemptible "them" than the N-word, no word drives a deeper moral and political wedge between the worthy and the wicked, no epithet more utterly *otherizes* its referent.

Nigga Theory instead appropriates the N-word's unparaphrasable power, the power it has to morally condemn and otherize criminals, especially violent black ones, and instead uses it as a term of art in a radically progressive theory of blame and punishment, a theory crafted to shake the foundations of all our conventional condemnations of criminals, including the most violent and forsaken black ones. I could adopt professor Kennedy's more genteel language and call this brand of Critical Race Theory "Bad Negro Theory," but "Bad Negro" doesn't otherize wrongdoers as forcefully or condemn them as contemptuously as the N-word. In the hands of black speakers and writers, the N-word can be a jagged-edged assault weapon that draws blood or a healing scalpel that sutures the places where blood flows. I reclaim this reclaimed word by both denying any substantive moral basis for using it to divide the worthy from the wicked and, at the same time, embracing its healing, bonding, unifying force.

This book also uses the racially charged N-word to keep race itself front and center in the discussion of mass incarceration, and to pointedly reject the canard pushed by leftists, liberals, and conservatives that class trumps race in our criminal justice system. Yet more proof that race takes priority came across my timeline as I was writing this Introduction: a viral video, in which a phalanx of cops physically assaults a black student at Columbia University because he looked like he did not belong in those hallowed halls of ivy. I've had many similar experiences.

What do they call a black man getting a Columbia degree?
A nigga.
What do they call one who has already earned said degree?
A nigga.
What do they call one like me who's a chaired law professor with degrees
from Harvard and Berkeley?
A nigga.

Word to black America—you might earn fancy degrees and make big cash, but you cannot cash in your face, for the face of crime in the eyes of law enforcement and civilians alike is black. As Jay-Z puts it in "The Story of O.J.":

> Light nigga, dark nigga, faux nigga, real nigga
> Rich nigga, poor nigga, house nigga, field nigga
> Still nigga, still nigga

To signal its sharp departure in style and substance from conventional morality and respectability politics, as well as to keep the independent importance of race at all times front and center, the central argument of this book, Nigga Theory, adopts a profane, transgressive, disruptive, and disreputable N-word-laden rhetoric steeped in irony, inversion, and oppositional black art of the kind crafted by politically conscious N-word virtuosos like Pac, Nas, Cube, and Hov.

I understand readers who nevertheless inwardly recoil at every utterance of the ugly epithet. I respect the N-word abolitionists who have protested some of my N-word-laden performances, exhibits, and speeches because, in their view, the word's racist roots make it inherently hateful and hence make some of my celebrations of its "virtues" misguided hate speech. I once shared that view myself. Like many others, I viewed the N-word as a variety of what the Supreme Court of the United States (SCOTUS) calls "fighting words," words that "by their very utterance inflict injury or tend to incite an immediate breach of the peace."[18] I quoted that language to Santa Monica police officers in my explanation of why a white male store clerk's application of the N-word to me during a verbal exchange provoked a reflexive backhand. I avoided charges and a mug shot, but it was not my proudest moment. And still, despite my longstanding visceral distaste for the violent insult, I have become convinced—by many radically progressive black writers, performing artists, poets, philosophers, and commentators—of the unique rhetorical efficacy of the N-word. When black folk use it with care and precision to disrupt and displace dehumanizing discourses *about* them, they ultimately enact their own transgressive, transformational word work.

◆

Nigga Theory refuses to reduce race to class (*Rich nigga, poor nigga ... still nigga*), while some progressive narratives carelessly conflate the two. "All of

Us or None" is a terrific grassroots organization of formerly incarcerated men and women whose name is the perfect slogan for a politics that centers incarcerated violent black offenders and refuses to leave them behind; but for Michelle Alexander, its importance lies in its ability to encourage political solidarity between blacks and poor and working-class whites.[19] For many on the left, the election of Donald Trump was a confirmation of the standard liberal account of why poor and working-class whites support racially illiberal politicians and policies. Economically distressed working-class white people, anxious about trade and lost manufacturing jobs and the decline in their overall economic level, especially after the 2008 Great Recession, felt financially "left behind" and so sought solace in the catharsis provided by hating and hurting Blacks, Latinos, Muslims, foreigners, in a word, *others*, and thus cast ballots for Trump to shore up their social status and threatened sense of social superiority, to give themselves a form of cultural and psychological compensation, a psychic benefit, that W.E.B. Du Bois calls the "public and psychological wage" of whiteness—an anodyne for their economic pain and suffering and anxiety.

Alexander agrees; she claims that conservatives garnered the votes they needed to create racialized mass incarceration by "appealing to the racism and vulnerability of lower class whites, a group of people who are understandably eager to ensure that they never find themselves trapped at the bottom of the American totem pole."[20] Thanks to the special susceptibility of poor and working-class whites to racist demagoguery, according to Alexander "a new system of racialized social control [namely, the New Jim Crow] was created by exploiting the vulnerabilities and racial resentments of poor and working-class whites."[21] In his polemic about the dangers of "identity politics," Mark Lilla makes a similar point:

> Marxists are much more on-point here...people who might be on the edge are drawn to racist rhetoric and anti-immigrant rhetoric because they've been economically disenfranchised, and so they look for a scapegoat, and so the real problems are economic.[22]

Even conservatives got in on the-bashing-the-white-working-class act, in Kevin D. Williamson's *National Review* article about the allegedly strong support for Trump among working-class whites. He states, "The white American underclass is in thrall to a vicious, selfish culture whose main products are misery and used heroin needles. Donald Trump's speeches make them feel good. So does OxyContin." The conservative commentator continues: "the truth about these dysfunctional downscale communities, is that they deserve to die."[23] Marxists, liberals, and conservatives found common ground after Trump's election in stereotyping and scapegoating working-class whites as broke and bitter and therefore especially prone to rabid irrationality.

This claim is deeply classist claptrap. It impugns the character of honest hardworking white people struggling to scratch out a living in America's casino economy and implies that economic suffering somehow robs white people of moral agency, clouds their conscience, makes them especially susceptible to ethno-nationalist demagoguery, and impels them to make racially illiberal choices. Of course many white working-class people voted for Trump, but even more middle-class whites did. The insecurity they felt was not primarily economic. The 2016 election of Donald Trump provides a rare opportunity to test and debunk the class-anxiety canard. On the campaign trail, Mr. Trump went beyond racially charged dog whistles and code words and unapologetically wore his racism on his sleeve, rising to political prominence by pushing "birtherism," a conspiracy theory that the country's first black president was not an American citizen.[24] He declared in his Presidential Announcement Speech that undocumented immigrants from Mexico were "bringing drugs. They're bringing crime. They're rapists. And some, I assume, are good people." During his campaign, he tweeted an image of a masked, dark-skinned man with a handgun alongside a set of points about deaths in 2015, including the wildly false and inflammatory claim that 81% of whites are killed by blacks (in reality roughly 82% of white murder victims are killed by whites each year). He vowed to ban Muslims from entering the United States while signaling potential support for a Muslim registry (raising the specter of Manzanar-style internment camps). He asserted that a Latino US District Judge, Gonzalo Curiel, presiding over civil fraud lawsuits against Trump University, could not be impartial because he was "of Mexican heritage." Amid protests over fatal police shootings of unarmed black people, he railed against a "war on police" and promised to institute a national "stop and frisk" policy that had already been struck down as unconstitutionally discriminatory in his own New York.[25]

Poor and working-class whites, the ones suffering the greatest economic distress in the four years leading up to Trump's election, were not more susceptible to his brand of white identity politics than better-off whites, and indeed, it was well-off whites who were more likely to support Trump. Research shows that even whites who voted for Obama in 2012 and switched to Trump in 2016 were motivated to do so by racism, not economic anxiety, and that racism can make people anxious about the economy rather than the other way around. White identity politics carried Trump to the White House, not economic anxiety. Simply put, race trumped class in 2016. White nationalism trounced economic equity. Racism was a much more powerful force in the election of Donald Trump than white working-class economic disenfranchisement.

Facts matter in the fight against racial oppression in America, including facts about voter motivations. Those who see economic and financial insecurity as the root cause of Trumpism and other kinds of racially illiberal demagoguery will seek to curb racism through policies that strengthen the social safety net. But universal basic income, "Medicare for all," or other redistributionist economic policies, although they deserve our support because they're morally right and economically feasible, will not win over Trump voters—these voters are more fearful of losing their dominant status as white people within a demographically diverse and ever-evolving nation than they are about economic issues. In fact, the studies show that Trump's supporters—again, most of whom were not poor or working-class—largely oppose policies that would reduce the economic distress of poor and working-class whites because, thanks to a decades-long campaign to destroy support for the safety net by racializing government programs with tendentious tropes of Cadillac-driving black welfare queens and the like, they view such policies as handouts for Blacks and other people of color. Deep-seated psychological resentment and racial anxiety rooted in a sense of group status threat are uniquely, independently, and irreducibly racial problems that demand racial solutions.

All too often, liberals pay lip service to the role of group status in the formation of political preferences, and yet they consistently lowball just how psychologically valuable it is to see one's self as part of the dominant social group—they too often grossly underestimate the value of what Du Bois identified as the psychic boon of whiteness. They believe that people's economic self-interest must logically take priority over other concerns. Alexander, for instance, argues that poor and working-class whites were persuaded by elites and capitalists to prioritize their racial status interests over their common economic interests with Blacks, "resulting in the emergence of new caste systems *that only marginally benefit whites* but were devastating for African Americans."[26] (Emphasis added.) But the data will show that the symbolic, psychic boon of whiteness—whites' sense of dominance over America's social and political priorities—is not some sop that "only marginally benefits whites." As University of Pennsylvania political scientist Diana C. Mutz points out, "what we know about American voters is that symbolic appeals matter a great deal."[27] Psychologically and emotionally, seeing one's self as part of a dominant group can feel real good.

There is nothing "illogical" about people finding symbolic considerations more urgent and compelling than material ones. It is not "illogical" to weigh substantial psychic satisfactions against significant economic frustrations and conclude that the former outweigh the latter. Taking pride in one's social identity, reveling in belonging to a certain social group—even an historically subjugated one—can bring as much psychic satisfaction to members of that social entity as great material compensation. As Maya Angelou puts it in "Still I Rise," despite being trod in the dirt, "I walk like I've got oil wells/ Pumping in my living room." It's dangerous for a racially oppressed people in America to ever underestimate the psychic boon for white people of belonging to a racial group that has enjoyed social dominance in this nation since its inception, a feeling for many that is emotionally equivalent to (Angelou again) having gold mines "diggin' in [their] own backyard." To grasp the nuances of this nation's primordial divide over race, we must never downplay its irreducible centrality and independent potency.

Of course, both race and class matter, and both are central to a radically progressive racial justice agenda, for civil rights without economic redistribution will leave far too many truly disadvantaged folks behind. But it's a grave mistake to view class-based policies as likely to reduce the racial resentments or status anxieties of white voters. Elected officials who embrace the misguided "economic anxiety" narrative in hopes of reducing the appeal of racist demagoguery may pursue policies that will do little to assuage the racial anxieties of whites who cast their 2016 ballot out of deep-seated fear that they were slowly losing their social standing in America and that Trump was the best candidate to reinforce this nation's racist hierarchy. When these voters hear about racialized mass incarceration or rampant police misconduct or "inclusion, diversity, and equity" in schools and workplaces, they're listening with ears attuned to demographic trends, cultural shifts, and anxiety about their own future. Unlike economic threats, status threats—anxieties about power, identity, and group superiority—strike at the heart of who and what one is, and what it means to identify as a white man, woman, boy, or girl in America. It may prove hard to economically "bribe" fearful whites to accept a somewhat higher standard of living in exchange for what many view as existential annihilation or, in the pungent phrasing of some ethno-nationalist scaremongers, "white genocide."

The economic anxiety explanation for Trumpism and white identity politics belongs to the category of what Paul Krugman calls zombie ideas—arguments that have been proven wrong, should be dead, but nonetheless "shamble relentlessly forward" because they serve a political purpose.[28] For some, the economic anxiety narrative serves to promote a redistributionist economic policy. For others, the economic distress excuse props up the legitimacy and moral authority of American democracy. So pundits and politicians persist in trotting out the brain-eating economic anxiety theory despite the slew of zombie-slaying studies that offer plain conclusions: helping white voters feel less economic vulnerability does not automatically make them less prone to support racist policies and politicians.

◆

The liberal New Jim Crow narrative also robs black folk of agency, treating racialized mass incarceration as an affliction foisted upon the black community by external actors rather than as what it actually is: a bottom-up phenomenon driven by moral condemnations of black wrongdoers by both nonblack and black citizens and elected officials. Think back to the height of hysteria about the crack plague and street crime, during the period when Blacks were being warehoused in prison blocks and jail cells at precipitously rising rates. Most members of the Congressional Black Caucus, responding to their constituents, voted in favor of the 1986 Anti-Drug Abuse Act, which fueled the War on Drugs by establishing for the first time mandatory minimum sentences for specified quantities of cocaine as well as a 100-to-1 sentencing disparity between crack (more associated with black users) and powder (more associated with white users) cocaine. Seven years later, a 1993 Gallup Poll found 82% of the Blacks surveyed believed that the courts in their area did not treat criminals harshly enough; 75% favored putting more police on the streets to reduce crime; and 68% supported building more prisons so that longer sentences could be given.[29] Widespread support for "get tough" crime policies among black citizens and politicians as prison populations exploded undermines the liberal New Jim Crow narrative's core claim. Black folk, despite bearing the brunt of mass incarceration, fueled our own hyper-incarceration by looking at criminal justice matters through conventional moral lenses tinted with our own respectability politics.

As Alexander notes, "violent crime tends to provoke the most visceral and punitive response" in concerned black citizens, who supported more prisons and longer sentences through these years.[30] This cannot be argued away, as Alexander tries to, by distinguishing between "support for" and "complicity with" racialized mass incarceration,[31] a distinction that dissolves under mild interrogation. Nigga Theory assumes that "law and order" black folk engage in meaningful moral reflection and make nuanced moral judgments, and are capable of critical self-reflection and self-revision, and thus open to persuasion, as people ready to think through what approaches to blame and punishment best serve the black community's interest in equal justice for all. Widespread moral condemnations of black criminals—especially violent ones like Willie Horton, the dark-skinned convicted murderer featured in an infamous 1988 presidential campaign ad who escaped while on work furlough and then raped a white Maryland woman and bound and stabbed her boyfriend—percolated into the policies and practices of nonblack and black "tough on crime" DAs, police chiefs, politicians, and other "official" drivers of racialized mass incarceration. As I've been saying in print and in person for over 20 years, prevailing values and moral norms about blame and punishment, especially the blame and punishment of violent or serious black offenders, were—and are—the taproot of racialized mass incarceration. Black folk, despite bearing the brunt of such incarceration, unwittingly became accomplices of the carceral state and complicit in our own hyper-incarceration by adopting the same regressive moral framework in criminal matters. In addressing the future, any theory needs to address black as well as white attitudes and understandings.

◆

To help humanize violent black offenders and keep them centered throughout our discussion, this book draws on one of America's most powerful, provocative, transgressive, and disreputable N-word-laden forms of political communication and art: Gangsta Rap, a particular bête noire of proponents of respectability politics, who heap scorn on the genre for the violence, misogyny, homophobia, and materialism commonly associated with it (Alexander, for instance, refers to gangsta rappers as "black minstrels"[32]). That there are mindless mercenaries, misogynists, and homophobes in gangsta rap cannot be denied (stand up Rick Ross et al.). But what also cannot be denied by anyone who actually listens to the music is the way some of its most popular and accomplished performers—Pac, Nas, Hov, and Ice Cube—spit lyrics laced with political commentary and invitations to sympathetically identify with black criminals, including violent black hustlers and gangbangers. Rather than passively accept being reduced to objects of derision and butts of jokes, these transgressive griots grabbed mics and dropped multiplatinum albums that penetrated pop culture with their own violent-black-offender narrative, the "narrative of a Nigga," if you will, complete with that narrative's own moral and political lenses. In style (lyrics liberally sprinkled with the disreputable N-word and other profane utterances), these songs rejected respectability politics; in substance, these performers rejected the "lovable Black People"/"condemnable Nigga" moral dichotomy. It's wrong to tar reflective and critical gansta rappers with the same brush as shallow and rudderless hacks.

In 2007, at USC's Bovard Auditorium before over 1,000 students, faculty, and alumni, Joanne Morris produced a play I wrote called *Race, Rap, and Redemption*, which was designed to explore issues of racial and social justice, oppression, unity, theology, and redemption through rap and hip-hop music, dance, song, and poetry. I will discuss this example of what Clifford Geertz calls "metaphysical theater" in some detail below, but for now will just mention that it deployed gansta rap in support of an iconic violent black criminal—a death row inmate named Stanley "Tookie" Williams, a convicted murderer and one of the people who helped flood the streets of our own South Central neighborhoods with crack and violence, a co-founder of the notorious street gang called the Crips. Because USC is located in South Central Los Angeles, crime is of more than academic interest to our scholarly community—on a first-hand basis, we pay the price of proximity to poor and crime-ridden neighborhoods and must continuously strike a balance between fear and compassion. Just before the event, Mr. Williams had been executed by the state of California. Governor Arnold Schwarzenegger had denied his 11th-hour petition for a reprieve. Incorporated into our reflections on whether we should "pour liquor for Tookie," (that is, express solidarity with him in the form of a libations ritual) were live performances of gangsta rap and gangsta rap-inspired song, dance, drama, cinema, sermon, and spoken word. As the video of the event shows,[33] on that night most of the Trojan community in attendance accepted the invitation to bond with even the "wickedest" black criminal by rising to their feet in empathy for and solidarity with other Tookies still sitting on death row.

Transgressive words and symbols and performances can change hearts and minds, but they can also cost those who take part in them their personal freedom or professional ambitions when, in the eyes of authorities or higher ups, edgy utterances cross from the cutting edge to the bleeding edge. For instance, my play included live performances by Ice Cube, whom police have repeatedly arrested for going on stage and uttering these provocative but unmistakably political lyrics:

> Fuck tha police, coming straight from the underground
> A young nigga got it bad 'cause I'm brown
> And not the other color, so police think
> They have the authority to kill a minority

Cube also performed that anthem—N-word-laden, profanely oppositional—in my Bovard production, triggering severe negative consequences for the interim law school dean, whose programming support made Cube's defiant performance possible. That dean suffered the wrath of our then-president and then-provost for aiding and abetting such an inflammatory performance in what they called "the tinderbox ready to ignite that is South Central L.A."[34] Nigga Theory traffics in transgressive utterances precisely because it is a way to examine the relationship between freedom of expression, academic freedom, transgressive art, unsayable words, words that wound, hate speech, racial justice, and social change. Nigga Theory necessarily stands against hate speech codes and against finding secret satisfaction in seeing someone "punch a Nazi" on viral videos, not because I have any particular sympathy for racists or Nazis, but because down that road lies destruction for black dissidents and dissenters whose oppositional words and symbols offend people with privilege and power.

◆

Racialized mass incarceration has been a river fed by many streams, but by far its biggest tributaries have been the moral, legal, and political lenses through which ordinary people both inside and outside the black community look at black criminals, especially serious or violent ones. Accordingly,

Nigga Theory weaves together critical reflections on morality, law, and language in the form of political communication.

It's the absence of doubt—the moral certainty that one is righteously doing the right thing—that deliberately kills people, by strapping on a bomb and walking into a crowd of tourists, for instance, or by strapping down a man in a chair and injecting, gassing, shocking, or shooting him to death. Nigga Theory argues for less certainty and for more epistemic humility in our moral discourse, and criminal condemnations of black wrongdoers on five different, interlocking levels.

First, drawing on Tommie Shelby's *Dark Ghettos: Injustice, Dissent, and Reform* and its Rawlsian critique of America's unjust basic social structure[35] (John Rawls insisted on reciprocity in his theory of justice), Nigga Theory asks whether or not denizens of dark ghettos *owe* a duty to obey the laws of an intolerably unjust social system. Those who justify punishing desperately poor black criminals on "paying a debt to society" grounds assume a social system in which the burdens and benefits of social cooperation are fairly (or at least not intolerably unfairly) distributed, and that laws benefit everyone. So, as a kind of debt for the benefits gained, everybody *owes* obedience to those laws; someone who breaks the law owes something to those who do not, because he has acquired an unfair advantage. Punishing him takes from him what he owes, exacts that debt, and thereby restores the equilibrium of benefits and burdens. Nigga Theory debunks this "Gentlemen's Club" picture of the relation between black folk and society, exposing the emptiness of the claim that the state—as The People's representative in criminal prosecutions—is morally justified in punishing truly disadvantaged black criminals to make them pay their "debt" to society.

Second, even if, under a Rawlsian analysis, the state retains the moral right to punish morally condemnable (albeit unjustly oppressed) black offenders, anti-black bias—buried, or not, in the cognitive unconscious of ordinary judges and jurors—undermines the reliability, impartiality, and fairness of such moral condemnations.

Third, the moral condemnations of any wrongdoer of any race cannot be trusted at a philosophical level because the phenomenon of moral luck—the radically counterintuitive findings of moral philosophers like Thomas Nagel and Bernard Williams that *all* praise, blame, and moral responsibility hinge on fortuity—undermines the rationality and legitimacy of all moral condemnation.[36] The "self" is a tissue of contingencies and one's moral status a crapshoot, and this provides a fresh framework and vocabulary for thinking about ancient questions of free will and blameworthiness.

Fourth, Nigga Theory considers the moral responsibility of the United States itself (again, *We the People*) for the criminal behavior of many violent black wrongdoers. It identifies two grounds for such responsibility: the general criminogenic social conditions (like extreme social disadvantage that the state fosters or lets fester), and federal and state policies that helped jumpstart the crack plague of the 1980s and 1990s. Federal and state governments bear major responsibility for crime caused by chronic unemployment, grinding poverty, crumbling schools, inadequate health care, food and shelter insecurity, hunger and homelessness, and the foreseeable carceral consequences. A violent offender's bad choice or criminal intent does not break the causal chain between racial oppression and criminal wrongdoing in black communities—it is a foreseeable link in that causal chain for which those who maintain our unjust social order bear responsibility.

Fifth, according to conventional legal theory, violent black offenders—black murderers, for instance—are merely "found" or discovered during the "fact-finding" process of a criminal trial by jurors acting as fact "finders." In reality, black murderers are not "found" like discoverable facts of nature, they are socially constructed, manufactured, minted, if you will, in DA offices, on benches, and in jury boxes by prosecutors, judges, and jurors. To expose where bias lives in the substantive criminal law and its processes, and how judges and juries socially construct black murderers, Nigga Theory refutes and remodels criminal law's prevailing paradigm of *mens rea* (criminal intent), the law's ancient and foundational requirement of moral blameworthiness. Under the *mens rea* requirement, a killing without malice is manslaughter rather than murder; a criminal killing with malice is murder. But in most criminal trials, a decision needs to be made by the jury about the existence of malice. Because ordinary people unconsciously and routinely make biased moral judgments of black wrongdoers, as studies have shown, they more readily find that a violent black offender acted with murderous *mens rea* than a similarly situated violent white one. Nigga Theory will cast serious doubt on the reliability, objectivity, and trustworthiness of criminal conviction as a test of the most morally blameworthy Blacks.

◆

And Nigga Theory is not just interested in the criminal courtroom. Whenever the moral turpitude of black wrongdoers becomes the topic of the moment on talk radio, in coffee shops, and around water coolers, another potential site for the biased social construction of wicked black criminals becomes active. As neurological studies have recently helped establish, the dominant brand of anti-black discrimination in post-civil rights era America is not active racial animus but unconscious racial bias. This analysis will show why epistemic humility should temper our contempt toward serious black wrongdoers inside and outside the courtroom.

Such humility can bring with it a new approach to justice. Instead of corrupt processes of assessing blame, we can have a complex, balanced understanding of causality. Instead of putting people to death we should be putting them right. Instead of seeking retaliation and retribution, we should set out to reform and restore. Instead of wreaking revenge, we should find ways to generate redemption.

◆

A Royal typewriter and the Queen's English. I personally witnessed their power to kick open the locked door of a black man's prison cell. Creative word work and symbolic communication—including transgressive, disreputable, and uncomfortable words and symbols—have the power to produce social change and promote racial justice. When Colin Kaepernick took a knee during the national anthem to protest lethal police misconduct against black people, his nonlinguistic form of symbolic communication was a political act with social and political consequences. In the last presidential election, the word "deplorable" became a fiercely contested form of political communication. A core question of Nigga Theory—because it is, finally, a theory of justice—is whether radically progressive black artists and writers can, *by fiercely contesting its meaning*, bend the N-word into an instrument of political communication that can promote solidarity with black criminals, including violent ones. A new radically progressive moral and political framework calls for a radically new rhetoric, one that in style rejects respectability politics and in substance rejects its moral dichotomies. Can the N-word figure in such a rhetoric? Moreover, in matters of transgressive words and symbols more generally, how can we tell the difference between the cutting and the bleeding edge?

Immediately after Ice Cube had performed "Fuck tha Police" and other classics in *Race, Rap, and Redemption*, the ill-fated Dean of our law school read him the following USC Law School resolution on stage in front of a packed auditorium of students and faculty. It recognizes Cube—and through him other politically relevant "gangsta" rappers—as a wordsmith and scholar. As I wrote the resolution, I knew the genre that Cube pioneered did not need the imprimatur of a major research university to vindicate its value as an effective form of oppositional political communication. Still, it felt good to see it get such recognition just the same.

Be It Resolved:
A Resolution under the seal of the USC Gould School of Law.

Whereas Ice Cube, a rap pioneer and virtuoso lyricist, has led a musical revolution with brutal, profound, and politically charged music,

Whereas Ice Cube's searing music rails against injustice and takes to task an oppressive social order that traps Blacks and other minorities in ghettos, robs them of opportunities for escape, and then makes them scapegoats for the System's own failures,

Whereas Ice Cube's latest masterpiece, Laugh Now, Cry Later, simmers with celebration, humor, irony, rage, reflection, and deep insights that are the hallmarks of timeless music and first-rate critical scholarship,

Now therefore be it resolved that the USC Law School hereby joins with Dean Ed McCaffery, Professor Jody Armour, and Professor Ron Garet in honoring Ice Cube on the occasion of his participation in Race, Rap, and Redemption at USC and recognizing his musical genius and his tireless commitment to racial justice.

Nigga Theory is words, it is word work, it is performance, it is an accounting, it is a recognition, it is a prayer, it is a demand for justice.

CHAPTER **ONE**

CONTINGENCY, IRONY, AND SOLIDARITY IN BLAME AND PUNISHMENT[37]

*T*he jagged-edged N-word's unparaphrasable power can focus attention on the strong but irrational and unreliable urge to morally condemn violent black criminals. And it can also invite law-abiding people to stand in political solidarity with such criminals.[38] It is a double-edged epithet that can serve to monsterize and push away a black wrongdoer as well as humanize and embrace him. When used as a metaphoric re-description, a "nigga" (with a lower-case "n") stands for black wickedness, a personification of black subjective culpability, and I will use it to probe the intersection of morality, race, class, and collective accountability in matters of blame and punishment. But when used as a unifying political performative, the word "Nigga" (with a capital "N") can be aimed at bringing together black criminals and non-criminals. It is here, as a unifying political performative, that its irony becomes most evident.

The common law uses, as a test for culpability and wickedness, the notion of a "depraved heart." Unprovoked, intentional killing is murder precisely because it evinces a depraved or extreme indifference to the value of human life.[39] But not all unintentional criminal killings are deemed manslaughter. In some cases, the jury is given the depraved heart metaphor and told to use it as the litmus test for a high level of subjective culpability—if a person, for instance, unintentionally administers a fatal dose of drugs, the jury is asked to decide if that person did so with a depraved indifference to the consequences, and therefore is guilty of murder rather than mere manslslaughter.[40] Over and over, juries find black wrongdoers to have depraved hearts at a much greater rate than white wrongdoers, and we know that they find this in simple photographs as well as from evidence at trial. This is how the justice system turns black people into "niggas"—by deciding, with extreme prejudice, that they have depraved or extremely indifferent black hearts. These moral condemnations have been conclusively shown to be illegitimate and error-ridden, lacking any sound basis. Our social construction of "niggas" in jury boxes and everyday life is riddled with such bias and irrationality, making "niggas" figments of our distorted mental processes and moral imaginations. Black criminality is *made* in court and *made* in America.

And what follows from this analysis is that a "nigga" is a personification of irony, always on the road to becoming a "Nigga." The word can be flipped, robbed of its power to coherently otherize or condemn a black wrongdoer, and used with sharp irony to call attention to the groundless injustice of morally condemning black offenders as niggas. And, moreover, in that same spirit, it can function as an urgent political call to bond with and support Niggas. We Niggas are made in America, too.

◆

I first professionally "dropped the N-bomb" at a Criminal Justice and Race Workshop for the Association of American Law Schools [AALS] during the 1999 Annual Meeting in New Orleans. In the company of sedate legal scholars, I performed an N-word-laden gangsta rap song by Ice Cube titled "The Nigga Ya Love to Hate," from his 1990 album *AmeriKKKa's Most Wanted*, spitting lines like "kicking shit called street knowledge—why more Niggas in the pen than in college?"[41] I told my audience that the baffling silences that our professional vocabulary could not fill compelled me to use this profane alternative, a way to iterate the voice of speechlessness underneath the rigor, precision, and eloquence of our scholarly marks and noises.

As criminal law professors, our primary professional vocabularies are those of *morality* and *law*—the two language games prosecutors and defense lawyers must master and deftly deploy—and thus I have thought a lot about the world of shared meanings these vocabularies create and the limits they impose. As the son of a black inmate and a close friend of many others, I would characterize my relationship with the language of blame and punishment inside and outside my law school classrooms over the past 20 years as *impossible*. I find the proud but calcified language of both the legal academy and conventional morality—"choice," "free will," "personal responsibility," "subjective culpability," "malice," "malignant heart," "moral agency," and *"mens rea"*—not adequate to my needs and purposes, to my sense of myself and my world, requiring me, as it plainly does, to view as wicked and irresponsible my closest friends, family, and the *up to* 90% of young black men in some inner-city neighborhoods who will end up in jail, on probation, or on parole at some point in their lives.[42] Any language whose words and logic lock up staggering numbers of truly disadvantaged Blacks on the grounds of their own moral deficiencies is a disabled and disabling device for grappling with meaning in moral and criminal matters, one that ignores or discounts savage inequalities in race and class, and that sweeps empirically demonstrable anti-black bias under the rug of jury verdicts and "findings of fact" about guilt and innocence. Prevailing legal and moral language blocks the access of "wicked" black wrongdoers to the empathy, sympathy, care, and concern of ordinary, law-abiding people. Such language actively stalls conscience in relation to wrongdoers' suffering, masking the pity and waste of mass incarceration and draconian punishment. Yet in my scholarly associations and in the legal journals I read, I see an entrenched moral and legal vocabulary content to admire its own paralysis, to accept with serenity its estrangement from the underprivileged and disadvantaged masses.

As James Boyd White points out, when words lose their meaning, a speaker must make a new language, remake an old one, or radically repurpose old words to serve new ends.[43] In my N-word-laden 1999 AALS performance of *AmeriKKKa's Most Wanted*, I radically reconstituted my cultural resources—my possibilities for making and maintaining meaning—in order to make them adequate to my needs. I repurposed "nigger" (and "nigga")—words Professor Kennedy rightly calls the "nuclear bomb[s] of racial epithets" in his 2002 book *Nigger: The Strange Career of a Troublesome Word*[44]—in its most condemnatory sense for critical and *conceptual* purposes, and in its most compassionate sense for unifying *political* purposes.

Conceptually, Nigga Theory uses the "morally deficient black man" sense of "nigga" to critique the categories, distinctions, and dichotomies of conventional morality and the substantive criminal law. A "nigga" is a personification of moral blameworthiness in the same sense that the "Reasonable

Man" is a legal concept that personifies moral innocence: a Reasonable Man makes "reasonable" mistakes and thus his shortcomings are exculpatory or mitigatory under many doctrines, including negligence, recklessness, self-defense, provocation, extreme emotional disturbance, and duress. Both a nigga and a Reasonable Man exemplify human characteristics, including human limitations and frailties—but in the case of a nigga, the deficiencies and limitations are generally viewed as not excusable, while in the case of the Reasonable Man, they (by definition) are excusable. In this sense nigga means precisely what black comedian Chris Rock meant in his laugh line, "I love black people, but I hate niggas!"—which as you recall struck a resonant chord with black audiences precisely because many did (and still do) view black wrongdoers as morally condemnable. Among its many effects, in its unironically pejorative sense, the word inflames that widely shared and deeply entrenched urge to retaliate and avenge, or, to dress it up in loftier language, to see blameworthy wrongdoers pay their debt to society. Legal philosopher Meir Dan-Cohen aptly dubs this urge to blame and punish wicked wrongdoers "the retributive urge."[45] Because millions of Americans of all races share that laughing black audience's contempt for black wrongdoers, so-called "niggas" inflame the retributive urge in millions of people of all races.

Under our substantive criminal law, an alleged wrongdoer can be "innocent" in one of two ways: by being innocent of causing the harm or by being morally innocent—that is, the wrongdoer can cause harm but do so without subjective culpability. Prosecutors, defense attorneys, judges, and jurors routinely debate and weigh the moral blameworthiness of wrongdoers because the substantive criminal law directs them to. As the Model Penal Code puts it, "crime does and should mean condemnation," but not everyone who commits a prohibited or criminal *act* is culpable. For instance, a driver can hit and kill a pedestrian, thus qualifying as a "wrongdoer" by committing the prohibited act of causing someone's death, but do so without subjective culpability if the victim darted from between parked cars and the driver's reactions, even if not perfect, were those of an ordinary or "reasonable person" in the same situation. Thus, if jurors conclude that a wrongdoer killed someone *without* the requisite subjective wickedness or "vicious will," they must return a verdict of not guilty. So the criminal law—through its *mens rea* requirement—routinely directs judges and jurors to distinguish between wicked and innocent wrongdoers and to differentiate degrees of wicked criminality for purposes of punishment. Under the law of homicide, for instance, a wrongdoer can suffer different punishments depending on whether he is found wicked in the First or Second Degree; voluntarily or involuntarily wicked; purposely, knowingly, recklessly, or negligently wicked; or wickedly depraved and indifferent. And thus, a jury could find a morally blameworthy black wrongdoer to be a nigga in the First or Second Degree; a Voluntary or Involuntary nigga; a purposeful, knowing, reckless, or negligent nigga; or a nigga with a depraved and malignant heart. In fact, most "official niggas"—blacks formally convicted of violent or serious crimes—have been found subjectively wicked in one of these ways beyond a reasonable doubt by a jury or other factfinder, and their criminal conviction provides assurance, backed by the full faith and credit of the US criminal justice system, that these violent and serious black wrongdoers deserve our most corrosive contempt and most extreme forms of retribution. Once I refute the moral and legal grounds for condemning black wrongdoers, any pejorative reference to them as "niggas" should ring hollow and shine an irony-laden light on the fact that some of our most self-righteous and contemptuous labels reinforce and perpetuate unwarranted moral evaluations of black wrongdoers.

Politically, Nigga Theory harnesses the ironic uses of the N-word to assert solidarity with black criminals whom the word seeks to vilify on misguided moral and legal grounds. A key insight of the law and literature movement is that the true center of value of a word, text, or performance of language—its most important meaning—is to be found not in any factual information that it conveys (not in what is *says*) but in what it *does*, specifically, in the community that it establishes with its audience. "It is here," says James Boyd White, "that the author offers his reader a place to stand, a place from which he can observe and judge the characters and events of the world."[46] Nigga Theory offers its reader a place to stand beyond the moral condemnations of black wrongdoers, a place from which it can be seen that a person's self is a tissue of contingencies whose moral record is determined by the union of fortuity and human frailty rather than solely through the workings of "free will." It is a place that prioritizes restoration, redemption, and rehabilitation over retribution, retaliation, and revenge. Hence, it is a place from which disproportionately poor black criminals can be understood not as wicked wrongdoers mired in self-destruction for which they alone are to blame, but as tragic social facts for which we as a class- and race-riven nation are accountable. A brush stroke in a new political landscape, the N-word's very meaning—its substantive content and range of application—is part of a fierce *political* contest over the meanings of "us" and "them," over the formation and transformation of individual and collective black identities.

Politically conscious black urban poets and N-word virtuosos—The Last Poets, Tupac Shakur, dead prez, Nas, Ice Cube, Jay-Z—vividly illustrate how the word can be used to embrace as well as push away, accept as well as reject, recognize as well as deny. In the hands of these poets, gangsta rap is an N-word-laden oppositional political discourse; it is language smitheryed—Toni Morrison's word[47]—to challenge conventional characterizations of black criminals, undermining those characterizations with ironies, inversions, and invitations to bond. Modeling solidarity, these oppositional black poets provide the inspiration for my metaphoric re-description of *mens rea* and moral blame. After all, as Richard Rorty observes in his philosophical essays on language through the lenses of Ludwig Wittgenstein, Donald Davidson, and Friedrich Nietzsche, viewing human history as the history of successive metaphors lets us "see the poet, in the generic sense of the maker of new words, the shaper of new languages, as the vanguard of the species," and the inspiration for revolutionary science, morality, and legal theory. The common insight animating the word work of these philosophers and "gangsta" poets—Nas and Nietzsche, Davidson and dead prez, Wittgenstein and Ice Cube, George Lakoff and The Last Poets—is that "truth" in matters of morality and justice is "a mobile army of metaphors," a ceaseless struggle over metaphorical re-description, a pitched political battle over the range of application of words and symbols.[48]

◆

As I have suggested, Nigga Theory refers to a group of interlocking proofs and performances aimed at destroying the moral and legal distinction between disproportionately privileged law-abiding blacks and disproportionately poor law-breaking ones, and, most importantly, promoting solidarity between them. To be sure, many of the proofs and performances underlying Nigga Theory have the potential to also promote solidarity among all law-abiders and all criminals regardless of race or class. However, black people bear the brunt of our blame and punishment practices, because they are disproportionately trapped in criminogenic conditions, because stereotypes and prejudice make black criminals especially likely to stoke the retributive urge in ordinary Americans, and because many misguided black leaders, lawmakers, scholars, and prosecutors have supported and still support the mass incarceration of black men and women.

Class plays a central role in the social construction of "niggas." As the careful studies of Ruth Peterson and Lauren Krivo on the links between race, place, class, and crime in the urban black community demonstrate, the vast majority of violent crimes Americans worry most about—murder, manslaughter, robbery, aggravated assault—are committed by "extremely disadvantaged" blacks, not the black bourgeoisie, whose crime rates are much closer to those of their white middle- and upper-middle-class counterparts.[49] In terms of violent crime, Bad Negroes are disproportionately truly disadvantaged blacks living in extremely disadvantaged neighborhoods. Good Negroes, by contrast, disproportionately come from the ranks of middle- and upper-middle-class blacks living in much better neighborhoods. The hills of View Park that I call home might be the Good Negro capital of America—it is brimming with well-to-do and hence relatively law-abiding Negroes. Known as the "Black Beverly Hills" and "Golden Ghetto," it is one of the wealthiest majority black areas in the United States.

For going on two generations now, the working-class and poor black neighborhoods that surround it—including South Central, The Jungle, Inglewood, Watts, and Compton—have hemorrhaged staggering numbers of young black men into prison yards and juvenile detention centers. The flow of poor Blacks from bleak streets to cell blocks turned torrential in the mid-1980s with the onset of the crack plague and enactment of laws like the Anti-Drug Abuse Act of 1986, which ushered in a new era of mandatory minimum sentences for possession of specified amounts of cocaine, as well as the infamous 100-to-1 sentencing disparity for powder and crack cocaine. Ironically or fittingly, depending on the interpretation of the observer, these laws were co-sponsored by Mickey Leland, chair of the Congressional Black Caucus, and Harlem congressman Charles Rangel, and they were supported by most members of the Congressional Black Caucus.[50] Truly disadvantaged black males took the brunt of these severe new sanctions. Thanks in part to the actions and attitudes of these and other middle-class black leaders toward poor black wrongdoers, nearly two generations of poor blacks have been severely hobbled.

Because of widespread class bigotry, many view the truly disadvantaged backgrounds of most Blacks who commit violent street crimes as further proof of their moral bankruptcy. In the eyes of millions of Americans, being broke, like being a criminal, means being morally deficient—millions blame poverty solely on blameworthy poor people, just as they blame wrongdoing solely on blameworthy criminals.

Over 50 years ago, Michael Harrington's extraordinarily influential book, *The Other America*, debunked the then-popular belief that America was a classless society by shining a light on the "invisible" poor, especially inner-city Blacks, Appalachian Whites, farm workers, and the elderly. But his explanation of poverty absolved middle-class America of accountability for the plight of the poor by attributing poverty not to macro level social factors like social inequality or the simple absence of jobs, but instead to the absence of proper values and dispositions in poor people themselves, that is, to their twisted proclivities and "culture of poverty." In Harrington's words, "there is ... a language of the poor, a psychology of the poor, a worldview of the poor. To be impoverished is to be an internal alien, to grow up in a culture that is radically different from the one that dominates the society."[51]

The celebrated Senator Daniel Patrick Moynihan advanced a similar view, attributing inner-city poverty to deficiencies in the structure of the "Negro family." Harvard urban government professor Edward C. Banfield—head of the Presidential Task Force on Model Cities under President Nixon and advisor to Presidents Ford and Reagan—put it this way, "the lower-class individual lives from moment to moment.... Impulse governs his behavior ... He is therefore radically improvident: whatever he cannot consume immediately he considers valueless.... [He] has a feeble, attenuated sense of self."[52] Such moral condemnation of the poor began long before the 20th century, of course—comparable judgments were made in the 18th and 19th centuries as well. But Moynihan, Banfield, and company helped turn classist stereotypes and bias into administrative fact.

In the Reagan years, the "culture of poverty" perspective ripened into plump orthodoxy; it became received wisdom that the cause of poverty was not macro-level social factors—like extreme social and economic inequality in the setting of a cultural belief system sociologists call the American Dream,[53] redlining, galloping unemployment caused by corrupt economic policy and the massive flow of jobs from dying rustbelt cities, crumbling schools, inadequate health care, or even the stampede of the black bourgeoisie from economically integrated black neighborhoods to economically segregated formerly white ones like my own in View Park—but rather the internal deficiencies of the poor, who, as Barbara Ehrenreich points out, were viewed as "dissolute, promiscuous, prone to addiction and crime, unable to 'defer gratification,' or possibly even set an alarm clock."[54] Bill Clinton famously formulated and implemented policies guided by "culture of poverty" thinking.[55] Indeed, much legislation enacted by both Democratic and Republican lawmakers today remains imbued with this perspective.

"Culture of poverty" thinking can subtly dovetail with stereotypes of black men as morally deficient, generating presumptions of their proneness to slack off, malinger, make excuses for personal deficiencies, and wait for handouts—presumptions that induce speakers to lecture predominantly black and predominantly white audiences differently. Often this meant reserving for black audiences admonitions about the importance of working hard, "breaking the cycle where a father is not at home," and, above all, taking personal responsibility for their lives, as in the case of President Obama's 2013 commencement speech at Martin Luther King, Jr.'s alma mater, Morehouse College. Morehouse is a selective, competitive, demanding all-male private liberal arts college in Atlanta that may be the nation's most famous historically black college or university; of course, in order to reach commencement day, most of these young black males had to demonstrate persistence, perseverance, seriousness of purpose, and a strong sense of individual responsibility. Accordingly, it is hard to imagine any large group of young black males in America less likely to be in need of reminders or chastisements about avoiding laziness and eschewing excuses going forward. Nevertheless, while acknowledging present-day racism and the "bitter legacies of slavery and segregation," the president admonished that, "as black men," "we" must accept "individual responsibility" for our lives and not blame racism for whatever obstacles we may face or failures we may suffer. More specifically, the president lectured these "Morehouse men"[56] that too many young black men make "bad choices."

"Growing up, I made quite a few myself," he said. "Sometimes I wrote off my own failings as just another example of the world trying to keep a black man down. I had a tendency to make excuses for me not doing the right thing."[57]

Because excuses reduce or negate personal responsibility for failures and bad choices, Obama—like many proponents of personal responsibility—flatly and categorically rejected them in his next sentence: "I understand there's a common fraternity creed here at Morehouse: 'Excuses are tools of the incompetent used to build bridges to nowhere and monuments of nothingness.'" The president then ended this passage with a punchy one-liner that could be a political slogan for, and mantra of, personal responsibility enthusiasts everywhere: "Well, we've got no time for excuses."

So from the standpoint of Nigga Theory, those who deny our collective accountability for the plight of both criminals and the poor—call them Deniers—are a multiracial, bipartisan group committed to the same logic of denial, a logic that discounts macro-level social explanations of crime and poverty. Deniers instead adopt (or give undue weight to) individual-level explanations centered on the "moral poverty" of the poor, and the "moral poverty" of criminals, and hence the hyper-concentrated "moral depravity" of poor black criminals, who are thus especially likely to stoke the retributive urge. Nigga Theory recognizes that poor black criminals belong to a special category of hyper-concentrated *otherness* that makes them easy to hate—a profound *otherness* that the words "nigger" and "nigga" capture with fierce felicity.

The retributive urge, even in the black community, to blame and punish black criminals, further stoked by the extreme otherization or niggerization of black criminals in popular stage acts, books, and op-eds by black entertainers, scholars, and commentators, makes it easier for many ordinary law-abiding Americans to agree with those who deny that racial oppression can cause serious wrongdoing. The instinctive retributive urge makes it harder for them to recognize the structural determinants of criminal choices. And hence they deny our collective accountability for the cataclysmic crack plague and its festering aftermath, a monumental, more than 30-year-long crime and incarceration disaster that has inflicted as much misery on the black community as a thousand Hurricane Katrinas slamming a thousand Ninth Wards. Our strong and deep urge to blame and punish black wrongdoers helps ordinary Americans deny our collective accountability for the foreseeable criminal acts of poor blacks stranded in forsaken neighborhoods brimming with guns and drugs. The inflamed retributive urge causes voters, jurors, judges, lawmakers, and others to ignore, deny, or downplay the role of macro-level social factors (for which we are collectively accountable) in both the production and construction of black criminals.

In sum, the better wrongdoers fit the "depraved nigga" stereotype the more they stir the retributive urge for blame and punishment. The more wrongdoers stir the retributive urge, the easier it is for Americans to deny a causal connection between the specific criminal acts of poor black wrongdoers and general macro-level social facts like racism and joblessness. And the easier it is to deny that macro-level social forces cause criminal wrongdoing, the easier it is to deny our collective accountability for the criminal consequences of being broke, black, and hopeless in post-civil rights America.

Nigga Theory rests on the hopeful and optimistic premise that once the moral basis for the retributive urge toward black criminals is shown to be illegitimate, irrational, and unreliable, it may become easier for fair-minded Americans to curb their punitive, retributive reflexes long enough to recognize the macro-level social factors that breed crime and poverty before passing judgment. If the urge to blame and punish "niggas" loses its footing in logic and fairness, then judges, jurors, and others will be able to see black wrongdoers not as radically "other" moral monsters to be damned, but rather as social facts to be deplored and, if necessary, incapacitated and, if possible, rehabilitated—never, as now, harshly punished in the name of retribution, retaliation, and revenge.

◆

We interrupt this hopefulness with a case in point and cautionary tale. Call it arresting irony or just improbable farce, but midday Black Friday, while laying out some of these lucubrations on "suspicious Negroes" on my laptop, I had an eerie nigga-alarm-laden visitation, complete with a portable steel cage and cocked assault weapons. I was ruminating in the rumpus room of our upper-middle-class hillside home in our economically gated all-black neighborhood when my dogs started barking, which at midday means The Mailman Cometh. Our dogs hate to hear the postman clang the door on our mailbox shut after stuffing it mostly with junk mail and come-on schemes—**M E G A B U C K S** *You Could Be Our Next Millionaire!*— that pander to the poverty surrounding this privileged enclave. (Buried in the small print are the impossibly long odds against winning: *505,000,000 to one.*) To spare the dogs that acoustic insult, as usual I walked over to the foyer, swung open the front door, and stepped outside to intercept the mail. But, by striding across our doorsill into a cloudless Southland afternoon, everything thrown into brilliant visibility by the impassive slant of our southwestern sun, I set off wailing sirens and scrolling nigga-alarms in the hearts and minds of a small cluster of Sheriff's deputies, provoking several to draw and train their handguns on my head and torso. "Freeze" and "Get your hands up" were their simultaneous but mutually contradictory commands—if you "freeze," of course, you cannot "get your hands up"—but as I was about to share this snarky observation with my gun-wielding interlocutors I noticed that the nearest one held his cocked firearm in a tremulous hand, a sign that he was in the throes of an instinctive and fuel-injected fight-or-flight reaction. It struck me that despite my gray beard, professorship, and two sons in college, I looked *otherwise* to them. By standing 6'5", weighing 200 pounds, and brazenly brandishing nappiness from crown to jowl, I was to these armed and alarmed officers a "big, black man" who "looked like a criminal." It turns out that here in the Good Negro capital of America, nappy performatives and celebrations of the African-American soul are worn at one's own peril.

With nigga alarms wailing, me and my impertinent performative were patted down and locked in the backseat of a police cruiser with the heavy-handed disrespect that is the common lot of "suspect niggas." As I peered through the police car partition cage, more deputies arrived, a sharpshooter posted up across the street, and a phalanx of officers swept through our home with drawn assault weapons. With implacable forces swirling around me, I inwardly moved toward the quiet "eye" of this sudden tempest, that unruffled region at a storm's center about which winds rage and rotate, but which itself remains calm. From this serene eye I gazed at the links between my own rolling "prisoner transport cage" and those wrapped in concrete and barbed wire called correctional institutions. In this stillness I heard echoes of long-ago captivities—plantations brimming with Blacks in bondage—commingling with current-day captivities of both black inmates and law-abiding Negroes who appear imminently dangerous to ordinary police officers equipped with guns and rolling cages.

I was eventually told that someone had reported hearing a gunshot, although the way echoes reverberate through these densely-populated hills, its location necessarily involved guesswork. As the sweep uncovered no evidence of foul play—just the sole other occupants of the home in addition to me: a playful chocolate Labrador and a gray-flannel Weimaraner—with a certain detached reflection I watched the deputies' "nigga alarm" sirens first de-escalate into "nigga alert" honks, then dissolve into "nigga advisory" drones, and finally melt into the melodious "safe negro" warble that for many years has been music to the ears of innocent but "suspicious" Blacks. The door of my custom-built cage swung open as "safe negro" scrolled across their ticker tape displays and I emerged like an Easter chick from its shell, stretching my legs and counting my blessings. Yet, had the Deputy's surge of adrenaline made his trigger finger any *twitchier*, or had his stereotypes about big, black men made it any *itchier*, our encounter could easily have ended not in a warble but a dirge.

As it was, all this nigga alarm cost me was several hours of work time. In *Negrophobia and Reasonable Racism*, I dubbed the social price Blacks must pay as targets of racial profiling, rooted in racial stereotypes and statistical generalizations, the "Black Tax."[58] Sometimes that tax is more than social—it taxes time, it garnishes productivity.

Bear in mind that nigga alarms, alerts, and advisories are predictions and risk assessments rooted in the beliefs, assumptions, and perceptions of ordinary men and women. Because the law defines the perceptions and responses of ordinary people as "reasonable," the detector's warnings reflect "reasonable" risk assessments of the dangerousness of ambiguous blacks. Of course, appearances can be deceiving, so law-abiding Negroes can trigger false alarms, alerts, and advisories in ordinary people. Nevertheless, in the eyes of the law such false warnings are "reasonable mistakes" as long as they are the kind that ordinary people would make under similar circumstances.

Self-defense claims illustrate how the substantive criminal law treats false nigga alarms. Self-defense doctrine privileges both private citizens and police personnel to use lethal defensive force against persons who reasonably appear to pose an imminent threat of serious harm. The reach of this privilege to shoot scary black males can be exceedingly long, as illustrated by cases like Bernhard Goetz, Amadou Diallo, Sean Bell, and Trayvon Martin. Professors E. Ashby Plant and B. Michelle Peruche have conducted experiments with police officers which showed that officers were quicker to decide to shoot an *unarmed* black target than a similarly situated *unarmed* white target.[59] Because such discriminatory reactions often occur in the cognitive unconscious, bypassing the actor's voluntary or conscious control,[60] racially liberal and well-meaning officers (and ordinary citizens) arguably cannot help shooting ambiguous Blacks more hastily. Because self-defense doctrine excuses ordinary mistakes rooted in ordinary human frailty, the law of self-defense thus allows ordinary police officers and civilians alike to use lethal defensive force more hastily against ambiguous but innocent Blacks than against similarly situated whites—precisely because racism is ordinary, because it is *reasonable*. So long as ambiguous black men make the trigger finger of ordinary citizens or law enforcement personnel in uncertain situations itchier or twitchier than that finger would be for similarly situated white men, more hasty applications of deadly force to black men will qualify as reasonable and privileged. Under current law, the quicker use of lethal force against Blacks by ordinary, "reasonable," and well-meaning police officers and private citizens is an inexorable expression of the Black Tax, one that black men must simply grin and bear, often without civil compensation or criminal vindication.[61]

◆

Allow me a brief side note. Interestingly, instead of criticizing the use of such profiling, many in the black community only critique its unfair use on them. It is not the practice they object to, but rather the fact that it is still too blunt an instrument, not sufficiently calibrated to exclude all Good Negroes. These critics add that the disproportionate misdeeds of Bad Negroes hurt the interests of good law-abiding Negroes by providing the statistical justification for the "Black Tax." As Ellis Cose chronicles in *The Rage of a Privileged Class*, the Black Tax is the bane of the existence of the black bourgeoisie and one big reason black Brahmins feel so enraged.[62] Indifferent as lightning, the Black Tax strikes both black haves and black have-nots, both Good and Bad Negroes. But unlike natural lightning, which in myth never strikes twice in the same place, bolts of Black Tax lightning repeatedly strike the same targets again and again. This phenomenon is shown by a Community Service Society of New York's analysis of 2009 stop-and-frisk data for the New York police: there were 132,000 stops of black men 16–24 in 2009 (94% of which did not lead to an arrest). According to Census Bureau data, only 120,000 black men of that age lived in New York City in 2009. Thus, "on average, every young black man can be expected to be stopped and frisked by the police each year."[63] Put differently, young black men in New York under this policy became law-enforcement lightning rods who could expect to be struck over and over by blue serge bolts of Black Tax lightning.

Some privileged blacks would not find the Black Tax so infuriating if it were more targeted, tailored, and regressive, that is, more limited to *poor* blacks, whose disproportionate misdeeds establish and maintain the statistical link between race and crime in the first place. Black Brahmin icon Bill Cosby stressed the class factor in his address at the NAACP on the 50th anniversary of *Brown v. Board of Education*: "Ladies and Gentlemen, the lower economic and lower middle economic people are not holding their end in this deal."[64] Statistically at least, these better-off critics of poor blacks have a point: the vast majority of black street criminals are from extremely disadvantaged neighborhoods. From this statistical perspective, by committing street crimes at such disproportionately high rates, poor black criminals make *blackness itself,* in the language of evidence law, *relevant* evidence of criminal wrongdoing or criminal intent. The disproportionate misdeeds of poor blacks—to paraphrase the evidence code—make the proposition that someone did or will do a crime statistically more likely to be true, given his blackness, than it would be without that factor. This cold but cogent math—chiefly bottomed on the criminal wrongdoing of blacks from truly disadvantaged neighborhoods—has prompted both my black Beverly Hills neighbors and the police to embrace something akin to a mapping of the link between race, place, class, and crime, something akin to a "nigga geography" or "nigga cartography."[65] Not surprisingly, there's an app for that—a service originally launched under the name "Ghetto Tracker" and relying on crowd-sourced information (locals rate which parts of town are safe and which ones are ghetto, or unsafe) to help people avoid unsafe areas.[66] For Good Negroes and police, "class" and "place" profiling—"spatial profiling"—is perfectly rational, reasonable, and right. Thus an enraged "privileged class" that rails against too blunt racial profiling *itself* routinely practices spatial profiling without compunction, or even a hint of irony. They don't want to abolish it; they just want a Black Tax break.

And yet, although I have attacked the Black Tax in books, blogs, and law reviews, a silver lining runs through it. Given that extreme disadvantage breeds street crime (and that truly disadvantaged blacks disproportionately committing street crime will continue to statistically justify the Black Tax), the implication is that the only way for enraged black Brahmins to sing less of the Black Tax blues is to destroy its statistical foundation by lifting poor blacks out of extremely disadvantaged neighborhoods, fixing their crumbling schools, and addressing other criminogenic social conditions that besiege them. In fact, whenever members of the black bourgeoisie are struck by bolts of Black Tax lightning (whenever, say, they nearly get tennis elbow from trying to flag down cabs that won't stop), their rage should give way to a "moment of Zen"—they should reflect on reasons for the disparities in crime rates in the hopelessness, frustration, alienation, and despair of truly disadvantaged Blacks stranded in neighborhoods abandoned long ago by the privileged class itself. The relatively law-abiding black bourgeoisie should view the Black Tax as a tithe that binds their fate to that of extremely disadvantaged Blacks, a relentless reminder that as long as "they" don't look good, "we" don't look good. That is the silver lining, at least in theory.

◆

But the Black Tax is also levied when a black person has already committed a prohibited act or *actus reus*—for instance, a black defendant in a criminal trial who clearly caused a death or some other serious social harm. At this point, the risk of wrongdoing has been realized, and if the jury believes beyond a reasonable doubt that the defendant committed a wrongful act, they set about assessing the defendant's moral fault, blameworthiness, and subjective culpability.[67] And again, of course, decisions about a black wrongdoer's wickedness, his *mens rea*, reflect the moral judgments, perceptions, and beliefs of ordinary men and women.

The click-clack sound of double barrel hammers cocking in rapid succession represents our *readiness* to condemn and ostracize wrongdoers if and when they fail to refute that ordinary inference of subjective culpability that accompanies a wrongful act.[68] As Professor George Fletcher observes, if someone commits a prohibited act—say, a jewelry store clerk opens a safe and turns over all the jewels to an unauthorized stranger, or a driver runs over someone lying in the street, or a State Department employee turns over vital state secrets to a foreign government—we typically infer from his wrongful act that he is wickedly dishonest, indifferent, or greedy. More succinctly, we typically infer a bad actor from a bad act. In this sense, someone who commits a prohibited act is presumptively blameworthy. And this is particularly true of black wrongdoers, in part because of the implicit biases we all have. Accordingly, a black wrongdoer is a *prima facie* nigga. This inference of wickedness can be defeated, if, for instance, the clerk, the driver, and the State Department employee can be shown to have committed their prohibited acts *at gunpoint*, and thus their wrongful acts are not the result of their dishonesty, indifference, or greed. All three could claim a full excuse of duress.[69] Excuses, in the words of George Fletcher, "preclude an inference from the act to the actor's character."[70] But can a *prima facie* nigga destroy the ordinary inference of wickedness that accompanies wrongdoing by claiming a valid excuse?

A wrongdoer may be unable to assert a valid excuse if the law does not recognize the kind of excuse he wants to assert, or if the jury does not think he deserves the benefit of a legally recognized excuse. In either case, without an effective excuse, he will be found wicked beyond a reasonable doubt. A *prima facie* nigga can seek to assert either a broad *partial* excuse like provocation or "extreme emotional disturbance," or a broad *full* excuse like duress or self-defense. In claims of provocation and extreme emotional disturbance, a wrongdoer is partially excused if a "reasonable person in the situation" would have been sorely tempted to lose self-control; in duress and self-defense, he is fully excused if a "reasonable person" in the wrongdoer's situation would have been overwhelmed by the threats or apparent threats. So both kinds of excuse turn crucially on the "reasonable person in the situation" test of subjective culpability.[71] The reasonable person test provides judges and jurors with a flexible legal vehicle by which they can excuse a wrongdoer on the moral ground that his circumstances, in the words of Mark Kelman, drove a wedge between his "contingent" self—the self that came forward under the unjust pressures of the situation in which he found himself—and some underlying "true" self that could have manifested itself and maintained control if not for those unjust pressures.[72]

The "reasonable or ordinary person in the situation" test of wickedness can be either rigid and "invariant" (i.e., a typical person drawn from the general population, average in mental, emotional, psychological, and dispositional makeup) or flexible and "individualized" (a typical person drawn from a social subgroup, like a typical battered woman or a typical person suffering from a post-traumatic stress disorder or a typical impoverished, poorly educated and chronically unemployed person).[73] By disregarding a person's own special cognitive and volitional capacities, the invariant one-size-fits-all approach imposes on individuals a legal standard that may be very difficult or impossible for them to meet; it weakens or destroys the link between legal guilt and moral blameworthiness and so may do violence to the criminal law's ancient *mens rea* requirement by imposing a kind of strict liability on wrongdoers. Accordingly, an individualized test of reasonableness is the more just and principled approach to blame and punishment. But because as a matter of practical politics, judges will not formulate a completely individualized reasonable person test that takes into consideration all of a defendant's circumstances and attributes, the underlying question of legal excuses can be distilled to this: "Should the 'reasonable person in the situation' test of blameworthiness in cases of duress and extreme emotional disturbance be individualized to make allowances for the wrongdoer's disadvantaged social background?" Alternatively, in instructing on the reasonable person standard: "Should courts instruct jurors on an 'ordinary impoverished black man trapped behind ghetto walls' test of reasonableness in claims of putative self-defense, duress, provocation, or extreme emotional distress?" Bear in mind that, at bottom, this assessment depends on jury sympathy. In the words of a Model Penal Code Comment on the reasonable person test in provocation cases: "*In the end, the question is whether the actor's loss of self-control can be understood in terms that arouse sympathy in the ordinary citizen.*"[74] Sympathy, or its absence, drives our moral judgments of wrongdoers at least as much as—if not far more than—reason or logic or categorical imperatives. But as the studies of in-group empathy bias I discuss later show, a *prima facie* nigga inspires no sympathy in many observers, commentators, or decision makers: individuals are not unsympathetic because they are Bad Negroes, they are Bad Negroes because they are unsympathetic.

Two other factors make many legal decision makers unwilling to recognize or credit broad excuses for *prima facie* Bad Negroes. Inasmuch as their victims are especially sympathetic because they are from socially marginalized groups, sympathy for victims may flatly trump that for victimizers.[75] And some argue that excuses insult the dignity of their intended beneficiaries—black criminals—by treating them like agencyless animals rather than as *persons*, that is, as moral agents capable of meaningful choice. Both these classic and oft-repeated reasons for rejecting most excuses (even limited and long-standing excuses like heat of passion on sudden provocation) are captured in the following comment by Professor Stephen Morse:

> I would abolish [the provocation defense] and convict all intentional killers of murder. Reasonable people do not kill no matter how much they are provoked, and even enraged people generally retain the capacity to control homicidal or any other kind of aggressive antisocial desires. We cheapen both life and our conception of responsibility by maintaining the provocation/passion mitigation. This may seem harsh and contrary to the supposedly humanitarian reforms of the evolving criminal law. But this ... interpretation of criminal law history is morally mistaken. It is humanitarian only if one *focuses sympathetically on perpetrators and not on their victims* and views the former as mostly *helpless objects of their overwhelming emotions and irrationality*. This *sympathy is misplaced*, however, and is *disrespectful to the perpetrator*. As virtually every human being knows because we all have been enraged, it is easy not to kill, even when one is enraged. [emphasis added][76]

Consistent with Morse's hostility to excuses, many courts arbitrarily—from the standpoint of the culpability principle—limit the scope of excuse claims *as a matter of law* so that wrongdoers never get to present them to a jury.[77] These artificial legal limitations on what kinds of extenuating factors a wrongdoer can get before a jury short-circuits the wrongdoer's ability to arouse jury sympathy.

Studies of unconscious discrimination—both in the form of attribution bias and ingroup empathy bias—show that ordinary people are more likely to reject excuses for Blacks than for similarly situated Whites.[78] In a classic experiment, Birt Duncan showed white subjects a videotape depicting one person (either black or white) ambiguously shoving another (either black or white). Subjects who characterized the shove as "violent" more frequently attributed the wrongdoing to personal, dispositional causes when the harm-doer was black, but to situational causes when the harm-doer was white.[79] In a recent study of juvenile offenders, George S. Bridges and Sara Steen found a pronounced difference in court officials' attributions of intent in crimes by black versus white youths; court officials are significantly more likely to perceive blacks' crimes as caused by internal factors and crimes committed by whites as caused by external ones.[80] The resulting absence of valid excuses means the jury will confirm the *prima facie* readings by finding the wrongdoer a blameworthy Bad Negro beyond a reasonable doubt.

From the standpoint of Good Negro Theory, any racial justice advocate who tries to "make excuses" for *a priori* blameworthy Bad Negroes is being unfaithful to the kind of "morality of means" that inspired Justice Marshall to refuse to make excuses for "thuggery when perpetrated by Blacks."[81] This suggests that distinguishing and distancing Good and Bad Negroes is an ethical obligation, one that imposes ethical limits on how racial justice advocates should treat black criminals and approach criminal matters. Under Good Negro Ethics, racial justice advocates who fail to morally and legally distinguish and distance black criminals from law-abiding blacks breach their most basic duty to *help* rather than *hurt* Black People. From the standpoint of Good Negro Ethics, black activists fail the community by defending black criminals, failing to sharply distinguish between Good and Bad Negroes, and failing to maximize the distance between them in the eyes of whites; it *hurts* Black People, they say, when racial justice advocates carry briefs for niggas.

According to classic Good Negro theory, excuses—such as an "ordinary impoverished black man trapped behind ghetto walls" test of the "reasonable man"—are bad policy for Blacks as a group because excuses keep criminal wrongdoers, including drug dealers and gangbangers, out of jail and on the street, where they can claim more mostly black victims. In short, "A thug in prison can't shoot your sister."[82] Randall Kennedy, a leading proponent of this point of view, puts it this way: "In terms of misery inflicted by direct criminal violence," Blacks "suffer more from the criminal acts of their racial 'brothers' and 'sisters' than they do from the racist misconduct of white police officers."[83] This wry remark may very well be true. It is not hard to imagine that a black gangbanger could inflict more pain and suffering on other blacks than a bigot with a badge and a gun. It may even be true that, to quote another champion of this viewpoint, "Racist white cops, however vicious, are ultimately minor irritants when compared to the viciousness of the black gangs and wanton violence."[84] From this perspective, calling destructive criminals like gangbangers racial "brothers" or "sisters"—words of solidarity and ingroup love—rings as false as calling viciously racist white cops "brothers" or "sisters."

From the utilitarian cost-benefit perspective of Good Negro Theory, many criminal matters pit the interests of "us" lovable and law-abiding Black People against "them" niggas. Thus, "colorblind criminal laws"—that is, laws silent on race and not enacted for the purpose of treating one racial group different than another—whose *effects* disproportionately burden niggas can be good social policy for law-abiding blacks. For instance, laws that punish crack offenders much more harshly than powder cocaine offenders (who more often are white or upper class) may *help* Black People more than they *hurt* niggas, say Good Negro Theorists, "by incarcerating for longer periods those who use and sell a drug that has had an especially devastating effect on African-American communities."[85] By the same logic, because urban curfews that disproportionately fall upon black youngsters also help some black residents feel more secure, such disparities may *help* Black People more than they *hurt* niggas. Similarly, because crackdowns on gangs that disproportionately affect black gang members also reduce gang-related crime, Black People may be *helped* more than niggas *hurt* by such racial disparities. And because prosecutions of pregnant drug addicts that disproportionately fall on pregnant black women also may deter conduct harmful to black unborn babies, Black People may be *helped* more than niggas *hurt* by such racial disparities. Viewing laws like these as "social policy" propositions, Kennedy concludes that "it is often unclear whether social policy that is silent as to race and devoid of a covert racial purpose is harmful or helpful to blacks as a whole since, typically, such a policy will burden some blacks and benefit others."[86]

Under this cost-benefit, utilitarian, welfare principle—and positing that *most* blacks in the aggregate are law-abiding—there is no reason to give any special weight to the justness or fairness of severely punishing black criminals more than they deserve to be, given their disadvantaged social backgrounds and human frailty. As David Lyons describes this utilitarian approach in *Ethics and the Rule of Law*, when interests conflict "we should serve the greater aggregate interest, taking into account all the benefits and burdens that might result from the decisions that are available to us."[87] By this logic, because the social, political, and safety costs of excusing black criminals fall on the larger law-abiding black population while the benefits of excusing them are reaped only by the smaller Bad Negroes contingent, recognizing general excuses for black wrongdoers fails the cost-benefit test. When the interests of these two subdivisions collide, the moral and legal principle that should settle the conflict, according to Good Negro Theory, is the welfare principle—the principle that laws are good if they increase the satisfaction of law-abiding Black People more than they increase the frustration of niggas. Utility matters more than compassion, mercy, forgiveness, or individualized justice. From this perspective, even if judges, jurors, voters, policymakers, and the rest of us impose draconian punishments on black wrongdoers, as long as these laws and other social practices *help* law-abiding Black People more than they *hurt* Bad Negroes, they are cost-justified and desirable, no matter how much they ignore extenuating and mitigating factors in a person's life. This utilitarian approach creates and perpetuates vast injustice, as we will see.

◆

At the conceptual level, the object of Nigga Theory is to attack every one of these values, beliefs, and assumptions and thereby expose the blame and punishment problem for what it really is—not a subjective culpability or personal responsibility problem but a political and social one, all the way down. Let's start with the assertion by proponents of personal responsibility that there is no moral equivalence between traditional Jim Crow and racialized mass incarceration because the former was about social oppression of innocent blacks, while the so-called New Jim Crow is about the self-destruction of black wrongdoers who are the authors of their own plight, which in turn implies that there is no collective responsibility for the carceral burdens they bear.

Deniers—those who deny that crime can be traced to our unjust basic social structure—reject our collective accountability on two standard grounds: (a) impersonal social forces cannot *cause* people to choose to do wrong, and (b) even if empirical evidence proves that such forces do *cause* voluntary wrongdoing in the sense of increasing the rate at which people make wicked criminal choices, such forces are not the "proximate cause" of crime.

The deniers assert that social forces cannot *determine* human action, that voluntary criminal acts cannot be *caused* by impersonal macro-level social factors like poverty and social inequality. We may *deplore* tsunamis, avalanches, or shark attacks, but we would not morally *blame* these impersonal destructive forces any more than we would blame a rock for falling on one's head, for we rightly reserve blame and praise for *persons* with wills and character traits.[88] Deniers contend that macro-level approaches offend the personal dignity of wrongdoers by treating them as things or events or Pavlovian bundles of conditioned reflexes without hearts or minds or wills. For proponents of personal responsibility, this is the Achilles heel of all macro-level explanations of wrongdoing and the flaw in the logic of all broad excuses for criminal misconduct. Such explanations and excuses, they contend, deny the personhood of criminals by treating them as bad "social facts" rather than bad *persons*.[89] Accordingly, personal responsibility champions tell us we must condemn black criminals to show them respect and damn them in the name of their own personal dignity.

Nevertheless, empirical evidence compels the conclusion that criminal wrongdoing *is* caused by social forces such as extreme social disadvantage. Social science proves the existence of a clear causal link between social facts and personal, private, individual acts. In his pioneering work, *Suicide: A Study in Sociology* (1897), Émile Durkheim showed how the seemingly most personal, private, and even "anti-social" decision of someone to end his own existence rather than continue to suffer a weary life—a decision ostensibly rooted only in individual psychology, private thought processes, and personal demons—actually reflects social currents and *at bottom* is primarily a social (not psychological or biological) fact. The social character of deliberate acts of violent self-destruction can remain hidden if we look only at separate individuals and their melancholy musings; but the social character of suicide leaps into bold relief when we look at *rates* of suicide. These suicide *rates* differ among societies, and among different groups in the same society, and they show regularities over time, with changes in them often occurring at similar times in different societies. "Each society," Durkheim observes, "is predisposed to contribute a definite quota of voluntary deaths."[90] These regular, predictable, stable patterns of "personal and private" decisions to shuffle off this mortal coil—in short, these systematic suicidal tendencies—cannot be explained purely in terms of psychological facts, individual mental states, or random aggregations of dire deeds. Rather, these patterns point to underlying causes that produce suicidal thoughts and acts in *groups* of individuals. The decisive question then is, "what factors explain these group-level patterns of voluntary self-destruction?" The suicide *rate*, he explains, is a "numerical datum" that measures and expresses each society's "aptitude for suicide," that is, "the suicidal tendency with which each society is collectively afflicted."[91] Hence, a foundational insight of sociology is that impersonal social forces *can cause* people to choose to engage in anti-social behavior.

The second formidable argument Deniers raise against America's accountability for undoing entire generations of Blacks through unnecessary and unwarranted mass incarceration runs thus: Even if we acknowledge what the empirical evidence clearly demonstrates, namely, that macro-level social factors can *cause* people to commit voluntary criminal acts in the sense of dramatically increasing the *rate* of wrongdoing in certain neighborhoods and for certain social subgroups, those criminogenic social forces may not be what lawyers and legal commentators call the "proximate" cause of the resulting crime.

A core tenet of American civil and criminal law is that for an individual or entity (such as the American government) to be accountable for harm resulting from destructive forces it unleashes (including destructive social forces), those forces must be the "factual cause" and the "proximate cause" of the resulting harm. Factual cause means that the resulting harm (here, for instance, disproportionate crime rates among truly disadvantaged Blacks) would not have occurred if the defendant (here America) had not unleashed certain destructive forces or criminogenic conditions like redlining, rampant joblessness, crumbling schools, inadequate health care, and the rest. But these social forces may not be the proximate cause of any criminal act if the culpable choices of criminal wrongdoers intervene between the extreme disadvantage, on the one hand, and the individual holdups, drive-bys, and street crimes, on the other.

For instance, if a gasoline truck and trailer unit spills a massive amount of gas on an open highway and malicious bystanders willfully kindle a conflagration with a book of matches, some courts refuse to hold the truck owner accountable for the resulting damage; courts conclude that the volatile spill was not the "proximate cause" of the resulting flames, even though it was clearly a necessary condition or factual cause of the fire. These courts say that the malicious match-strikers are the "superseding," "efficient," or "proximate" cause of the fiery destruction, thus shifting the entire responsibility for the flames to the willful wrongdoers and away from the truck owner whose volatile spill set the stage. For these courts, results (here, fiery destruction) that follow from the voluntary actions of the subsequent persons (here, the malicious match strikers) are caused by them *alone*.[92]

This notion is sometimes called the doctrine of *novus actus interveniens*. Under the *novus actus* doctrine, later voluntary human action "displaces the relevance of prior conduct by others and provides a new foundation for causal responsibility."[93] Glanville Williams provides the classic defense of the doctrine:

A person is primarily responsible for what he himself does. He is not responsible, not blameworthy, for what other people do. The fact that his own conduct, rightful or wrongful, provided the background for a subsequent voluntary and wrong act by another does not make him responsible for it. What he does may be a but-for cause of the injurious act, but he did not do it. His conduct is not an imputable cause of it. Only the later actor, the doer of the act that intervenes between the first act and the result, the final wielder of human autonomy in the matter, bears responsibility (along with his accomplices) for the result that ensues.[94]

From this perspective, the violent and nonviolent criminal acts of Blacks trapped in dark ghettos are caused *solely* by them.

To clarify this point, consider the 30 years encompassing the crack plague and its still festering aftermath in light of the massive gas spill example just discussed. According to Senate transcripts and other reliable sources,[95] in the critical period between 1982 and 1988, high ranking US officials during the Reagan and George H.W. Bush administrations made well-documented decisions to fight communism by prioritizing foreign policy over drug enforcement. Thus these government officials helped jumpstart and fuel the crack plague by knowingly—albeit not conspiratorially—helping flood poor black neighborhoods with cocaine and guns in furtherance of national security. In other words, US officials helped supply many books of matches in the form of guns and drugs to young black males wading through waist-deep combustible criminogenic conditions like extreme and concentrated social disadvantage.

But whereas combustible gas spills provide *opportunities* for malicious acts, combustible criminogenic conditions do more: they penetrate the mental states of those immersed in them—they mold mental states. Specifically, extreme and hyper-concentrated disadvantage produce the hopelessness, resentment, hostility, and alienation that *motivate* law-breaking, while an ample supply of guns and drugs, at least partly traceable to US foreign policy priorities in the critical early years of the crack epidemic, provide the *means* and *opportunities* for hopelessness and hostility to find expression in law-breaking. In short, at the level of motivations and opportunities, we bear collective responsibility for the foreseeable consequences of our unjust social structure and policy priorities.

This is precisely where Deniers invoke the *novus actus* doctrine as a "proximate cause defense," asserting that the wicked decisions of the individuals slogging through combustible social currents to spread fiery destruction negate our collective accountability for their abundantly foreseeable and statistically inevitable match-striking. They insist that each wrongdoer's personal and individual "moral moment" severs the link between social forces and criminal acts, and establish criminal intents and vicious wills and depraved hearts as the proximate causal agents, and these wicked inner states, Deniers continue and many courts consistently agree, cut off our collective accountability for the criminal acts produced by our collective existence.

◆

Sometimes courts and juries and legislatures are perfectly willing to say that blameworthy intervening action does *not* break the chain of causation, so long as the subsequent wrongdoing was *foreseeable*. In State v. Bier,[96] for instance, when the defendant's wife said she wanted to commit suicide, he placed a loaded, cocked pistol within her reach, and she used it to kill herself.[97] The defendant's conviction for negligent homicide was upheld on appeal—foreseeability was enough to establish proximate cause.[98] A driver who negligently leaves his car idling and unattended can be the proximate cause of death or serious bodily harm resulting from a car thief on a joy ride—the foreseeability of thieves and joy rides establishes proximate cause.[99] The owner of an apartment building in a crime-ridden location who fails to install locks on entrance doors or provide exterior lighting can be the proximate cause of robberies, rapes, and other violent assaults on tenants by intervening human agents who intentionally act to produce the forbidden result: foreseeability establishes accountability.[100] One drag racer can be liable for causing the death of his racing partner despite his partner's voluntary choice to drive recklessly.[101] In a game of Russian roulette, the surviving player will be liable for killing his partner even though the deceased freely chose to put the gun to his head and squeeze the trigger, again on grounds of foreseeability.[102] And finally, courts routinely ignore or reject the *novus actus* or intervening-act doctrine and hold drug suppliers accountable for the foreseeable, though freely chosen, acts of their purchasers, including their purchasers' drug overdoses and resulting deaths.[103]

So just like everyday morality, the law does not follow a hard, fixed rule about causation and accountability when subsequent voluntary human actions intervene. Rather, the law remains ceaselessly torn between two competing perspectives. Pulling one way is the perspective that underlies the *novus actus* or intervening act doctrine—indeed underlies all retributive approaches to blame and punishment—namely, the view that humans are solely and fully responsible for their freely chosen actions. This is enthusiastically endorsed by tough-on-crime advocates, who feel any departure from this principle of sole and full responsibility puts us on the slippery slope to social determinism and the complete abdication of personal responsibility. Pulling the other way is the perspective endorsed by advocates for the damned, a perspective that sees wrongdoing as caused by a combination of preceding social facts *and* the wrongdoer's ordinary human frailty. Voluntary human action is voluntary *and* caused by preceding forces and factors. Pendulum-like, the law and our everyday moral intuitions swing back and forth between these competing conceptions of causation and accountability.

This raises the pivotal question: where do we draw the line between societal accountability and personal responsibility? What factors determine which way the causation pendulum swings in the minds of ordinary judges, jurors, and lawmakers? The most important is the perceived wickedness of wrongdoers, because that arouses the urge for vengeance and retribution in ordinary people—the more wicked wrongdoers seem, the more they stir "the retributive urge" to blame and punish; the more they stir "the retributive urge," the more likely ordinary people are to view them as "independent intervening causes" or "superseding causes" of criminal harms.[104] Contrary to what we might expect, then, judgments about wrongdoers' blameworthiness come first, and only then conclusions about whether preceding forces and factors caused the results. This sounds backward and counterintuitive because we expect that we would exhaust all questions of causation accountability, and only then, after finding that A *caused* B's death, do we weigh A's blameworthy wickedness. Nevertheless, the everyday reality of our actual decision-making is that we routinely blame individuals *before* we decide whether to call them "independent," "superseding," or "efficient" causes of criminal actions; in other words, we first decide about the wrongdoers' wickedness and moral turpitude—we decide whether they are guilty or innocent—and only then do we assess whether preceding forces and factors are a proximate cause. However counterintuitive this pattern may initially sound, it pervades all moral and legal thinking. In the words of Meir Dan-Cohen:

> The statement that A caused B's death may, in ordinary speech, be as much a conclusory statement, based on the prior tacit judgment that A deserves to be punished for B's death, as it is an independent statement of fact which leads to that conclusion.... [T]he conclusion that A deserves to be punished may be directly and intuitively generated by *the retributive urge*, preceding and merely rationalized by the finding of a sufficient causal relationship between A's acts and B's death.[105]

In short, the retributive urge—rooted in contempt for wicked and blameworthy wrongdoers—routinely determines how we think about causation and determine accountability.

The question of whether A was the sole or superseding cause of B's death, then, boils down to the question of whether punishing A is necessary to satisfy the retributive urge he arouses in us. If the fact of B's death at the hands of A does not produce a strong retributive urge—that is, if we are willing to partially or fully excuse A for bringing about the prohibited result—then we are more willing to call other factors preceding or surrounding A's act (including macro-level social factors) the proximate cause of B's death.[106] Conversely, the more we view wrongdoers as wickedly depraved, the more they stir the retributive urge for vengeance and retribution, the easier it is for us to conclude that their voluntary wrongdoing breaks the causal chain between earlier factors and their crime, shifts responsibility for crime entirely to them, and absolves us as a nation of accountability for the abundantly foreseeable results of our own social forces and currents.

All of this has particular consequences for this project, and for Nigga Theory more broadly. Quite simply, the more we view wrongdoers as that most distilled and concentrated form of wickedness—morally condemnable niggas—the easier it is for us to deny accountability for their plight, for moral judgments drive our conclusions about causation and thus drive our conclusions about our collective accountability for the criminogenic effects of extreme disadvantage. In other words, Niggerizing black wrongdoers helps us deny our accountability for the foreseeable effects of being extremely poor, hopeless, and black in America.

But still, a core aspect of Nigga Theory is hope. Once the moral basis for the retributive urge is shown to be illegitimate, irrational, and unreliable, it may become easier for fair-minded Americans to curb (at least temporarily) their urge to condemn long enough to recognize and acknowledge the causal links between crime and our own macro-level social forces. And this can pave the way for us to accept collective accountability for the crack plague and its consequences, and our continued mass incarceration of people of color. Macro-level perspectives—which an inflamed retributive urge obscures—can help law-abiding Americans see the common humanity in wrongdoers by helping us think beyond the boundaries of good and evil and praise and blame in criminal matters. Of course, it flatters those of us who are prosperous and law-abiding to believe that our material well-being and good name reflect virtue and pluck, not luck. But from the macro-level perspective, such thinking is unwarranted, however widespread, and pregnant with political implications for our treatment of the truly disadvantaged.

CHAPTER **TWO**

MORAL LUCK IN THE SOCIAL PRODUCTION
OF "NIGGAS"

Po' niggers can't have no luck—
—Nigger Jim, **Adventures of Huckleberry Finn**

*I*T CANNOT BE DENIED that luck permeates our lives in countless ways. Some enjoy good luck in their upbringing or hit the genetic lottery. Others, in Immanuel Kant's words, "by a particularly unfortunate fate or by the niggardly provision of a step-motherly nature," do not fare as well.[107] Because luck lacks a moral compass—no moral principle determines its social distribution—many experience life as profoundly unfair. Good luck happens to seemingly bad people, bad luck to seemingly good. Some stumble into money, others toil ceaselessly but stay poor. Consider my neighborhood: View Park residents are among the luckiest Negroes in the race. From atop these affluent hills, Black Brahmins literally look down upon less advantaged neighborhoods— The Jungle, South Central, Inglewood, Watts, Compton—filled with residents who have the riches of Hills Negroes in sight but out of reach. Lucky children of View Park Negroes will on average grow up in safer neighborhoods, attend better schools, eat healthier food, receive better health care, and enjoy more social and economic opportunities than black children from surrounding neighborhoods. Luck gives the kids in the Hills a head start, while holding those at lower street levels back. Because many factors beyond our control determine our "street level," the distribution of street levels in a community reflects the distribution of social and economic luck.

But what does such social and economic luck have to do with moral blameworthiness and personal responsibility? Can luck make people who they are and determine what they do? If we learn that *somehow* luck determines what people actually do and whether we praise or blame them, our moral judgments of them begin to look irrational and illegitimate. "Without being able to explain exactly why," moral philosopher Thomas Nagel points out, "we feel that the appropriateness of moral assessment is easily undermined by the discovery that the act or attribute, no matter how good or bad, is not under the person's control."[108] One of our strongest moral intuitions is that a lucky or unlucky coin toss cannot determine a person's moral standing (say, heads Bad Negro, tails Good) or his moral and criminal responsibility for what he does (say, heads we blame him, tails we don't). As moral philosopher Bernard Williams argues, "Anything which is the product of happy or unhappy contingency is no proper object of moral assessment, and no proper determinant of it, either."[109] Simply put, a moral judgment of someone is *personal*—we feel indignation and contempt toward persons for their acts, but not toward things or events or happenings, because only persons can *control* the acts for which they are blamed—only persons have moral agency.

Unlucky poor people beset by bad social and economic luck—especially those who remain law-abiding and take pride in their Good Negro status— may feel especially tempted to see the moral universe as luck-free. They may find reassurance and comfort in the thought that, at least in the moral arena, they do not have to worry about things beyond their control determining how others judge them or how they judge themselves. If morality is immune to luck, then bad luck cannot determine what even the unluckiest poor person does, turning her actions into events; nor can bad luck determine who she is *in her heart* (her motives, intentions, cares, concerns, and aversions), turning her into an externally determined *thing* without moral agency. Put differently, if morality is immune to luck, then those mired in bad social and economic luck can find *in morality* a source of social approval and self-respect immune to luck—a safe haven for a self hounded by unhappy contingency. Under this comforting view of morality, there can be no moral lottery or crapshoot, because a successful moral life is equally open to all sane and rational adults. This apparent immunity of morality to luck offers, in the words of Williams, a quantum of "solace to a sense of the world's unfairness."

Nevertheless, if careful reflection leads inexorably to the conclusion that luck—something beyond our control—actually determines what people do and whether we praise or blame them, then our moral judgments begin to look irrational and illegitimate, and whatever solace there is in believing that one's moral worth is immune to luck evaporates. A person's lack of control over the result of a coin flip makes that test of praise and blame patently irrational and illegitimate. This insight informs the most basic requirement of the substantive criminal law: the voluntary act requirement.

The Model Penal Code defines an "act" as a "bodily movement, whether voluntary or involuntary."[110] By this definition, sometimes our acts are beyond our control; for instance, someone having a seizure, convulsion, or other reflex movement cannot control her acts. Under the voluntary act requirement, someone suffering a seizure—and as a result, for instance, causing a car accident—cannot be criminally responsible for her acts or their effects because they are beyond her control. To talk of blaming or excusing someone for the harmful effects of a sudden seizure, notes Professor Jeffrie Murphy, "make[s] no more sense than would talk of excusing a rock for falling on one's head."[111] Before we ever reach the question of someone's subjective culpability, we must first find an "act" under her control for which she can be responsible. Take away a wrongdoer's control over what she does, and what she does—even elaborate bodily movements that cause another's death with great precision—looks like an *event* that *happens* to a *thing* rather than an *act committed* by a *person*.

For instance, in a famous case, a certain Ms. Cogdon left her bed in the middle of the night, "fetched an axe from the woodheap, entered [her beloved daughter] Pat's room, and struck her two accurate forceful blows on the head with the blade of the axe, thus killing her." Because she was sleepwalking when she killed Pat, she was acquitted (in the words of Norval Morris) "because the act of killing itself was not, in law, regarded as *her act* at all."[112] Because it was beyond her control, it was not the act of a person—*her act*—but rather an event that happened to a thing. We never get to the question of whether she should be excused for what she actually did because in a real sense she did not *do* it—questions of responsibility come before questions of subjective culpability. For instance, if Pat suddenly awoke and shot Ms. Cogdon to avoid getting the axe, Pat would be responsible for her voluntary act of killing Ms. Cogdon, but she would not be blamed for the killing because no subjective culpability or *mens rea* accompanied her voluntary act. Blame requires both responsibility for the act and subjective culpability. Control establishes responsibility for an act and distinguishes bad persons and their acts from bad things and events and states of affair, all of which can be deplored, but none of which can be blamed like persons can. Understanding this logic clarifies the link between moral responsibility and luck. If luck—a factor beyond our control—determines what we do, and if what we do determines our moral responsibility, then our moral standing hinges on luck.

◆

Let's apply this analysis to cases of vehicular homicide. Millions of times a day drivers across America carelessly speed or fail to keep a proper lookout in order to attend to their navigation or audio systems, to talk, text, search, or surf (sometimes simultaneously), or to eat, primp, preen, discipline unruly kids, all while wielding one- to three-ton minivans, sedans, trucks and SUVs—massive metal and glass missiles on wheels. Fortunately, despite innumerable close calls and near misses, most distracted or speeding drivers cause no harm, so most neither look back on their careless acts with compunction nor suffer the condemnation of their neighbors—*so long as no one gets hurt.* But occasionally someone's speeding or inadvertence kills; a child, for instance, happens to dart into the careless driver's path. Assuming proper attention or speed would have prevented the tragedy, instantly a gulf—a yawning moral and legal chasm—opens between "us" careless but lucky motorists and "them" careless but unlucky killers. Specifically, "us" careless but lucky drivers (and other social perceivers) morally condemn "them" careless and unlucky killers, even though in a significant sense both lucky non-killers and unlucky killers *do* the exact same thing, engage in exactly the same voluntary acts, take exactly the same excessive risks. The moral and legal difference between careless non-killers and careless killers depends entirely on a factor—a fortuitous darting child—neither could control. For *doing* the exact same thing, lucky distracted drivers and speeders might get a traffic ticket while unlucky ones can get the indelible stigma of a felony conviction for vehicular manslaughter and years of jail time.

In cases of so-called involuntary (i.e., negligent or reckless) manslaughter, for any given level of carelessness, we have two similarly situated groups of risk-takers, equal in risk-creation and subjective culpability or *mens rea*, yet only the unlucky get branded and punished. For any given level of careless wrongdoing, *luck alone* determines what they have done and so what they are judged for. Neither careless criminals nor equally careless non-criminals can control the single factor that drives the moral and criminal wedge between them, namely, the *results* of their equally negligent or reckless conduct. Thus, each year luck alone distinguishes millions of careless non-felons who remain in good moral standing from a handful of equally careless, officially blameworthy felons.

Similarly, a father sprinting back to his car on a sweltering summer day after realizing that he mistakenly left his sleeping infant in the back seat knows before he gets there that the rest of his moral life hangs on whether he gets there to find the child dead or alive. The final result of his inadvertence—which can depend on external determinants entirely beyond his control such as the temperature, the cloud cover, or an observant passerby—will determine his moral and criminal status. No matter how swiftly he sprints, morally he is at the mercy of luck.

Moral luck exposes a paradox—a pair of warring intuitions—embedded deep in the concept of responsibility. One set of intuitions tells us that heads-Good-Negro-tails-Bad-Negro coin tosses cannot determine a person's culpability; another set tells us that careless people who kill are more culpable than ones who do not. Even though reflection and logic tell us that the only difference between the careless actor we condemn and the one we don't is a factor over which neither had any control, as soon as we come face to face with actual victims, whether through contemporaneous observance or pictures and vivid descriptions, we cannot help blaming the unlucky actual killer more than those lucky motorists whose carelessness did not kill or injure anyone.

Anytime we make the consequences of what people do the basis for blaming or praising them, we let luck arbitrarily distinguish between people who are identical in subjective culpability. And this is as true of intentional as careless killings. Take two intentional shooters, one who kills while the other does not, only because the intended victim happened to be wearing a bullet proof vest or to slip on a banana peel as the gun's hammer hit its firing pin. Murderers are regarded as criminally and morally worse than attempted murderers, even if only luck separates them. Like the speeders, both shooters are doing the same thing, aiming and shooting, but only the wrongdoing of the "unlucky" shooter kills.

It might seem we could resolve the paradox, reconcile our intuitions, simply by blaming and punishing people the same whenever they do the same thing, run the same risks, irrespective of results. So the lucky and harmless would be blamed just *as much as* the unlucky and lethal, or the unlucky and lethal would be blamed just *as little as* the lucky and harmless. If we blamed the lucky just *as much as* the unlucky, along with speeding tickets, highway patrol officers would have to issue speeding motorists indictments for the moral and criminal equivalent of vehicular manslaughter, say, "attempted negligent or reckless homicide," where an attempt is punished the same as the completed crime.[113] With the help of traffic cameras, in mere months there could be cell blocks brimming with people who never actually killed but who did the same things as convicted careless killers, like speeding, dialing, tuning, and texting. We balk at this. If we blamed the unlucky *as little as* the lucky, officers would issue a mere traffic citation to someone whose culpable speeding or culpable inadvertence caused his three-ton SUV to kill a cluster of kids in a crosswalk. As we observe the bloody aftermath, we balk again.[114] Neither way of reconciling the intuitions seems acceptable.

Whenever we run a moral boundary between people who *do* the exact same thing, who create the same risks, and blame one group of actors more solely on the basis of events beyond their control (on the basis of something *they* did not *do*), we are no longer judging them as persons, as moral beings who can control what they are blamed and praised for. As Ms. Cogdon, the axe-wielding somnambulist, reminds us, control—moral agency—is what distinguishes bad persons and their acts from bad things and events. Moral judgments are not evaluations of events or things, only of persons and their actions. Because persons are responsible only for what they do, they must be judged for what they do, subtracting from what they do anything that merely happens, any factors beyond their control. But in cases of criminal negligence and criminal recklessness, we shift our evaluation from persons and the acts they control to tragic consequences beyond their control, making those fortuitous consequences the basis for driving a moral and legal wedge between equally careless actors.

Moral luck thus undermines the legitimacy of our moral judgments—and hence the distinction between "Good Negroes" and "Bad Negroes"—in two additional ways: as circumstantial and as constitutive luck. First consider how "moral circumstantial luck"—luck in the choices and moral tests our circumstances present to us—invalidates the moral distinction between me and the kids I grew up with who became felons. Let's say that when my childhood friend, LJ, sold the drugs that resulted in his felony conviction, he flunked the moral test posed by his circumstances. He may have felt great situational pressures from poverty and social inequality, but let's say we blame him anyway, on the grounds that the situational pressures merely exposed his character flaws and dispositional deficiencies, that the pressures were not sufficient to support any excuses or mitigations such as duress or extreme emotional disturbance. Accordingly, we find him morally responsible and subjectively culpable for his wrongful act.

Looked at this way, moral deficiencies are like manufacturing defects, say, a hairline fracture in a soda bottle. In my torts class, we learn from a famous exploding bottle case that 1) no bottle manufacturing process is perfect, 2) manufacturing defects are inevitable in most large-scale production processes, 3) statisticians can with mathematical precision predict the defect rates, and 4) most important for present purposes, not every bottle with a manufacturing defect explodes, only those exposed to high levels of internal pressure or external shock. Absent high levels of pressure or shock (say, had the bottles been filled with a less-carbonated beverage or been kept from striking the edge of a table), many defective bottles never explode and cause injury. Because they produce no harmful consequences, such manufacturing defects may remain cloaked in fortuity, forever latent. By the same token, not all persons with LJ's posited character flaws commit street crimes, only those—or at least disproportionately those—exposed to the peculiar pressures and shocks of living in bleak streets under dire circumstances. This reality sets the stage for circumstantial luck to determine moral responsibility. Persons with the same moral deficiencies can end up with totally different moral and criminal records solely because luck plunks them down in different circumstances.

Take two homeowners, Timorous and Pusillanimous, with the same moral character defect—say, cowardice. Pusillanimous is also parsimonious, so he does nothing to upgrade his house, while Timorous hires a general contractor to work on his. Timorous sees a big black man on his property and there have been a rash of home invasion robberies in his neighborhood lately, some involving black assailants. As the ambiguous black man approaches, a terrified Timorous raises his hunting rifle in sincere self-defense. The shot he fires kills what turns out to be an innocent employee of his new general contractor. Under these circumstances, a homeowner has a valid self-defense claim as long as he showed ordinary fortitude in what he did (for instance, he might be excused for his mistake if he fired his rifle as the ambiguous victim was entering the house in what could reasonably be misconstrued as a stealthy or furtive manner). But Timorous, a cowardly homeowner whose excessive fear and trembling cause him to shoot far more hastily than would persons of ordinary fortitude (say, when the ambiguous black figure first steps into Timorous' long gravel driveway) will be found unreasonable and in most jurisdictions convicted of second degree murder. Had he not found himself in that uncertain situation, the unreasonable killer's cowardly disposition may never have caused criminal harm (or perhaps even come to light) and he would have remained a good law-abiding citizen like Pusillanimous rather than a convicted murderer.

Just as resultant luck arbitrarily makes some careless drivers more blameworthy than others, circumstantial luck arbitrarily makes some morally deficient persons more blameworthy than others who are just as morally deficient. Although all cowardly homeowners and speeding motorists are morally deficient, luck determines whose moral deficiency causes harm and thus who can be morally blamed for what they have done. For our careless motorists, fortuity forged the fatal link between their culpable indifference and the unjustifiable killing of a pedestrian; for our cowardly homeowners, bad luck links their culpable disposition to the unjustifiable killing of a supposed assailant. In other words, it is moral bad luck for a cowardly person to find himself in high-pressure circumstances that expose his flaw, moral good luck for someone else just as cowardly to be spared such circumstances.

German Nazis and American slave owners forcefully illustrate moral circumstantial luck. Any of the ordinary citizens or concentration camp guards of Nazi Germany, like any of the ordinary citizens or slave owners in antebellum America (including "gentlemen slave-owners" like Thomas Jefferson and George Washington), could have heroically opposed the odious regimes in which they found themselves. Instead, most of them failed the moral test they faced and behaved badly, upholding and participating in the morally indefensible. Nagel invites us to compare an actual German Nazi to another German with the same character traits as the Nazi but whose company (for business reasons) relocated him to Argentina before the Nazis came to power. The relocated Argentine German might lead "a quiet and harmless life in Argentina" while his dispositional twin back in Germany served as an officer in a concentration camp. An ordinarily anti-Semitic German in the Forties was able to avoid taking innocent Jewish lives due to factors beyond his control—another case of moral good luck. That many people, vast majorities in some cases, can with cool deliberation participate in enormous moral atrocities like slavery and the Holocaust suggests that the "character flaw" some circumstances reveal may be ordinary human frailty, rather than aberrational depravity—in the language of products liability, such circumstances may reveal a design defect, one buried deep in human nature.

"Good Negroes" who morally condemn "Bad Negroes" without knowing how their own dispositional deficiencies would hold up in nightmare worlds of filth and hunger and violence and extreme suffering can, like the Argentine German, claim one crucial distinction between themselves and actual perpetrators—although the economically privileged Good Negro and relocated Argentine German could have (or even would have) behaved just as badly as the Bad Negro and German Nazi in the same situation, the Good Negro and relocated Argentine German simply did not, and thus, are not similarly responsible. A person can only be morally responsible for what she does. So from the standpoint of moral responsibility for actual criminal acts, there is a difference between Good and Bad Negroes and between the relocated Argentine German and the Nazi—the good Negro and Argentine German never actually cause deaths or participate in killings. The same was true in our analysis of lucky and unlucky speeders—only unlucky speeders, not their equally careless but lucky counterparts, actually cause deaths for which they can be responsible. It is irrational to blame the frail and unlucky and not the equally frail but lucky ones who would have done the same thing but who just happened not to be tested and exposed.

Nazis, slave masters, and violent gangbangers are clearly responsible for the harms caused by their vicious wills and bad intentions, but at the same time they are just as clearly *not* responsible for being thrown into a situation that exposed their frailties. Our control over whether our vices and frailties are exposed, over whether they cause harm, is in this sense no greater than Ms. Cogdon's control over whether her bodily movements caused harm. In Nagel's pithy words, a person is "not morally responsible for what he is and is not responsible for." Nevertheless, as soon as we stop rationally reflecting on this indubitable moral truth and look at a concrete case, we can't help condemning. You cannot tour the gas ovens of Auschwitz and not feel condemnation for "ordinary Nazis"; you cannot tour the slave fortresses in Ghana, contemplate the unspeakable horrors of the Middle Passage, and not feel indignation toward slave masters and their accomplices; you cannot walk the streets of South Central LA and hear a bereaved parent weeping over the body of a slain child and not feel contempt for the responsible gangbanger.

♦

An especially potent brand of moral circumstantial luck comes from the "spaces and flows" in which we find ourselves—that is, from our spatially distinct neighborhoods and the flow of jobs, people, and social currents through them.[115] Call this luck in the strains and moral tests presented to us by the flow of macroeconomic and other social forces through our neighborhoods and school districts, "moral spatial luck." Moral spatial luck subverts the moral distinction between me and LJ and the other young black men I grew up with—for convenience, call them *my brothas*—by setting the stage for them to succumb to provocations and temptations while sparing me those hard tests and thus paving my path to prosperity and a spotless criminal record.

Here's how. Once prison removed my paternal influence, just like *my brothas*, I routinely sailed up and down Park Street in Akron, on whose south corner stands the Haven of Rest Rescue Mission for the homeless and on whose north corner sits a hotspot for stabbings, shootings, drugs, and prostitution called (fall from) Grace Park. As a frank reminder to neighborhood residents of their own dim future, the street that Park intersects with to create these corners of concentrated poverty and crime is named Prospect. Just like *my brothas*, I sailed up and down this prospectless street with hostility, resentment, frustration, and hopelessness. Thus, in character traits and internal dispositions, they and I were flip sides of the same coin: we all dreamed the American Dream of prosperity symbolized in those days by homes in the suburbs and cars with "diamonds in the back" (in the words of Curtis Mayfield), even as we watched the legitimate means of getting our piece of that Dream choke and die before our eyes as every rubber plant in Akron shuttered its windows and even our iconic Goodyear blimp began berthing in distant hangars.

Had I remained stranded in that crime-ridden neighborhood in that forsaken rustbelt city (seething with resentment over the growing chasm between my diamond-in-the-back dreams and dwindling legitimate means), I strongly suspect that I too would have "chosen" to commit crimes and my moral record would have been dramatically and indelibly downgraded: "Tails, Bad Negro."

What kept me from failing the hard moral tests of our circumstances was the fortuitous intervention of two Great Society programs for "at risk" youth—Upward Bound and A Better Chance (ABC). I happened to hear about Upward Bound in time to apply; *my brotha*, LJ (a better student at the time), heard about it too late. Luck—not pluck—landed me and not LJ in Upward Bound. Upward Bound in turn led me to A Better Chance, which shipped me to a boarding school on The Main Line, a historical bastion of "old money" and sprawling estates in the western suburbs of Philadelphia. Consequently, while LJ remained mired in America's cynically deindustrialized heartland,[116] I hobnobbed with highly oxygenated Main Line blue bloods at keggers, gala fundraisers, and pep rallies. Of course, I "put in work" once I got the chance, routinely pulling all-nighters to keep up with the competition in the classroom and on the hardwood at Lower Merion High School; but it cannot be denied that the circumstantial luck of landing in two small and disappearing War on Poverty programs, and spending my high school years in privileged neighborhoods and school districts, contributed at least as much to the things I get and take credit for as my own work ethic or academic aptitude. In more ways than we dare imagine, morally we are at the mercy of luck.

This unequal distribution of moral good luck and moral bad luck—more specifically, of moral *spatial luck*—could lead ordinary people trapped in bad luck neighborhoods and school districts to experience life as profoundly unfair. Even the most diligent and intelligent student can apply himself to his studies with monk-like devotion, only to discover in the end that his high school diploma is a nearly worthless piece of paper in the college admissions process, because the public secondary school it comes from suddenly has no accreditation. This was the fate of Crenshaw High School, situated to draw teens from both poorer black neighborhoods and the hills of View Park, Baldwin Hills, and Windsor Hills, but which in fact draws mainly from poorer neighborhoods, because Hills Negroes often opt for Westside and private schools. Crenshaw was stripped of its accreditation for nearly six months in 2005 and 2006 by the Western Association of Schools and Colleges because of "great concerns regarding student achievement, the implementation of a curriculum and instructional program aligned with California academic standards, and the capacity of the school to address other critical areas."[117] Thanks to moral spatial luck, "virtue" was not vindicated in South Central and the link between legitimate means and the American Dream proved a cruel hoax.

Thus, any given student from Crenshaw, emotionally invested in the Weberian cultural belief system called the American Dream, thanks to bad spatial luck, is stuck in a neighborhood public school without accreditation and lacks access to that Dream. The divorce of legitimate educational means from the

American Dream imposes much greater strain and harder moral tests on this student than does the happy marriage between means and ends enjoyed by my Lower Merion High classmates and me, freeing our minds to focus on which selective colleges—Amherst, Williams, Wesleyan, Swarthmore, Haverford, the Ivies, or the Seven Sisters—would punch our tickets to prosperity. Certainly not all, but at least some statistically significant percentage of us Main Line and Lower Merion High Good Negroes would have cracked and revealed our own latent character flaws under the more taxing moral tests confronting Crenshaw students. Their neighborhood severs the means-ends connection by providing schools incapable of implementing a curriculum and instructional program aligned with even minimal California academic standards.

◆

Hidden in the Hills between La Brea Avenue and Crenshaw Boulevard, the *Los Angeles Times'* Bob Baker describes View Park as "a garden island in an urban sea, a plush community of high-priced homes and meticulously landscaped lawns." Walking these tranquil sidewalks, whose concrete slabs have been gently heaved in places by the swelling roots of trees, one can easily get the notion that there is nowhere better to go—there is a gentility to these blocks that becalms lives. Toni Morison once characterized "industrious Philadelphia Negroes" as "the proudest people in the race,"[118] but that distinction may now belong to the industrious Negroes of View Park, who have been known to look down on even slightly less wealthy but still upper-middle-class Blacks next door in Baldwin Hills; according to Baker, such still quite privileged but slightly less prosperous blacks "draw a raised eyebrow of disdain from View Park residents":

> "Baldwin Hills," one [View Park resident] sniffs with good-natured exaggeration, "is an eyesore"—a mere *tract* of homes, smaller and newer, with tiny or non-existent front yards.... When the county wanted to put a little asphalt and ivy jogging park in View Park in the 1970s, a number of residents argued against adding benches, drinking fountains, or restrooms. According to one politician's account—denied by community leaders—the reason was to discourage "those people" from Baldwin Hills, many of whom have just as much money as those people in View Park, from driving up the hill to use the park.[119]

In the 1940s and 1950s View Park was home to well-to-do Whites who had hoped to safeguard the narcotic gentility of their blocks through covenants not to sell to Blacks or Jews. But in 1948 the Supreme Court held in *Shelley v. Kraemer* that neither federal nor state courts could enforce racially restrictive covenants under the Equal Protection Clause. Consequently, *Shelley* enabled a substantial number of prosperous black families in the early 1960s to buy homes in previously white View Park. As prosperous Blacks trickled in, the trickle out of well-to-do Whites soon swelled into a wave of "white flight."[120] According to the *Los Angeles Times* story, "Within eight years, three-quarters of [Whites] had sold their homes to black lawyers, physicians, entrepreneurs and entertainers, often at cut-rate prices. By 1970, Blacks outnumbered whites nearly three to one. By 1980 the ratio was nine to one." The influx of lawyers, physicians, and other prosperous blacks created the conditions for the class-conscious cartography and spatial profiling of poor Blacks by their privileged counterparts that I discussed earlier.

In *The Truly Disadvantaged*, William Julius Wilson concisely described how economic segregation through middle-class migration and spatial separation produced social disorganization in poor black neighborhoods, the same kind of social disorganization that breeds crime according to many empirical studies:

> [T]he growing problem of joblessness in the inner city ... [is] partly created by the changing social composition of inner-city neighborhoods. In the 1940s, 1950s, and even the 1960s, lower-class, working-class, and middle-class black urban families all resided more or less in the same ghetto areas, albeit on different streets. The exodus of black middle-class professionals from the inner city has been increasingly accompanied by a movement of stable working-class blacks to higher-income neighborhoods in other parts of the city and to the suburbs. Confined by restrictive covenants to communities also inhabited by the urban black lower classes, the black working and middle classes in earlier years provided stability to inner-city neighborhoods and perpetuated and reinforced societal norms and values. In short, their very presence enhanced the social organization of ghetto communities.[121]

One powerful implication of Wilson's analysis is that landmark civil rights movement legal victories like *Shelley* mainly helped middle-class Blacks, not the truly disadvantaged or "black underclass." Worse still, these civil rights victories in some cases actually deepened the plight of the truly disadvantaged. For instance, before civil rights "victories" like *Shelley*, restrictive covenants created high density black communities with high levels of *economic integration*, that is, high levels of spatial overlap between black professionals and poor Blacks. These high levels of economic integration could reduce "social disorganization"—a factor causally linked to higher crime rates—by sustaining "the basic institutions in the inner city (including churches, stores, schools, recreational facilities, etc.) in the face of prolonged joblessness."[122]

But the mass migration of more mobile middle-class Blacks to neighborhoods like View Park helped isolate and concentrate disadvantage in existing black neighborhoods, thereby increasing economic segregation, social disorganization, and hence crime rates in the neighborhoods left behind. Yana Kucheva and Richard Sander reached conclusions consistent with this view in their analysis of the relationship between *Shelley* and the hyper-concentration of criminogenic disadvantage in poor black neighborhoods:

> What we see in our analysis, thus far, is all of a piece: restrictive covenants near ghettos were particularly prevalent (and, until *Shelley*, particularly effective) in middle-class communities of single-family homes. Middle-class Blacks were the most eager challengers of these covenants, and the ones with both the greatest means and strongest desire to move out of existing ghettoes. After *Shelley*, middle-class Blacks migrated to previously covenanted communities in large numbers, increasing substantially both the black homeownership rate and the level of intra-black economic segregation. The newly-entered communities consistently resegregated, so the aggregate level of black/white segregation did not change much, but the post-*Shelley* world had a much more geographically dispersed black population.[123]

It logically follows from these empirical findings that the black bourgeoisie, by destabilizing older black neighborhoods through their departure, increased the crime rate in those neighborhoods and made them more susceptible than ever to major crime waves. For the crack plague of the 1980s and 1990s, the ground zero were the economically segregated neighborhoods in Los Angeles with high concentrations of poor and working-class Blacks—South Central, Watts, The Jungle, Compton, Inglewood. Through our own "black flight" from economically integrated black neighborhoods into economically segregated, previously white neighborhoods like View Park in the 1960s and 1970s, mobile middle-class Blacks in Los Angeles fueled the higher crime rates in neighborhoods we abandoned and now regard with suspicion. This pattern of "black flight" and economic segregation is far from unique to LA, occurring also in cities like Chicago and St. Louis and many other urban, northern cities. Thus the deterioration of poor black neighborhoods across America into criminogenic tinder boxes of resentment, frustration, hopelessness, and suppressed violence cannot be attributed simply to racial prejudice in Whites or internal deficiencies in Blacks (like a "culture of poverty" or "welfare dependency").[124] It must be largely attributed to macroeconomic social forces (like the mass exodus of automobile, rubber, steel, and other "low-skilled" manufacturing jobs to lower-wage areas in the South or overseas) and to the mass exodus of the black bourgeoisie to previously white neighborhoods like View Park, Baldwin Hills, Windsor Hills, and Ladera Heights. The combined effect of two distinct flows—namely, the flow of manufacturing jobs South and overseas and the flow of the black middle class from traditional black neighborhoods into previously white ones—left poor Blacks stranded in geographical spaces filled with undiluted disadvantage and criminogenic social disorganization.

Thanks to moral spatial luck, relatively few View Park young people—fortune's favorites—have met or will meet the Black Criminal Litmus Test and be found a nigga. The math is simple: a grossly disproportionate number of the "violent crimes" Americans worry most about—murder, manslaughter, forcible rape, robbery, and aggravated assault[125]—are committed by Blacks from families below the poverty line. Because of demonstrable links between concentrated disadvantage and crime rates, poor neighborhoods have a much higher percentage of "dangerous Blacks"—Blacks who have committed or pose a heightened risk of committing violent street crime—than prosperous ones. To be more concise, someone from a poor black neighborhood poses a greater risk of street crime than his Golden Ghetto doppelganger.

The participation of my three sons in sports set the stage for my lessons in urban social maps and spatial profiling. Although my sons have grown up exclusively in View Park, from kindergarten through High School they all have played AAU basketball, Little League baseball, and Pop Warner football. On these teams they have formed close friendships with black kids and families from much less privileged nearby neighborhoods. Naturally, then, their teenage house parties include teens from Watts, Compton, Inglewood, and South Central. However, some of my fellow View Park homeowners, expressing safety concerns and claiming to speak for the neighborhood, vocally objected to my sons' parties for this very reason—in their words, "we do not want Compton up here." In strikingly similar language, a Black Sheriff's Deputy cautioned my sons and their event planners that, "we do not want South Central up here."[126]

Place names like South Central and Compton are synonymous with hard moral tests and hence moral bad luck. The South Central "we do not want up here" includes a neighborhood just down the hill from View Park known to local residents as The Jungle, which originally earned its name for its tropical trees and foliage (tranquil palms, banana trees, and begonias thriving amid tropical-style postwar apartment buildings), but whose name now suggests a jungle of a different kind, one with tattered palms standing amid ruins, and ruthless gangs vying for survival. The 2001 box office hit *Training Day* made The Jungle the very archetype of crime-ridden West Coast urban decay. It depicted Palmwood, one of the Jungle's many curvilinear dead end streets, as crawling with Bloods and snipers brazenly brandishing assault weapons from rooftops—a scene reminiscent of the mad jungle sequences in Conrad's *Heart of Darkness* and Coppola's *Apocalypse Now*. Once The Jungle's soaring crime rate made its name intolerably ironic, residents 20 years ago prevailed upon the Los Angeles City Council to rename the crime-ridden area Baldwin Village, in the poignant hope of linking its name to its respectable and geographically contiguous neighbor, Baldwin Hills.[127]

◆

Proponents of a politics of respectability and personal responsibility in criminal matters have one remaining forceful argument against the conclusion that the only difference between disproportionately middle-class Good Negroes and disproportionately poor Bad Negroes or "niggas" is circumstantial or resultant luck. Their forceful counterargument, simply put, is that not *all* Good Negroes are middle- and upper-class, and not *all* Bad Negroes are poor; not all those we praise are haves, and not all we condemn, have-nots. Indeed, often a critic of Bad Negroes will preface his criticisms with a moving account of the poverty and other circumstantial obstacles the critic himself overcame on his way to a successful moral life, making him living proof that a "man of character" can avoid doing bad things even under strong situational pressures. From this standpoint, even the most difficult circumstances leave room for praise and blame. There were Germans who saved Jewish lives during the Holocaust and White Americans who fought against chattel slavery in Jefferson's and Washington's day—good character, it seems, can sparkle like a jewel in a dung heap and motivate a person to do the right thing despite external circumstances.

Let's assume—just for the sake of argument—that poor Blacks who remain law-abiding despite the shocks and pressures of poverty have "good character," while poor black criminals have "bad character." For instance, assume Bad Negroes are greedy, cold, ungenerous, unkind, vain, and conceited while their Good (but disadvantaged) Negro counterparts are conscientious, considerate, generous, kind, modest, unselfish, caring, and compassionate. Assume that because of their superior moral character, Poor but Good Negroes suffer the slings and arrows of social and economic misfortune with patience and forbearance and without breaking the law.

It cannot be denied that blaming and praising people on the basis of moral character—or, as it is sometimes put, on the basis of who they are and what is in their "hearts"—is a common practice. In courtrooms, for instance, jurors are given ample opportunity in their jury instructions to directly assess the character of the accused in judging his guilt or innocence. One of the most basic excuse claims in the substantive criminal law is that the defendant's unjustified act should be attributed to his situation rather than to a bad character trait—this is the excuse claim at the heart of criminal negligence, recklessness, voluntary manslaughter, depraved heart murder, duress, putative self-defense, and all other doctrines that make guilt hinge on whether the wrongdoer acted like "a reasonable person *in the situation*."[128] Under the Model Penal Code, to convict under any of these doctrines, the jury must attribute the unjustified act to a character deficiency rather than a situational pressure.[129] So Poor but Good Negro critics who blame Bad Negroes for their character deficiencies can find ample support for their moral attitude in law and everyday life—they can say to their moral inferiors, "I am not *like* you. I am not greedy, cold, ungenerous, unkind, vain, or conceited, so I did not form the same bad intentions or act on the same bad motives as you. I do not share your character flaws, your 'inclinations, capacities, and temperament.' Because I am not the *kind* of person you are, I do not look at your contemptible moral record of criminal wrongdoing and say to myself, 'there but for the grace of God or good luck go I.' Because I've been there and *not* done that, I am living proof that we are not 'morally at the mercy of luck.' I do not sympathetically identify with you and hence morally condemn you without reservation."

The fatal flaw in this moral analysis is that the kind of person one is, one's character, is determined primarily by factors beyond a person's control: genetic make-up, pre-natal care, early childhood development, caregiver and parental rearing practices, family structure, schools, peers, personal assaults and traumas, and a multiplicity of other fortuitous experiential factors. The substantive criminal law makes allowances for some of the resulting "dispositional deficiencies," if they are deemed to be beyond the wrongdoer's control. When a woman suffering from battered woman syndrome kills her sleeping spouse and claims self-defense, for instance, even if the jury concludes that the act was not legally justified because the threat was not imminent or there were less drastic alternatives, in many jurisdictions she must be excused for the unjustified killing if a reasonable person suffering from the same post-traumatic stress disorder would have overestimated the threat of a sleeping man and, through learned helplessness, underestimated her ability to escape the abusive relationship. The test of subjective culpability in these cases is whether the battered woman acted like a reasonable person endowed with her cognitive and volitional deficiencies. The same is true of Negrophobes—people whose hypersensitivity to Blacks results from a personal history of violence at the hands of Blacks. Bernhard Goetz, the celebrated subway vigilante, included this argument in his successful self-defense claim after shooting four unarmed but arguably threatening black teenagers on a New York subway. The Goetz jury, using an individualized test of reasonableness that allowed them to consider his "prior experiences,"[130] concluded that his response to the four black youths was that of a reasonable man in the situation. The individualized test gave them ample discretion to measure his response by that of a "reasonable person who has been mugged before by black assailants" or of a "reasonable Negrophobe."[131] Further, in the area of criminal negligence, the courts can individualize the test of reasonableness to make allowances for the peculiar inner deficiencies of a wrongdoer: Thus, in *State v. Everhart*, the defendant, a young girl with an IQ of 72, gave birth in her own bedroom and, thinking that the baby had been born dead, wrapped it from head to foot in a blanket. The baby smothered to death. Under the non-individualized, generalized "reasonable person" test she was convicted of involuntary manslaughter, but the appellate court reversed the conviction by applying an individualized "reasonable person with an IQ of 72" test. Under the all-purpose "reasonable person in the situation test" at the heart of many legal excuses, the "reasonable person" can be individualized and endowed with the wrongdoer's dispositional, volitional, and cognitive deficiencies. The moral intuition supporting each of these individualized tests of reasonableness is that a person cannot be blamed for an inner deficiency—cognitive, volitional, or dispositional—that she did not choose, was not responsible for acquiring, and essentially had thrust upon her. Simply put, the substantive criminal law sometimes makes allowances for bad luck in the creation and development of one's peculiar inclinations, capacities, aversions, character traits, and actions.

Another source of character traits beyond someone's control is the childrearing practices of one's parents—whether and how much she was physically disciplined (struck or beaten) as a child, for instance. Recent research shows that such corporal punishment "psychologically damages the child, increases social violence in general, [and] leads to children's increased aggression and anger. Parents who were beaten go on to beat their own kids."[132] Severe child abuse—in closets, basements, attics, and broad daylight—can instill bad character traits and dispositions. Tragically, battered and exploited children abound in desperate economic circumstances and many criminals were battered children. In the words of Bob Herbert, "Victims of child abuse are likely to be kids from poor and often profoundly twisted families...Often their [lives] are case studies in unrelieved torment, sickening to hear about, sordid beyond belief."[133] The biological and environmental determinants of character and personality traits can be multiplied endlessly, each new determinant further reducing the area of moral agency and hence eroding our moral judgments of wrongdoers.[134]

Once we recognize how many factors beyond our control determine our "inclinations and capacities," our personality and character traits, we begin to recognize the many ways in which "who we are in our hearts" is a tissue of contingencies and so not a proper object of moral assessment. To be sure, bad traits may be the product of earlier choices and to some extent may be amenable to change through critical self-reflection and self-revision, but as Nagel notes, they are "largely a matter of constitutive bad fortune."[135]

◆

The most enthusiastic proponents of personal responsibility in criminal matters may resort to one last common argument for heaping blame and contempt on wrongdoers—they may make "choice" their last stand. A person can always *choose* to control his impulses to act on whatever bad character traits have been "thrust upon him," these "Choice Theorists" declare. The envious, conceited, and cowardly can control themselves, even if it takes a "monumental effort of will." Choice is the seat of personal responsibility and object of moral assessment, and so no matter the circumstances, if the wrongdoer *chooses* to do wrong, she can be blamed *purely* on the basis of her bad choice. Even if under the circumstances it would have been *extremely difficult* for an ordinary person to avoid losing control and giving in (for instance, say, a father walks in on a daycare provider sexually molesting his preschooler and kills in a blind rage), in the words of Stephen Morse, "even enraged people generally retain the capacity to control homicidal or any other kind of aggressive or antisocial desires."[136] In morally evaluating others, Choice Theorists insist, choice is a sufficient condition of moral responsibility; as long as it not impossible for a person to choose not to break the law, they contend, we must criminally condemn wrongdoers on the basis of their choices rather than their character.

Nevertheless, contrary to such assertions and prescriptions, the criminal law does partially excuse people who intentionally kill others in response to provocations or circumstances that would sorely test the self-control of ordinary people with ordinary character traits. Even though it was not impossible for such persons to choose not to kill, as long as the provoking or disturbing circumstance would sorely test the self-control of "a reasonable person" with ordinary character traits, the killing is mitigated from murder to manslaughter. This makes a person's *character* rather than his *choice* the primary object of blame or praise. Whether it is "extremely difficult" to choose the right course of conduct depends on a person's background personality and character traits. For instance, acting with ordinary fortitude in a given situation may be a piece of cake for a brave man, manageably difficult for a typical person, but *extremely difficult* for a coward, yet the coward would lack an excuse because cowardice is not an ordinary character trait of ordinary people.[137]

For this reason, under common law and Model Penal Code approaches to "heat of passion" and extreme emotional disturbance excuses, it is not enough that the wrongdoer found it extremely difficult to do the right thing or acted "under the influence of extreme emotional disturbance." Finding control extremely difficult just meets a threshold requirement. Assuming the jury finds that he was emotionally overwhelmed when he killed, for him to be partially excused they must also conclude that the circumstance would have triggered an emotional disturbance in, or sorely tested the self-control of, a "reasonable person in the situation." If his emotional disturbance and loss of self-control can be attributed to a blameworthy character trait, it cannot partially excuse his criminal act. In the landmark case of *Maher v. People*, for instance, the wrongdoer shot his wife's illicit lover in the ear and claimed heat of passion. The court stressed that the focus of the provocation excuse is the character of the accused:

> But if the act of killing, though intentional, be committed under the influence of passion or in heat of blood produced by an adequate or reasonable provocation...and is the result of the temporary excitement, by which the control of reason was disturbed, rather than of any wickedness of heart or cruelty or recklessness of disposition: then the law, out of indulgence to the frailty of human nature, or rather, in recognition of the laws upon which human nature is constituted, very properly regards the offense as of a less heinous character than murder, and gives it the designation of manslaughter.[138]

The court then goes on to give a character-based explanation for why not everyone overwhelmed by rage or other extreme emotional disturbance is partially excused:

> Nor...must the provocation, in every case, be held sufficient or reasonable, because such a state of excitement has followed from it; for then, by habitual and long continued indulgence of evil passions, a bad man might acquire a claim to mitigation which would not be available to better men, and on account of that very wickedness of heart which, in itself, constitutes an aggravation both in morals and in law.[139]

This same pattern of character-driven moral judgment runs throughout criminal law.

Consider another devastating blow to the claim that choice rather than character is the seat of personal responsibility and object of moral assessment: that essentially choice is not necessary for blame. We routinely blame and punish wrongdoers who lack awareness of wrongdoing. Thus, as happens frequently in the setting of date rapes, a man may sincerely but stupidly believe that an unwilling woman consents to sexual intercourse—he honestly but stupidly thinks "no" means "yes," for instance, and acts without adequate care and concern for her subjective willingness. In the words of Catharine MacKinnon, "many (maybe even most) rapes involve honest men and violated women."[140] His sincere belief that the unwanted sex was consensual may prove that he never chose to do wrong—he could not choose rape if he honestly believes the sex is consensual. He could, of course, be aware of a risk of being mistaken and therefore chose to do wrong in the sense of choosing to take excessive risks of seriously harming another person. Recklessness involves choice. But he cannot choose to commit rape or choose to take excessive risks of raping if he honestly lacks awareness that there is even a risk that the sex is nonconsensual. Nevertheless, in most American jurisdictions, if his honest but mistaken belief is not also reasonable, he is guilty of rape. And this moral judgment makes sense if the reason he lacks awareness of wrongdoing is lack of care and concern for others. The condition of a man's heart—his cares, concerns, aversions, and values—can determine the contents of his head: vices like conceit, self-absorption, coldness, and insufficient care and concern for others can keep risks to others from ever crossing a wrongdoer's mind. Whenever we blame people for inadvertent negligence, which we do throughout criminal law and everyday life, we look past the wrongdoer's lack of awareness and lack of choice and focus exclusively on his character; we ask *why* the wrongdoer lacked awareness and what that *why*, that reason or excuse, says about the kind of person he is. Accordingly, in support of retaining inadvertent negligence as a basis of criminal liability, the Model Penal Code Comment states that "moral defect can properly be imputed to instances where the defendant acts out of insensitivity to the interests of other people, and not merely out of an intellectual failure to grasp them." We condemn the unwitting wrongdoer if a person with ordinary levels of sympathy, care, and concern for others would have been aware.

Thus it is clear that choice is neither necessary nor sufficient for blame in law or everyday life. Instead, character is the real object of many, if not most, of our ordinary moral and legal judgments—we blame people on the basis of their traits and dispositions rather than their "free will." And this conclusion brings us right back to the decisive role of moral luck in the formation of our moral character traits, and to Nigga Theory's position on the illegitimacy of our moral condemnations of wrongdoers. In the end, a Bad Negro is a moral paradox—a product of moral luck—and a paradox should not provide a plausible platform for hate, contempt, and moral indignation.

CHAPTER **THREE**

LAW IN THE SOCIAL CONSTRUCTION OF "NIGGAS"

S THE BLACK CRIMINAL Litmus Test of a nigga reliable? In other words, is conviction a reliable test of a black person's blameworthiness? Criminal conviction can *seem* like a reliable "nigga detector" by the following logic:

» Because wrongdoers enjoy a constitutionally-protected presumption of innocence in criminal trials, the jury is generally instructed that the State must prove beyond a reasonable doubt not only that a wrongdoer committed a prohibited act but that he or she did so with a certain level of blameworthiness or subjective culpability or *mens rea*.

» Accordingly, a criminal conviction generally means that a jury found the wrongdoer to be morally blameworthy (that is, to have acted with the necessary *mens rea*) beyond a reasonable doubt.

» Hence, criminal conviction establishes accurately and reliably—i.e., beyond a reasonable doubt—that a black person deserves blame and contempt.

The problem with this argument, as we have seen, is that jurors' judgments of black blameworthiness—and thus their *mens rea* findings about

Blacks—are racially biased. And if jurors' moral judgments about Blacks are racially tainted, if black wrongdoers systematically suffer harsher moral evaluations than similarly situated Whites, they will more often satisfy the *mens rea* requirement for criminal conviction. And the racially-biased moral assessments of ordinary prosecutors, judges, and jurors ensure that black criminals are manufactured in the adjudication process, that black criminals are "constructed" and not merely "found" in the bias-laden fact-finding process of a criminal trial. This in turn means that a criminal conviction is unreliable evidence of blameworthiness in any cases involving blacks. Studies on attribution bias and ingroup empathy bias, discussed below, do indeed show that black wrongdoers systematically suffer harsher moral appraisals than similarly situated white wrongdoers.

◆

Those trained in American law schools have learned to think about the *mens rea* requirement in ways that conceal its central role as a vehicle for factfinders to make frontal moral judgments of wrongdoers, moral judgments riddled with racism. This is why paradigms matter—looking at things through the wrong ones can conceal where racial bias lives in the substantive criminal law and the adjudication of just deserts.[141] The prevailing paradigm of *mens rea* in the substantive criminal law should be overhauled because it does not adequately serve the most basic function of a sound paradigm—it does not explain many phenomena within its scope. Worse still from a racial justice perspective, the prevailing paradigm, like a conceptual cataract, obstructs a clear view of where bias lives both in black letter law and in the processes by which factfinders apply the black letter to Blacks.

The following analysis will provide a clear picture of how under current law biased moral judgments of a wrongdoer can directly and indirectly determine whether factfinders "find" the necessary *mens rea* for criminal conviction. Once the conceptual cataract has been removed through this more coherent interpretation of *mens rea*, a clear and simple truth comes into focus: bias lives in the *mens rea* requirement and in how judges and jurors apply it to black wrongdoers.

◆

The legal requirement of *mens rea* or subjective culpability is meant to assure that the punishment fits the blame. In its liability function, the requirement shields morally innocent wrongdoers from any punishment, and in its grading function the requirement subjects the less culpable to less punishment and the more culpable to more. But because the subjective culpability or "desert" of an offender can be and often is measured by his character, the *mens rea* requirement often calls on jurors to judge the character of the wrongdoer. In *Rethinking Criminal Law*, George Fletcher points out that "[a]n inference from the wrongful act to the actor's character is essential to a retributive theory of punishment"[142]—that is, a theory under which it is unjust to punish a person who does not deserve punishment and unjust to punish him more than he deserves (and deserts for punishment purposes are measured by subjective culpability). As he more fully states it:

(1) punishing wrongful conduct is just only if punishment is measured by the desert of the offender, (2) the desert of an offender is gauged by his character—i.e., the kind of person he is, (3) and therefore, a judgment about character is essential to the just distribution of punishment.

Excuses can disrupt this process, for they invite the jury to attribute a wrongful act to an actor's situation rather than her character, or, in Fletcher's words, an excuse can "preclude an inference from the [wrongful] act to the actor's character."[143] Otherwise, the actor's act reflects the actor's character, and that determines the punishment.

That *mens rea* findings often turn on whether jurors attribute the wrongdoer's act to his character or to his situation maps directly onto a body of social psychological research called attribution theory. Fritz Heider, "the father of attribution theory," focused his research on what he called "naïve" or "commonsense" psychology, the kind employed by ordinary people, including jurors and court officials. For Heider, people were like amateur scientists, trying to understand other people's behavior (here the behavior of wrongdoers) by piecing together information to explain its causes. Heider describes how ordinary people ("social perceivers") answer the "why" questions that arise when they interpret another's (wrongdoer's) conduct. When trying to decide why wrongdoers behave as they do, people either attribute the wrongdoing to internal, dispositional factors or external, situational ones. An internal attribution is the inference that a wrongdoer is behaving a certain way because of something about him or her, such as the person's attitudes, character, or personality. An external attribution is the inference that a wrongdoer is behaving a certain way because of something about the situation he or she is in. Research indicates that wrongdoers whose acts are viewed as stemming from external factors are generally held less responsible than those whose acts are viewed as stemming from internal factors. In a very influential study, however, Julian B. Rotter found that when people explain the behavior of others, they systematically tend to overlook the impact of situations and overestimate the role of personal factors. Because this bias is so pervasive, and often so misleading, it is called the fundamental attribution error.[144]

This is pregnant with implications from a racial justice standpoint, and perhaps more pregnant are studies showing differences in people's attributions about the causes of wrongful behavior by white versus black wrongdoers. In a classic experiment, psychologist Birt Duncan found that violent acts tended to be attributed to internal causes when the harm-doer was black, but to situational causes when the harm-doer was white.[145] In another study, sociologists George S. Bridges and Sara Steen found:

> Being black significantly reduces the likelihood of negative *external* attributions by probation officers and significantly increases the likelihood of negative *internal* attributions, even after adjusting for severity of the presenting offense and the youth's prior involvement in criminal behavior.[146]

In addition, they found that to the extent that court officials attribute black crimes to internal causes and white crimes to external causes, "they may be more likely to view minorities as culpable and prone to committing future crimes."[147] Thus, differential attributions about the causes of crime by Blacks and Whites contribute directly to differential evaluations of subjective culpability and dangerousness.[148] And from there, of course, we are led to differential findings of guilt and differential sentencing.

The demonstrable race-based differences in attributions implies that in assessing *mens rea*, factfinders more readily find the requirement met for blacks than for similarly situated whites, and they will more readily attribute a black defendant's commission of the *actus reus* to his character than they will his similarly situated white counterpart. Which means that criminals—including even murderers—are constructed by factfinders in the adjudication process. Imagine a black and a white actor, each of whom intentionally kills another person under similar circumstances and claims provocation. The *mens rea* for murder is "malice"—unlawful killings committed with "malice" are murder and those without malice are manslaughter. Malice means (among other things) an unprovoked intention to kill; thus, an adequate provocation negates malice. Accordingly, if jurors find that the defendant intentionally killed in the heat of passion, triggered by an adequate provocation, they will find no malice and hence convict him only of manslaughter, but if they do not find an adequate provocation, they will find malice and convict him of the more blameworthy kind of criminal homicide, murder. Under one common approach, the provocation, to be adequate, must be such as might cause *a reasonable or ordinary person in the same situation* to "lose self-control and act on impulse and without reflection."[149]

It is here that there is room for biased moral judgments and social construction because it is here that judges and jurors make attributions. As Model Penal Code reporters Jerome Michael and Herbert Wechsler observed:

> Provocation ... must be estimated by the probability that [the provocative] *circumstances* would affect *most men* in like fashion.... Other things being equal, the greater the provocation, measured in that way, the more ground there is for attributing the intensity of the actor's passions and his lack of self-control on the homicidal occasion to the extraordinary character of the *situation* in which he was placed rather than to any extraordinary deficiency in his own *character*.[150]

Again, they must determine whether to attribute the act to external, situational factors or to internal, dispositional ones.

As differential attributions about the causes of crime by Blacks and Whites lead to differential evaluations of subjective culpability, murderous black criminals are socially constructed at a far greater rate than murderous Whites. "Wickedness of heart or cruelty of disposition" is attributed to black wrongdoers at a greater rate than Whites in similar situations. Hence, black murderers are not merely found in the adjudication process, they are socially constructed through the racially biased moral evaluations of everyday prosecutors, judges, and jurors.

The Wechsler and Michael analysis of murderous *mens rea* and the provocation mitigation not only recognizes the central importance of the "character vs. situation" or "internal vs. external" distinction in jurors' assessments of subjective culpability, it also points out the kind of information that ordinary people (including ordinary jurors) rely on to decide between an internal and external explanation or attribution, namely, information about how *most people* would respond to the provocation at issue: Provocation, they point out, "must be estimated by the probability that [the provocative] circumstances would affect *most men* in like fashion."[151] The reasonable person test makes information about the reactions of *most people* decisive not only in provocation cases, but also in cases involving criminal negligence and recklessness and a host of other defenses. In the words of Mark Kelman, implicit in the reasonable or ordinary person test is the moral norm that "blame is reserved for the (statistically) deviant"[152]— typical beliefs and reactions generally qualify as reasonable ones. Hence, the reasonable person test directs factfinders to consider information about typical reactions in assessing a wrongdoer's blameworthiness.

Attribution research suggests that people give great weight to how typical an actor's reactions are in deciding whether to attribute them to external or internal factors; Harold Kelly's Covariation Principle, for instance, finds that when forming an attribution, people rely on consensus information, that is, how different people respond to the same stimulus.[153] The reasonable or ordinary person test, then, by calling on factfinders to consider consensus information in assessing defendants' subjective culpability, provides a very common legal vehicle for the formation and application of internal or external attributions and explanations by judges and jurors who are adjudicating a wrongdoer's just deserts.[154]

Moreover, the Model Penal Code makes it clear that the point of the word "situation" (in phrases like "reasonable person in the actor's *situation*") is to furnish factfinders with a discretion-laden doctrinal vehicle for excusing those reactions of an actor that can be attributed to his "situation" (and hence do not reveal internal, dispositional defects) and blaming the actor for those reactions that do reveal character defects (because they cannot be attributed to situational pressures). Thus, the Code makes the test for heat of passion whether the defendant acted "under the influence of extreme emotional disturbance for which there is reasonable explanation or excuse," and then directs that the determination of the reasonableness of the explanation or excuse shall be made "from the viewpoint of a person *in the actor's situation*."[155] In clarifying this formulation, the Comments state:

The word "situation" is designedly ambiguous.... There thus will be room for interpretation of the word "situation," and that is precisely the flexibility desired.... In the end, the question is whether the actor's loss of self-control can be understood in terms that arouse *sympathy* in the ordinary citizen. Section 210.3 faces this issue squarely and leaves the ultimate judgment to the ordinary citizen in the function of a juror assigned to resolve the specific case.[156]

It is worth noting the Code's recognition of a link between attributions and sympathy. To the extent that we attribute an actor's misbehavior to her situation, we are more disposed to sympathize with her: "There but for the grace of God go I" suggests recognition that, because of ordinary human frailty, in the same situation, I, the person passing judgment, might commit the same act. Conversely, the more we sympathize, the more disposed we may be to attribute her misbehavior to her situation. (So sympathy could drive attribution or attribution could drive sympathy or sympathy and attribution could be bi-directional and mutually influence each other.) By the same token, to the extent we attribute her misbehavior to her character, we may withhold sympathy, for we may think that we could not possibly commit the same act in the same situation. We see the act not as an expression of ordinary human frailty but rather as an expression of her extraordinary weakness or depravity. To the extent that we sympathize with wrongdoers, it may be possible to feel some sense of solidarity with them despite their plight; but without sympathy we can more readily view them as inalterably different, alien, other. Attribution processes (especially attributional stereotypes) may strongly affect how we define "us" and "them" in relation to criminals, and whether we opt for a politics of compassion or a politics of condemnation in criminal matters.

Because empathy and sympathy constitute a critical basis of jurors' blameworthiness or *mens rea* determinations, let's consider the empirical case for widespread anti-black empathy bias that makes jurors less likely to sympathetically identify with them in criminal prosecutions. One data source comes from neuroscientific studies. "Ingroup empathy bias" has a neural basis in the brain that researchers have captured using functional magnetic resonance imaging (FMRI). FMRI measures brain activity by detecting the changes in blood oxygenation and flow that occur in response to neural activity—more active brain areas consume more oxygen, and blood flow increases to the active area to meet this increased demand.[157] FMRI can produce an activation map, or NeuroImage, displaying which areas of the brain are active during a particular thought, action, or experience. Recent studies in social neuroscience show that "empathy for [another's] pain is supported by neuroanatomical circuits underlying both affective and cognitive processes."[158] These studies reveal distinct neural mechanisms for empathy and altruistic motivation. Specifically, one area of the brain or "neural matrix" (including bilateral anterior insula and anterior cingulate cortex) is thought to support the emotional or affective ingredients of empathy while another area (including parts of medial prefrontal cortex, or MPFC) is thought to underlie cognitive components of empathy, "such as the capacity to take another person's perspective." According to these findings, "the capacity to understand and share another's pain is supported by both affective (e.g., affect resonance) and cognitive (e.g., perspective-taking) mechanisms in the brain" and these mechanisms can be mapped using functional magnetic resonance imaging.

While their brain activity was being monitored with FMRI, 14 black and 14 white subjects were shown scenes depicting either black or white individuals "in a painful (e.g., in the midst of a natural disaster) or neutral (e.g., attending an outdoor picnic) situation." During scanning, participants indicated how much empathy they felt for the person in the target image using a four-point scale (1=not at all to 4=very much). Outside of the scanner, subjects also rated how much money and how much time they would be willing to donate to help each target. In addition, participants were given behavioral exit surveys after scanning to test their disposition for "perspective taking" (that is, the reported tendency to spontaneously adopt the psychological point of view of others in everyday life) and to test their love for, identification with, and loyalty to their social ingroup (using the Multigroup Ethnic Identity Measure or MEIM).

As in other social neuroscience studies of empathy, researchers found that, irrespective of race, subjects showed empathy for humankind in general through greater neural activity within anterior cingulated cortex and bilateral anterior insula when observing the suffering of other humans.[159] However, only black subjects showed extraordinary empathy for the pain of black victims—they had greater response within the medial prefrontal cortex (MPFC, which registers empathy) when perceiving Blacks in distress. Unlike Whites, Blacks "recruit medial prefrontal cortex when observing suffering of members of their own social group." Across subjects, activity within the MPFC when perceiving the pain of ingroup relative to outgroup members predicted a subject's higher empathy ratings and greater willingness to donate money and time to help the distressed victim. These findings suggest that there are distinct neural mechanisms of empathy and altruistic motivation in the brain and that the brain mechanisms (or neurocognitive processes) associated with an observer's self-identity underlie extraordinary empathy and altruistic motivation for members of one's own social group.

Researchers have also used electroencephalography (EEG) to capture white brains spontaneously displaying insensitivity to Blacks and other outgroups. When people are sensitive to the feelings, intentions, and needs of others, Jennifer N. Gutsell and Michael Inzlicht found, they "resonate with them by adopting their postures, intonations, and facial expressions, but also their motivational states and emotions."[160] The body actions and facial expressions of another activate the observer's neural networks that govern the same physical actions and expressions. The observer's neural networks *mirror* those of the object as the observer vicariously participates in the experiences of people, they observe by mentally simulating their actions and expressions and beyond—in many cases physically mimicking their expressions, gestures, and body postures. Such vicarious activation of the observer's neural system for action during perception of others' actions and expressions is called "perception-action-coupling." According to this perception-action model of empathy, such mirroring is the way the observer's brain understands the other's actions, intentions, and emotions. This perception-action link is made possible by "shared neural networks"—neural mechanisms that allow observers to mirror the actions and emotions of those they observe, "thereby synchronizing the inner states of both individuals." These shared neural networks are the basic building blocks of empathy.

Other research has identified shared neural networks for perception and the experience of disgust, pain, touch, and facial expressions. The system of neurons making up these shared networks are often called "the mirror-neuron system."[161] This mirror-neuron system enables observers to mentally simulate actions and emotions of others (that is, to experience perception-action-coupling), thereby increasing interpersonal sensitivity and laying the foundation for empathy and social understanding.[162] Accordingly, sensitivity or indifference to the actions, thoughts, and feelings of ingroup and outgroup members should be reflected in the shared neural networks that make up the mirror-neuron system.

The disturbing discovery of researchers is that the mirror-neuron system underlying the capacity of observers to mentally simulate the actions, intentions, and emotions of others is biased against outgroups, especially disliked outgroups.[163] For instance, while observing others in pain, people show less activity in brain areas associated with the experience of pain when observing ethnic outgroup members in pain than when observing similarly situated ingroup members. An even more basic and general bias against outgroups keeps Whites from mentally simulating simple, gross motor responses like those associated with reaching for a glass, picking it up, taking a small sip of water, and then putting the glass back in its place. An observer's ability to mentally mirror another person's gross motor responses is "the physiological process thought to be at the core of interpersonal sensitivity." Such a fundamental bias against mentally simulating the actions of members of outgroups, say researchers, "would not only make it difficult to empathize with outgroup members' suffering, but also to understand their actions and intentions."

EEG has been used to measure mirror neuron activity by recording "mu rhythm suppression" in observers while they passively observe ingroup and outgroup members. The "mu rhythm" is generated by the area of the brain involved in voluntary motor control. Mu rhythm or "mu waves"—waves in the frequency range of 8–13 Hz—attain maximal "amplitude" or "power" when individuals are at rest.[164] Early studies showed that the amplitude of "mu waves" could be *suppressed,* their power diminished, by execution, observation, or imagination, that is, by a subject's own physical movement or by his observation of others performing actions or by imagined movement. "When mu power decreases during observation of an object other, the subject's motor neurons are active and the subject is presumed to be simulating the object's action."[165] Thus, more mu activity or power (i.e., less mu suppression) reflects less motor cortex activity; less mu activity or power (i.e., more mu suppression) reflects more motor cortex activity. Today, mu suppression is a common measure of motor cortex activity and has recently been used to measure activity in the mirror-neuron-system by looking at motor cortex activity in subjects while they observed others performing actions.

Gutsell and Inzlicht used EEG to look at the mirror-neuron system while people passively observed ingroup (other white) and outgroup (black, South Asian, and East Asian) members. The subjects (or observers) in the experiment were 30 white, right-handed Canadian (University of Toronto Scarborough) students (13 female; mean age of 18.46). Researchers measured suppression of EEG oscillations in the 8–13 Hz "mu" frequency at scalp locations over the primary motor cortex, the area of the brain associated with gross motor responses. They found that observers showed increased mu suppression when passively observing ingroup members, this motor cortex activity suggesting that they were mentally simulating the actions of ingroup members. Critically, however, participants did not show significant mu suppression when observing outgroup members, indicating no activity over motor areas when they observed outgroup members, suggesting that they did not mentally simulate the actions of these others. Gutsell and Inzlicht conclude that "those neural networks underlying the simulation of actions and intentions—most likely part of the 'mirror-neuron-system'—are less responsive to outgroup members than to ingroup members" and "people experience less vicarious action and their associated somatic and autonomic states," the basic building blocks of empathy, "when confronted with outgroups than with ingroups."[166]

The reasonable person approach to *mens rea*, therefore, since it invites and enables factfinders to sympathetically identify with wrongdoers, is necessarily imbued with ingroup/outgroup bias. These neurophysiological insights expose the many and varied opportunities in the substantive criminal law and its processes for the social construction of black criminals. If a white juror and a black juror have different neural responses to black and white defendants, and those neural reactions are constitutive of the necessary sympathetic identification required for an accused wrongdoer to get the benefit of a full or partial excuse, then an objective finding of *mens rea* is impossible.

Thus, the malleable reasonable person test enables biased moral judgments about black wrongdoers in two different ways. First, it enables differential juror attributions about the causes of crime by Blacks and Whites, and that can lead to differential evaluations of the subjective culpability of Blacks and Whites not only in provocation cases, where it drives the social construction of black murderers, but across the entire body of substantive criminal law, from criminal negligence to self-defense, where the malleable test drives the biased social construction of black criminals in general. Further, the elastic reasonable person test provides a doctrinal vehicle for jurors to construct criminals in racially biased ways on the basis of ingroup empathy bias. And as I'll show below, other common approaches to *mens rea* (other than the reasonable person test)—approaches that may seem more factual and rule-governed, such as "awareness," "premeditation," and "intent"—can be equally malleable and thus can provide just as much room for the biased social construction of black criminals. Only through radically overhauling the prevailing *mens rea* paradigm can we shed light on the enormous number of opportunities that exist in criminal trials for jurors' racially biased moral judgments to result in the biased social construction of black criminals. And once we fully appreciate how bias-ridden our constructions of black criminals are, how unreliable criminal conviction is as a test of black blameworthiness, hopefully we will be better able to recognize racialized mass incarceration and the draconian sentences that have helped fuel it as the grave social injustices that they are.

◆

Trained under the prevailing *mens rea* paradigm, many American lawyers think of *mens rea* as an "aware mental state"—like "purpose," "knowledge," or "conscious disregard"—that must accompany the prohibited act or *actus reus*; in other words, it refers to an actor's subjective awareness of wrongdoing. Under this theory, known as "mentalism," only if an individual is aware of engaging in prohibited conduct can we regard it as being a choice of his or an expression of his will. Thus choice theory is sometimes related to Kant's view of the "will" as the locus of moral worth and proper object of moral criticism.[167] One cannot *choose* to do wrong if he lacks awareness of wrongdoing, and *choice* is the bedrock of personal and criminal responsibility for many courts and commentators.[168] Under this familiar approach, *mens rea* is seen as a "descriptive" requirement, because it describes an aware mental state.[169]

Descriptive requirements (rules, elements, and tests) stay close to predesignated and dispositive "facts" that jurors can "find" without needing to make moral judgments. In the case of an adult having sexual intercourse with a person less than 15 years of age, the "fact" of the victim's age determines criminal liability, and factfinders can determine whether that requirement was met without making a moral judgment about the defendant. There is much less room for bias in finding such "facts" or applying such descriptive requirements.[170] In contrast, nondescriptive or normative requirements (standards, elements, and tests) direct factfinders to make moral judgments in establishing their findings. A statute defining murder as an unintentional killing accompanied by "a depraved and malignant heart" turns on a nondescriptive, normative requirement. The depravity and malignancy—in a word, the wickedness—of the wrongdoer's heart determines criminal liability here and factfinders cannot determine the wickedness of his heart without making a moral judgment of him. In jury instructions that provide factfinders with nondescriptive and normative standards, factfinders are *directed* to make a frontal evaluation of his moral blameworthiness before returning a guilty verdict.

The dominant *mens rea* paradigm may be fairly characterized as both "mentalist" and "descriptivist." Its mentalism lies in its assumption that criminal culpability for wrongdoing lies only in an aware mental state, specifically, an intent to do wrong or at least a conscious awareness of wrongdoing; its descriptivism lies in its assertion that the *mens rea* tests contained in the jury instructions do not direct, invite, or enable factfinders to morally judge the wrongdoer. The legal directives used by jurors who sit in judgment on wrongdoers, according to descriptivists, avoid the background moral issue of the wrongdoer's wickedness and focus instead on the factual (or empirical) issue of whether the wrongdoer acted with an aware mental state. For descriptivists, once the issue of guilt or innocence has been reduced to that of the presence or absence of an aware mental state, there is no need for the factfinder to make any kind of direct moral judgment of the wrongdoer to convict him. For descriptivists, viewing *mens rea* tests as equivalent to an "aware mental states" requirement minimizes the factfinders' discretion and thus the legal room they have for biased social constructions of black wrongdoers.

In this respect, the distinction between descriptive tests of *mens rea* like "purpose," "knowledge," and "aware mental states" and normative ones like "depraved and malignant heart" tracks the more familiar one between rules and standards. In the words of trial lawyer Kathleen Sullivan:

> [L]egal directives take different forms that vary in the relative discretion they afford the decision maker. These forms can be classified as either 'rules' or 'standards' to signify where they fall on the continuum of discretion. Rules, once formulated, afford decision makers less discretion than do standards.... A legal directive is 'rule'-like when it binds a decision maker to respond in a determinate way to the presence of delimited triggering facts.... A legal directive is 'standard'-like when it tends to collapse decisionmaking back into the direct application of the background principle or policy to a fact situation.[171]

Inasmuch as the *mens rea* requirement binds factfinders to focus only on the "facts" of aware mental states, then, it is "rule"-like and descriptive; conversely, inasmuch as it frees them to exercise discretion in morally judging the defendant's subjective culpability, it is "standard"-like, nondescriptive, and normative.[172]

If, indeed, the *mens rea* requirement were descriptive and "rule"-like as proponents of the prevailing paradigm assert, then there is much less room in the criminal law for racially-biased moral judgments. Bias thrives on juror discretion, which is greatest when factfinders are asked to make direct moral judgments on the basis of discretion-laden, open-ended normative and nondescriptive standards. Such standards give maximum elbow room to conscious and unconscious bias. But, descriptivists argue, as *mens rea* is no more than an aware mental state, it may be viewed as an empirical fact—a discoverable fact of nature—whose existence factfinders can ascertain without any moral judgment, as they can ascertain a person's blood pressure or pulse, leaving jurors and judges few doctrinal opportunities, they claim, for biased moral judgments based on "ingroup empathy biases," or "race-based attributions," or other distortions entrenched in our cognitive unconscious. As a result, this dominant paradigm cannot recognize or acknowledge the enormous role racial and other social bias plays in the legal and social construction of black criminals—the paradigm effectively conceals where bias lives in jury instructions and the adjudication process. It must be replaced.

◆

Once jurors determine that a defendant has committed a prohibited act *with mens rea*, he may still escape liability by raising a "*mens rea* defense" of justification or excuse. In the words of Paul Robinson and Jane Grall:

> [M]ens rea describes only a subjective state of mind required by the definition of an offense. One who has the necessary *mens rea* may nonetheless be blameless because of a general defense, such as insanity, self-defense, or duress, that precludes moral culpability. By adopting a narrow concept of *mens rea*, which refers only to elements of an offense definition, one does not necessarily reject a normative view of criminal liability.[173]

From this standpoint, if a harm-doer has a valid excuse or justification for consciously committing a prohibited act, he lacks *mens rea* in its *broad* sense—that is, in its "all-encompassing usage, which treats the term '*mens rea*' as synonymous with moral fault."[174]

Thus the traditional model of *mens rea* bifurcates blameworthiness, creating a two-pronged conception and analysis of subjective culpability in the adjudication process. The first, definitional or "narrow" *mens rea* of aware mental states such as purposely, knowingly, or recklessly committing a prohibited act, and the second "broad" *mens rea*, comprised of "defenses"—that is, excuses and justifications such as duress or provocation—and calls on factfinders to make discretionary, moral judgments based on non-descriptive standards. Each culpability prong turns on fundamentally different kinds of legal directives and calls for radically different kinds of judgments (factual in the first prong, moral in the second) from the factfinders.

This cleavage in the *mens rea* requirement into definitional *mens rea* (aware mental states) and "defenses" makes it possible for descriptive mentalists to reconcile their narrow, descriptive conception of the *mens rea* requirement with its historical, doctrinal, and functional role, that of ensuring that criminal liability turns on blameworthiness. Because the category "defenses" includes all the considerations relevant to *broad mens rea* or "all-encompassing moral fault," it may seem that without losing anything important the term "*mens rea*" can be limited to and treated as synonymous with *narrow mens rea*. Thus, a descriptive, factual, non-normative approach to *mens rea* focused only on aware mental states would not mean the law does not care about the subjective culpability of citizens it blames and punishes. It does care. It just saves its inquiry into the defendant's general moral blameworthiness for the defenses. Nevertheless, the promise to give full or principled or even coherent attention to the wrongdoer's general blameworthiness in the "defenses" and "excuses" prong of the *mens rea* analysis is never made good. Primarily for reasons of policy and social welfare (rather than justice to the individual), courts, legislatures, and commentators severely circumscribe defenses like duress and provocation and filter out mitigating factors like a wrongdoer's "disadvantaged social background" in ways that leave defendants with very few doctrinal opportunities to argue that they are not blameworthy.

Furthermore, it is simply wrong to say that excuses, justifications, motives, causes, non-descriptive standards, and normative or moral judgments do not figure in definitional *mens rea*. To the contrary, they are at the core of *mens rea* tests required by the "offense definition" of countless crimes. For instance, of the four "kinds of culpability" (*mens rea* tests) of the Model Penal Code (purpose, knowledge, recklessness, and negligence), half (specifically, negligence and recklessness) explicitly require factfinders to use the malleable and nondescriptive "reasonable person standard" to determine a wrongdoer's subjective culpability—that is, to determine whether the motives or causes of his harmful act support a claim of justification or excuse. And in rolls bias.

Of course, referring to negligence and recklessness as excuses is unconventional; conventionally, these levels of culpability are viewed as requirements—preconditions—that must be met before there is a crime to excuse. Thus, for criminal homicide, it might seem that the prosecution must first prove that the defendant negligently, recklessly (or intentionally) killed the victim, for only then is there a criminal homicide to excuse. So *in form* negligence and recklessness (and intent) seem like "inculpatory" elements, while excuses and defenses like duress and self-defense seem like "exculpatory" elements. But negligence and recklessness often *function* as excuses; legally they are exculpatory elements masquerading in inculpatory clothing.

For instance, under the MPC, a person acts negligently when he fails to appreciate that his conduct creates a substantial and unjustifiable risk, and when his lack of awareness "involves a gross deviation from the standard of care that a reasonable person would observe in the actor's situation."[175] The "unjustifiable risk" element calls for a judgment of whether the conduct itself is excessively risky, but this goes to *actus reus* (prohibited conduct) not *mens rea* (subjective culpability). Justifications center on acts, excuses center on actors.[176]

State v. Everhart clearly illustrates this crucial distinction between ingredients of the negligence definition that require factfinders to morally appraise the *act* and those that require them to morally appraise the *actor* and her excuses. In *Everhart*, the young girl with an IQ of 72 accidentally smothered her baby to death. To convict the girl of criminal negligence, the prosecution had to prove that wrapping the baby in the way she did, under those circumstances, was an unjustified (excessively risky) act. Assuming the factfinders conclude that his act was unjustifiably risky (which it clearly was in this case), the law directs them to determine whether the person who created those excessive risks (someone we can now call the "wrongdoer") did so with subjective culpability or *mens rea*. That is, to prove criminal negligence, the prosecution must show not only that the defendant engaged in excessively risky conduct (wrongdoing), but also that her mental and emotional shortcomings, her cognitive and volitional failings, were *not* those of a "reasonable" or "ordinary person in the situation." This is the "excuse" dimension of negligence. Under this ingredient, someone who runs excessive risks without wickedness—i.e., without differentiating herself from ordinary people "in her situation"—is excused for her unjustifiably risky act. If the court viewed her IQ of 72 as a morally relevant excuse, it can make her low IQ part of her "situation" for purposes of the "reasonable person in her situation" test. The court in *Everhart* followed precisely this analysis, holding that because of the defendant's low IQ and the accidental nature of the death, the prosecution failed to prove culpable negligence.

Even in torts, where some commentators claim that negligence only focuses on acts and their justifications, not actors and their excuses, the reasonable person test clearly directs jurors to excuse some excessive risk-takers and condemn others. Under the emergency doctrine, trial judges in effect instruct juries that they may excuse an actor for an unjustified act if he acted under the taxing cognitive and volitional pressure of an emergency. As Dan Dobbs points out, the only logical application of the emergency doctrine occurs when there is wrongdoing—when the act inflicted more evil than it prevented. If the defendant's conduct would be reasonable even without considering the pressure of the emergency, then the emergency doctrine is irrelevant, for there is no wrongdoing to excuse. For instance, assume an emergency that confronts a defendant with a sudden and pressure-filled choice between causing death and causing property damage. If the defendant chooses the presumptive lesser of available evils—property damage—he is doing exactly what he would be expected to do even with hours of calm deliberation and decision. However, nothing about the choice being sudden and pressure-filled performs any independent moral or legal work. In such a case, as Dobbs observes, "it is right to hold that he is not negligent and not liable, but wrong to suggest that the emergency doctrine has anything to do with the decision." [177]

Clearly, then, the function of the emergency doctrine is to highlight for the factfinders that the "reasonable person in the situation" test excuses *ordinary* expressions of human frailty in the face of certain situational pressures. The cognitive and volitional deficiencies caused by the situational pressures excuse an unjustified act when the actor was "*reasonably* so disturbed or excited that the actor [could not] weigh alternative courses of action."[178] But, paradoxically, the most compelling evidence that the emergency doctrine provides for the existence of an excuse function at the heart of the reasonable person test in negligence decisions is that courts increasingly reject the emergency doctrine itself, since judges already always instruct the jury that the defendant is held to the standard of the reasonable person in the situation. "Emergency, if one exists, is one of the circumstances, and lawyers are free to argue to the jury that the defendant behaved reasonably considering the emergency (*or any other circumstance*)."[179] Accordingly, courts increasingly see emergency instructions as unnecessary and unfair.

The upshot of this analysis is that, in everyday operation, the general reasonableness standard functions as a legal vehicle for excuse claims in negligence, civil or criminal.[180] In fact, the reasonableness test does double duty, functioning as a legal vehicle for two separate levels of excuse claims: the general first-level or "objective" excuse claim, covering mistakes and accidents of ordinary people caused by emergencies and other external situational pressures; and the second-level or "individualized" excuse claim, covering mistakes and accidents of atypical people—like the young girl with an IQ of 72 in *Everhart*—caused by an idiosyncratic deficiency, one afflicting a limited subdivision of the population. As H.L.A. Hart observes, if the criminal law punishes those who could not help themselves by refusing to adjust the reasonable person test to the individual capacities of the wrongdoer, then it punishes the morally innocent. In such a case "criminal responsibility will be made independent of any 'subjective element.'"[181]

◆

The way "recklessness" is determined provides another window into the way the prevailing paradigm fails to recognize how much room core *mens rea* requirements provide for the biased social construction of black criminals. Under the MPC, a person acts recklessly when he *consciously* disregards a substantial and unjustifiable risk, as well as when his disregard "involves a gross deviation from the standard of conduct that a law-abiding person would observe in the actor's situation."[182] As with negligence, the factfinders must first determine whether the conduct was unjustifiably risky, then, assuming an affirmative answer to that question, whether such conduct was accompanied by subjective culpability, that is, whether the wrongdoer was consciously aware of his excessive risk-taking and, if so, whether such conscious wrongdoing represents a "gross deviation" from what "a law-abiding [read: reasonable] person ... in the actor's situation" would have done. Once more, factfinders will not find recklessness if they attribute the defendant's unjustifiable risk to the "situation," or if they empathize with her, and thus do not find a gross deviation from the reasonable person standard. But those who attribute the defendant's unjustifiable risk to her lack of a "law-abiding" disposition, or other character flaw, will more readily find a gross deviation and hence recklessness.

Consider, for instance, the case of *Parrish v. State*, 97 So.2d 356 (Fla.

Dist. Ct. App. 1957), in which a man in a car with companions pursued his ex-wife through the city streets of Jacksonville, FL in the early hours of the morning. He was armed with a bayonet and was apparently attempting to carry out his threat to kill her. He caught up with her at one point and broke her car window with his bayonet, but she maneuvered her car to elude him. Continuing her escape, she went through a stop sign at a high rate of speed and struck another car. She subsequently died of the injuries.

The ex-husband was convicted of second-degree murder. Suppose, however, that the ex-wife had survived but the driver of the car she struck had been killed. Could *she* be convicted of negligent or reckless homicide? First, whether this raises a question of negligence or recklessness depends on whether she was aware of the risk of injury to others as she ran the stop sign. This could go either way, as her defense attorney could say (and the factfinders could conclude) that fear flooded her consciousness to the point that she was completely oblivious of such risks, or the counsel representing the interests of her victims could perhaps persuasively contend that she was aware of *some* degree of risk. (As we will see, this awareness line between negligence and recklessness is thin and permeable.) The next issues would be, first, whether the risk she created was unjustified, and second, whether the risk she took, "considering the nature and purpose of [her] conduct and the circumstances known to [her], involves a gross deviation from the standard of care that a reasonable person would observe in the actor's situation."[183] However justified the conduct appears under this original statement of facts, we could alter them in various ways until they struck us as not sufficient to actually justify the conduct. Then we would have an "unjustified act" and the question would become whether she should be excused for excessively risky conduct. Under the MPC's approach, the distorting effect that fear can have on an ordinary person's awareness could lead jurors to excuse her unjustified act, as could any post-traumatic stress disorders she may have developed at the hands of her abusive ex-husband.

Because negligence and recklessness establish the minimum requisite levels of culpability for a vast array of crimes, the standard organizing distinctions—inculpatory vs. exculpatory elements, definitional elements vs. defenses, *mens rea* vs. excuses, aware mental states vs. reasonable person standards, descriptive directives vs. normative standards—collapse, as does the descriptivist dream of a non-normative approach to *mens rea*. Factfinder discretion is broad, and thus there are ample opportunities for the racially biased social construction of criminals in the adjudication process. In cases of negligence and recklessness, especially, the prevailing paradigm's distinctions between narrow, descriptive, definitional *mens rea* and broad, nondescriptive *mens rea* defenses dissolve into incoherence. Jurors must weigh a host of different factors simultaneously in reaching an unavoidably moral judgment about whether to attribute excessively risky conduct to the circumstances (and exculpate) or to the actor's bad character (and inculpate).

Negligence and recklessness cannot be treated as minor anomalies. Negligence is a common ground of criminal liability, and in some legal arenas, such as rape, constitutes the dominant approach—in the words of one casebook, "Most of the recent American cases permit a mistake defense, but only when the defendant's error as to consent is honest and *reasonable*."[184] And recklessness, the all-purpose and possibly most common *mens rea* requirement under the Model Penal Code and throughout the common law,[185] figures centrally in an enormous number and variety of crimes.

As a result, black wrongdoers are looking at double-barreled bias from jurors who must determine their guilt or innocence: "ingroup empathy bias" makes it less likely that white jurors will sympathize with a black wrongdoer and find that he acted like a "reasonable person," and "attribution bias," too, makes it less likely that jurors of all races will find that a black wrongdoer meets the reasonable person test, and more likely that they will attribute her behavior to her character rather than her situation.

Even the aware mental state requirement itself, through hidden and often unconscious manipulation of factual descriptions—that is, through the process of "interpretive construction"[186] of the underlying facts—functions like a flexible and discretion-laden standard, often shot through with racially-biased moral judgments. This is not just where bias lives in the criminal law and its processes—it is where it hides. The concept of "interpretive construction" will help us root out bias in seemingly factual judgments and descriptive standards like woodlice from under the lumber pile.

Under the dominant paradigm, factfinders easily and inconspicuously manipulate or "interpretively construct"—or what I will call "play the accordion" on—the legal facts in a case. Even well-meaning and conscientious jurors can consciously or unconsciously play the accordion on the facts of a criminal case and thereby "find" that he possessed the requisite mental state of awareness and premeditation, thereby allowing biases in the adjudication of just deserts to socially construct black criminals.

◆

Let's begin with a fact pattern that frequently arises in criminal law textbooks—a case of Russian roulette. Assume that in a park after school a 16-year-old wrongdoer produces a handgun from his backpack and proposes to a friend that they place a live round in one of the gun's six empty chambers, spin the cylinder, and each take turns pointing the revolver at the shin of the other and pulling the trigger. The cylinder would be spun again after each turn. Either participant could end the game at any time by saying the word "chicken" and calling off the contest—in which case the other player would be the winner. After five or ten turns where the hammer drops harmlessly on an empty chamber, the wrongdoer takes his turn, spins the cylinder, points the gun at the victim's lower leg, and fires a live round into his tibia.

Let's say the jury believes the wrongdoer when he says that (1) he had firmly resolved not to call off the game or "chicken out," but also that (2) he did not subjectively desire to shoot the victim; rather, he sincerely hoped and subjectively desired that the other player "chicken out" before someone suffered a gunshot wound. In that case, to prove the wrongdoer intended to cause the victim's injury, the prosecution must prove that he knew with substantial certainty one of the two of them would be shot. In turn, whether the shooter "intended" to cause this injury (in the "he knew it would result from his conduct" sense of intent) depends entirely on how the jury frames or interpretively constructs the facts. At the instant he squeezed the trigger, the shooter could only be aware of a 1-in-6 chance of injuring the victim; so if we frame the *actus reus* or prohibited conduct narrowly as only encompassing each discrete turn in the game (that is, if we interpret the facts from the standpoint of each individual squeeze of the trigger), the shooter's act cannot be characterized as accompanied by any knowledge-based or constructive intent to injure the victim. In contrast, if we frame or "interpretively construct" the facts broadly (that is, if we view the *actus reus* as the entire course of conduct and see both players as firmly resolved not to "chicken out"), the victim's injury can be characterized as an intended consequence of the shooter's conduct—he knew with substantial certainty that eventually, inevitably, someone would be shot. In other words, the jury's determination of the actor's intent at the time he squeezed the trigger depends on how the facts are interpretively constructed; that interpretation determines the outcome of the case, not the window dressing of an "intent" requirement.

Some thoughtful authorities on the nature and scope of the constructive intent requirement disagree. Professors James A. Henderson and Aaron D. Twerski, for instance, argue that we need to recognize a distinction between "the proximate consequences of discrete acts, on the one hand, and the inevitable consequences of general courses of conduct, on the other." They contend that the concept of "intended consequences" should not be applied to a course of repetitious conduct—such as batting in the lineup on a major league baseball club throughout a long season—undertaken by an actor, because over the course of such conduct "some types of unhappy consequences are, sooner or later, virtually certain to occur."

> For a batter in the major leagues, hitting foul balls into the stands, thereby striking patrons, is certain to occur from time to time across many thousands of swings of a bat. Yet, in connection with any given swing, not only does the batter not desire to hit a foul ball when he swings the bat, he does not believe that such a consequence is certain—or even very likely—to follow. The player understands at the outset of the baseball season that foul balls will inevitably occur; but the "act" referred to in the phrase "one intends the consequence of an act" is the discrete act of swinging a bat at a pitched ball, not the deliberate undertaking of the course of conduct involved in batting regularly in a major-league lineup. Properly conceptualized, intent focuses on discrete acts, not general courses of conduct.[187]

This clever distinction proves my point, however: choosing to broadly or narrowly describe the facts can make a case "easy" or "hard" and preordain its outcome. In *Hines v. Morrow*, for instance, the defendant negligently permitted a railroad crossing to become full of potholes.[188] A car became mired in the mud at the crossing. The plaintiff attempted to step out from between the two vehicles but found that he could not because his wooden leg had sunk into a mud hole. A coil from a tow rope caught the plaintiff's good leg, causing it such serious injury that it had to be amputated below the knee. On appeal, the defendant argued that the condition of the crossing was not the proximate cause of the plaintiff's injury, that is, he argued that it was not foreseeable that the victim would suffer injury in such a bizarre and freakish way.

In cases that turn on a flexible test like "foreseeability," lawyers and fact-finders put the rabbit in the hat (predetermine the outcome) when they interpretively construct the facts and pull it out again (confirm the predetermined outcome) when they wed the substantive law to those "found" facts.

As Clarence Morris has pointed out, had the court focused on the details of the events, the defendant might have proved the absence of foreseeability and prevailed.[189] Instead, the court adopted a broader interpretive focus in line with the plaintiff's description of the facts:

> The case, stated in the briefest form, is simply this: [Plaintiff] was on the highway, using it in a lawful manner, and slipped into this hole, created by [defendant's] negligence, and was injured in undertaking to extricate himself.... [To the defendant's argument that it] could not reasonably have been foreseen that slipping into this hole would have caused the [plaintiff] to have become entangled in a rope, and the moving truck, with such dire results ... [the] answer is plain: The exact consequences do not have to be foreseen.

This kind of interpretive legerdemain lies behind the intuitive appeal of the authors' foul ball analogy. A demystifying counter-analogy could be a shooter who fires not a single shot from a single action rifle into a crowd, but one who, armed with an automatic AK-47 with a long ammunition belt, takes aim at a crowd. Imagine that the ammunition belt he feeds the AK-47 contains a hundred randomly selected rounds, 99 of which are blanks and only one of which is "live." If we interpretively construct the facts by narrowing the time frame to each discrete shot and disjoining (or disaggregating) each shot from its predecessor and successor, we might conclude that he did not "intend" or "know with substantial certainty" that he would injure anyone in the crowd. Indeed, we can even assume that the shooter connects the AK-47 to an automatic timer and abandons it, so that it only fires one round from the ammunition belt per day or week, result-ing in great temporal distance between the *discrete* acts. Nevertheless, our intuitions would demand that he be responsible for an intentional injury when the "live" round is finally discharged into the crowd. Whether we expand or narrow the relevant time frame—how we play the interpretive accordion—depends on such moral intuitions, which means these moral intuitions *produce* the outcome, not the knowledge or constructive intent requirement, which merely serves as a conclusory label that does no real independent normative work.

◆

For an act to be judged reckless, the Model Penal Code requires that the actor "consciously disregard a substantial and unjustifiable risk" that some circumstance exists or that some result will occur. Does this formulation require the actor to be aware (1) of the risk, (2) that it is substantial, *and* (3) that it is unjustifiable? Or does it only require the actor to be aware of *some* risk, which the jury finds to be substantial and unjustifiable? Or does it require the actor to be aware of a *substantial* risk, which the jury finds to be unjustifiable? As one casebook correctly observes, "Grammatically, the Model Penal Code appears to require conscious awareness as to all three of the crucial factors. But is this interpretation tenable in practice?"[190] Certainly such an interpretation seems required by the conception of *mens rea* championed by mentalists and choice theorists—only if an actor was aware that his conduct was unjustified could it be said that he was aware of wrongdoing and consciously chose to do wrong. Simply being aware of creating "substantial" risks proves nothing about an actor's awareness of wrongdoing; as the MPC Comment points out, "Even substantial risks, it is clear, may be created without recklessness when the actor is seeking to serve a proper purpose."[191] If subjective culpability means awareness of wrongdoing and choosing to do wrong, the wrongdoer must necessarily be aware that the risk is unjustifiable. And yet, no such interpretation is tenable, for it would insulate from criminal liability anyone whose idiosyncratic values, beliefs, and attitudes lead them (perhaps unconsciously) to honestly conclude that conduct most of us would find outrageously risky either was (1) not very risky or (2) promoted interests so weighty that its social utility outweighed its social costs (that is, it "served a proper purpose"). Sanford H. Kadish and Stephen J. Schulhofer make this point with the following hypothetical:

> Consider a person who regards himself as an extraordinarily skillful driver. Finding himself in a hurry, he drives in a manner that creates an outrageously high risk of killing someone. He believes, however, that there is little risk because of his expertise as a driver. He drove negligently, but did he drive recklessly?[192]

To exculpate on this ground would amount to excusing him because of his mistake or ignorance of law, in violation of the principle that such mistakes and ignorance are no excuse. Thus, the "awareness and choice" approach to subjective culpability does not jibe with a plausible interpretation of the awareness requirement in recklessness.

Requiring the actor to be aware of a "substantial" risk which the jury finds to be unjustifiable is not tenable, either. Just as "substantial risks ... may be created without recklessness when the actor is seeking to serve a proper purpose," conversely, even very small—i.e., insubstantial—risks may be created with recklessness when the actor seeks to serve a patently improper purpose.[193] In shooting a gun into the air to celebrate a Lakers win, an actor may be aware of creating only a tiny risk that the bullet will hit someone when it falls back to earth. But because the creation of such a risk is so egregiously unjustifiable and constitutes such a gross deviation from the reasonable (or law-abiding) person standard, if it causes an innocent death, a jury could have little difficulty finding the actor reckless. Substantiality remains geared to unjustifiability and does little work independent of it. Jurors who are instructed to "find" awareness of a substantial risk before convicting someone who has created what they see as an outlandishly unjustified (albeit small) risk can simply conclude that he was aware of a substantial risk precisely because of its outlandishness and his subjective culpability in creating it. Nothing in the Code or Commentaries defines what constitutes a substantial risk nor prohibits such discretionary judgments by factfinders. On the contrary, in the words of the Comment:

> Some standard is needed for determining *how* substantial and *how* unjustifiable the risk must be in order to warrant a finding of culpability. There is no way to state this value judgment that does not beg the question in the last analysis; the point is that the jury must evaluate the actor's conduct and determine whether it should be condemned.[194]

The Comment recognizes that both the substantiality and unjustifiability criteria are flexible, nondescriptive legal directives, each calling on factfinders to make a "value judgment" in determining whether it has been met. The substantiality criterion does no independent work either in defining whether the risk was excessive or whether the actor's awareness of creating an excessive risk was reckless.

A finding of recklessness, it therefore seems, only requires the actor to be aware of *some* risk, risk that the jury finds to be unjustifiable. As discussed above, the jury's inquiry into whether the risk was unjustifiable concerns the *actus reus* ingredient in recklessness—excessively risky conduct is prohibited conduct. The *mens rea* or subjective culpability inquiry requires a determination of whether or not acting with such awareness constituted a gross deviation from the behavior of a reasonable person in the actor's situation. But because we are all aware of *some* risk in just about everything we do (from getting behind the wheel of a car to getting out of bed), this element also does little independent work as a basis for distinguishing between negligence and recklessness. It amounts to a featureless generality—"awareness of some risk"—that hovers over all human activity and hence can easily be "found" (or not) at the discretion of the factfinders.

For instance, a two-year-old child named Morgan Pena was killed by a driver who was attempting to dial a number on his cell phone. The driver surely was aware that failing to keep a proper lookout increases risks to pedestrians like Morgan and that a proper lookout is impossible while his eyes and attention are on his keypad. Nevertheless, the driver "apparently failed to appreciate the full extent of the danger his conduct created." The driver was cited for careless driving and running a stop sign, "but he was not charged with a more serious offense because the police determined that he was not reckless."[195] Professor Kimberly Ferzan refers to this level of culpability as "opaque recklessness"—"awareness of some risk but failure to appreciate how substantial it was."[196] Opaque recklessness "is probably a regular feature of dangerous behavior, and it arguably lies somewhere between the Model Penal Code notions of recklessness and negligence."[197] Amorphous, indeterminate, "in between" states of awareness like opaque recklessness—states of awareness that may accompany the majority of unintentional homicides and other crimes—leave it to the unguided discretion of the factfinder whether to find the harm-doer responsible for recklessness or negligence, and it is that unguided discretion that allows ingroup and outgroup biases to wreak havoc with equal justice under the law.

To avoid a vague (and amorphous to the point of vacuous) awareness test, we could frame the risk he must be aware of more narrowly—that is, rather than saying he must be aware of the general risk of driving while talking on a cell phone, we could say he must be aware that driving in such a manner poses risks to pedestrians, or more specifically still, that such driving poses a risk to the particular pedestrian who was in the crosswalk when the actor's car entered it. If the risk is framed very broadly, the awareness requirement may be easily met; but if the risk is framed very narrowly, then the awareness requirement may not be as easily met. No legal directive tells the factfinders at what level of generality they must frame the risks, and thus the frame of the relevant risk can be stretched or squeezed like an accordion, with the awareness requirement dancing to whatever tune gets played by the jury's interpretive construction of the facts. A finding of awareness (or lack thereof) by ordinary jurors may often serve as a conclusory label that then becomes the justification or rationalization for the initial and underlying negative evaluation.

For instance, in *People v. Hall*,[198] the harm-doer, while skiing, flew off of a knoll and collided with the victim, who was crossing the slope below. Hall, a "trained ski racer who had been coached about skiing in control and skiing safely," "for some time over a considerable distance" travelled too fast for conditions in an out-of-control fashion—"back on his skis, with his ski tips in the air and his arms out to his sides to maintain balance." A witness, himself a ski instructor, "said that Hall was bounced around by the moguls on the slope rather than skiing in control and managing the bumps." Hall admitted that he first saw the victim "when he was airborne and that he was unable to stop when he saw people below him just before the collision." The People charged Hall with reckless manslaughter ("recklessly causing the death of another person"), requiring the prosecution to prove that Hall "consciously disregarded"—was aware of—a substantial and unjustifiable risk that, in the court's words, "by skiing so fast and out of control he might collide with and kill another skier unless he regained control and slowed down." [199]

These facts initially seem to support a slam-dunk finding of awareness of excessive risk-taking. Yet in a later trial, the jury rejected the charge of reckless manslaughter and convicted only of the lesser offense of negligent homicide.[200] Colorado statutes follow the Model Penal Code's definitions of manslaughter and negligent homicide, so "the crucial factor distinguishing these levels of culpability is awareness." In other words, the jury had to conclude that Hall met the elements that negligence and recklessness have in common—namely, substantial and unjustified risk-taking that grossly deviates from the kind of risk-taking that a reasonable person in the situation would undertake—but that he lacked awareness of doing so.

One can only suppose that the jury found only negligence—despite abundant proof that Hall was aware of creating unnecessary risks—because to them a manslaughter conviction simply seemed too severe; on their intuitive grading scale, he only deserved to be blamed and punished for negligence. That is not to say that they consciously disregarded their duty to apply the law to the facts. I assume that most factfinders in most cases do not practice jury nullification. Rather, they may have sincerely concluded that Hall lacked the *requisite* awareness of the *requisite* risk at the time of the fatal collision. Nevertheless, their conclusion about his lack of awareness was probably directly and intuitively generated by urges and values and sympathies that preceded and were merely rationalized by their finding about his mental state.

In practical application, the concepts of *awareness* and *wickedness* often reverse the roles assigned to them in moral and legal theory. Looked at from the "common sense view of justice that blame and punishment are inappropriate and unfair in the absence of choice,"[201] one might expect the conclusion that A should be blamed for recklessly causing B's death to be based, in part, on the factfinder's judgment that A was at least subjectively aware of creating an unjustified risk of causing B's death. Because there can be no choice without awareness and no recklessness level of wickedness without choice, there can be no recklessness level of wickedness without awareness. However, in practice, the conclusion of factfinders that A deserves to be blamed and punished for recklessness may be directly and intuitively generated by evaluative judgments or retributive urges rooted in conscious and unconscious psychological processes, and a finding of fact about awareness may often really be a value judgment about the wrongdoer's more culpable level of wickedness masquerading as a factual judgment about the presence or absence of an aware mental state.

In the end, the determination that an actor's beliefs or reactions constitute a "gross deviation" from those of a "reasonable person in the actor's situation," gives lots of latitude—"gross" being about as nondescriptive and open-ended as directives get—for the factfinder to play the interpretive accordion by means of malleable nondescriptive standards to the tune of jurors' (often unspoken or even unconscious) urges and intuitions.

◆

Another malleable "aware mental state" is "premeditation." Premeditation—conscious reflection by the harm-doer on his intent to kill—seems to require a simple factual judgment from the juror, namely, whether the harm-doer actually reflected on his murderous intent. Yet many courts hold that some premeditation is required while simultaneously holding that "no time is too short" for the requisite premeditation to occur.[202] In *Young v. State*, for instance, an argument erupted over a card game, escalating into a scuffle during which the defendant shot two men in the chest with .22 caliber gun. Upholding the defendant's conviction on two counts of premeditated (first-degree) murder, the court reasoned that "[no] appreciable space of time between the formation of the intention to kill and the act of killing" was required and that "[p]remeditation and deliberation may be formed while the killer is 'pressing the trigger that fired the fatal shot.'"[203] It is a transparent fiction to maintain that premeditation can occur in the nanoseconds it takes to squeeze a trigger; if a mental process that can be fully realized in a small fraction of a second can be called meditation and reflection, it essentially collapses the distinction between intentional and premeditated acts. The Arizona Supreme Court reached this same conclusion in a case where the Arizona legislature tried to define premeditation as an intention that "precedes the killing by any length of time to permit reflection" with the further clarification that "[p]roof of actual reflection is not required." The Court reasoned that eliminating proof of actual reflection eliminates the difference between intentional killings that are first-degree murders and those that are second-degree. Because real legal consequences ride on the formal distinction between premeditated (first-degree) and merely intentional (second-degree) murders, the way the Arizona legislature tried to define premeditation, concluded the Court, was unconstitutional because arbitrary and capricious, in violation of due process. To salvage its constitutionality, the court interpreted the statute to require proof of actual reflection.[204]

Be that as it may, in the many jurisdictions where no appreciable space of time between intent and the act of killing is required, the rule simply gives the jury the unfettered discretion to make a *mens rea* grading judgment about the defendant based on their assessment of his deserts. If they think he does not deserve maximum condemnation and punishment, they can conclude that less than a second between the formation of the intention and its execution is not enough time for actual reflection on the intention to kill, but if they think he does deserve the maximum, then—in keeping with the "oft repeated statement ... that 'no time is too short for a wicked man to frame in his mind the scheme of murder'"[205]—they can conclude that he did adequately meditate the intent in the instant it took to squeeze the trigger.[206] By building a "wicked man"/"good man" distinction into the standard, the bias factors are obviously compounded.

◆

Also exacerbating the often unconscious tendencies to attribute black wrongdoing to character flaws rather than situational factors is the quite conscious belief by many Americans that Blacks have defective characters that render them prone to criminality.[207] This supposed bad black character increases the likelihood that any particular black wrongdoer acted with the requisite *mens rea* for criminal guilt. Thus, in *People v. Zackowitz*, the defendant's wife broke into tears after being insulted by one of four men at work repairing an automobile on a city street. The enraged defendant, Zackowitz, warned the men that "if they did not get out of there in five minutes, he would come back and bump them all off."[208] Once back at their apartment, his wife disclosed the content of the insult—one of the men had propositioned her as a prostitute. With rekindled rage, Zackowitz returned to the scene of the insult with a pistol in his pocket. After words and blows—the defendant kicked the victim, Coppola, in the stomach, Coppola went for defendant with a wrench—there was a single fatal shot. On the key question of Zackowitz's state of mind at the moment of the killing, the question was not whether he intended to kill but whether that intent was formulated before the shot (before "he went forth from his apartment"), making the crime first-degree murder, or whether the intent to kill was first formulated during the fight, making it murder in the second-degree. As proof of premeditation, the prosecution pointed to three pistols and a teargas gun Zackowitz kept in a radio box in his apartment. The prosecution did not claim that Zackowitz brought the pistols or teargas gun with him to the encounter. The only relevance of the weapons was to prove "that here was a man of vicious and dangerous propensities, who because of those propensities was more likely to kill with deliberate and premeditated design than a man of irreproachable life and amiable manners." In his appellate brief, the District Attorney defended the admissibility of the evidence on precisely this ground, stating that "the possession of the weapons characterized the defendant as 'a desperate type of criminal,' a 'person criminally inclined.'" In Cardozo's words, "[a]lmost at the opening of the trial the People began the endeavor to load the defendant down with the burden of an evil character." He was put before the jury as "a man of murderous heart, or criminal disposition."[209] The jury found that Zackowitz acted with premeditation and sentenced him to death.

Justice Benjamin N. Cardozo, writing for the SCOTUS majority, ultimately reversed the judgment of conviction, but first admitted that evidence designed to show "bad character" or criminal propensity *is* relevant, in the Rules of Evidence sense ("'Relevant evidence' means evidence having any tendency to make the existence of any fact that is of consequence to the determination of the action more probable or less probable than it would be without the evidence"). Quarrelsome defendants, he admits, are "more likely to start a quarrel than one of milder type," and "a man of dangerous mode of life more likely than a shy recluse."[210] He assumes that evidence of bad character or criminal propensity tends to show that the defendant was more likely to have acted "in conformity therewith."[211] *McCormick's Handbook* agrees, stating that evidence designed to show the defendant had "bad character" and thus was more likely to be guilty of the crime "is not irrelevant."[212] It is rational to consider character in assessing blameworthiness for the same reason it is rational to consider race in assessing the likelihood that someone has or will engage in criminal activity. Defenders of racial profiling contend that blackness itself indicates propensity, at least in the statistical sense—that Blacks thus pose a greater risk of crime than non-Blacks. In surveys, most Americans agree with the statement that "Blacks are prone to violence." Both evidence of "bad character" and "evidence" of blackness—and its associated propensities—can be viewed as increasing the likelihood of actions in conformity therewith. Bad character evidence and "rational" racial profiling practices rest on the same statistical logic. Cardozo attacks this logic, however, as inadequate to justify allowing even relevant evidence of "murderous propensity" to get to the factfinder. "Character is never an issue in a criminal prosecution unless the defendant chooses to make it one," he declares.[213] The underlying reason for keeping relevant evidence of the defendant's character and propensities away from the factfinder, he says, "is one, not of logic, but of policy," specifically, the policy of protecting the innocent by preserving the rationality and accuracy of the fact-finding process. Recast in the language of the Federal Rules of Evidence, Cardozo views otherwise relevant evidence of the defendant's bad character as inadmissible because its prejudicial effects *categorically* outweigh its probative value:

> The natural and inevitable tendency of the tribunal—whether judge or jury—is to give excessive weight to [such evidence] and either to allow it to bear too strongly on the present charge, or to take the proof of it as justifying a condemnation irrespective of guilt of the present charge.

Cardozo worried that if the jury believed that, generally speaking, the accused has "an evil character" or is a "man of murderous disposition,"[214] they would too readily conclude that he premeditated his intent on the occasion of the murder, or that even if he did not premeditate his intent on that particular occasion, he still deserves to be blamed and punished "consistent with guilt in its highest grade." Again, recast in the language of the

Federal Rules of Evidence, the prejudicial effect of character evidence arises because the jury is likely to give the evidence too much weight (overestimate its probative value) or because the evidence will arouse undue hostility toward one of the parties.[215] Prejudice, used here as a term of art, includes (but means more than) conscious bias, the kind that tempts jurors to disregard an instruction from the judge on what elements the prosecution must prove for conviction. This amounts to jury nullification.[216] The kind of prejudice contemplated by the Rules of Evidence can also arise from the impact of certain evidence on mental processes that occur without the factfinders' conscious awareness or control. For instance, prejudice arising from the impact of character evidence on the factfinders' cognitive unconscious may determine how they interpretively construct the facts or otherwise manipulate malleable and discretion-laden legal tests. It should come as no surprise that when the substantive criminal law, through jury instructions, requires the jury to perform an intellectual feat that runs counter to the jury's moral intuitions and gut reactions and other inclinations, the jury may unwittingly follow its inclinations rather than the black letter laid down in the jury instructions. Thus, as Justice Jackson admonishes, "The naïve assumption that prejudicial effects can be overcome by instructions to the jury ... all practicing lawyers know to be unmitigated fiction."[217] And in the words of another court:

[O]ne cannot unring a bell; after the thrust of the saber it is difficult to say forget the wound; and finally, if you throw a skunk into the jury box, you can't instruct the jury not to smell it.[218]

Empirical research corroborates these concerns: studies find that if jurors are exposed to a defendant's record of prior convictions for similar offenses, it significantly increases the likelihood of conviction, and that cautionary instructions eliminate little or none of the prejudicial effects that flow from such evidence.[219] Similarly, studies found that exposure to a legally inadmissible confession significantly increased the chance of a guilty verdict despite weak other evidence, and that instructions to the jury to ignore the confession had no measurable effect on the probability of conviction.[220] Again, the jury may strive to "approach their task responsibly and to sort out discrete issues given to them under proper instructions,"[221] but courts and codes generally recognize that certain kinds of evidence, like bad character and criminal propensity evidence, are likely to have an improper impact on the legal outcomes. Specifically, the jury gives such evidence "excessive weight," which implies that such evidence causes jurors to convict more often than they would if they were not improperly influenced in a way detrimental to the accused. Bad character and criminal propensity evidence, in the words of Justice John Marshall Harlan in *Winship*, increases the risk of "factual errors that result in convicting the innocent."[222] Jurors may not think they are giving certain evidence "too much weight," may strive not to do so, and may even be prompted to resist the temptation or human tendency to do so by instructions from the judge. Evidence is nevertheless excluded as prejudicial when it is likely to subvert the rationality and accuracy of the fact-finding process. Thus, according to McCormick, character evidence "is not irrelevant, but in the setting of jury trial the danger of prejudice outweighs the probative value."[223] And when the Judicial Conference of the United States, the policy-making body of the federal judiciary, was chaired by Chief Justice Rehnquist, the Conference decried new rules permitting evidence of bad character and criminal propensity in prosecutions for child molestation and sexual assault, pointing out that the new rules posed a "danger of convicting a criminal defendant for past, as opposed to charged, behavior or for being a bad person."[224] As the Judicial Conference noted, its conclusion that evidence of bad character and criminal propensity distorts the rationality, accuracy, and fairness of the fact-finding process reflects a "highly unusual unanimity" of the judges, lawyers, and academics who make up its advisory committees.

The rationality-subverting effect of evidence of character carries negative implications for black people on trial. In cases involving black defendants, their pigmentation and identity performance are proof of their bad character or criminal propensity.[225] The propensities (or proclivities) associated with Blacks are established as stereotypes early in the memories of factfinders, in early childhood, and can function as conscious beliefs (especially when supported by statistics) or unconscious sets of associations; so in a real sense, in the courtroom (as well as on the street), a black actor wears evidence of his "bad character" and criminal propensity on his face. Accordingly, the prejudicial effects of evidence of bad character and criminal propensity pointed out by the Federal Rules of Evidence, McCormick, Rehnquist, the Judicial Conference and many others, may routinely influence the adjudication of black blame and punishment.

When we put together our understanding of the gravitational pull exerted by value judgments about defendants' character on the factfinders' judgments about every other element of a charged offense, with our understanding of the role of negative stereotypes about black character traits in the perceptions and judgments of jurors and other social decisionmakers, we see how much room there is within the rules and standards themselves for bias to thrive. As *Zackowitz* teaches, the seemingly factual judgment about whether the defendant actually reflected on his intent may often be—or merely reflect—a moral appraisal of the killer's character and deserts, with a finding of premeditation merely serving as a conclusory label for the determination that "he was a man of murderous heart, of criminal disposition."[226]

The deck is stacked. The substantive criminal law directs jurors to make explicitly character-based assessments of the defendant's deserts, character, and subjective culpability. Instructions given to juries include: "the dictate of a wicked, depraved and malignant heart," "an abandoned and malignant heart," "a depraved heart regardless of human life," and "that hardness of heart or that malignancy of attitude qualifying as 'depraved indifference'"[227]; factfinders can *diagnose* a harm-doer's depraved heart even from inadvertent or negligent risk creation[228]; the harm-doer need not even be aware of running excessive risks to be convicted of murder; the malice for murder need not include an aware mental state; different factfinders could convict the *same* inadvertent killer of negligent homicide, manslaughter, or murder solely on the basis of different diagnoses of the condition of his heart at the time of the excessively risky conduct; the depraved heart approach turns on "the degree of the jury's moral abhorrence" to the killing and killer even though such a test "remits the issue to varying and highly subjective judgment calls of the judge or jury."[229] The accumulative effects of these judgment calls is racialized mass incarceration.

The leaner, modern *mens rea* language of the Model Penal Code, with its precise delineation of levels of culpability, has been hailed as a vast improvement over the vague and value-laden traditional definitions of *mens rea* which required proof that the harm-doer acted "willfully," "maliciously," "corruptly," and "wantonly." These traditional *mens rea* formulas were criticized as conveying "more atmosphere or emotion than concrete meaning."[230] To distinguish between manslaughter and unintentional murder, instead of proof of a depraved heart, the Model Penal Code requires proof of recklessness "in circumstances manifesting *extreme indifference to the value of human life*." But this test of unintentional murder requires a judgment call just as subjective as "depraved heart." The jury's moral abhorrence is still the touchstone. The leaner, more modern, less vituperative language of the

Model Penal Code can lull the unwary into a false impression that modern approaches require the factfinder to make fewer direct moral judgments of the harm-doer. The unacknowledged truth is that there is as much room for "subjective judgment calls" in the modern terminologies and approaches to *mens rea* as there was in the traditional formulations—it's the same old value-laden and discretionary wine in high-tech terminological bottles. At many levels of narrow, definitional *mens rea* analysis—negligence, reckless-ness, depraved heart malice, extreme indifference—the rule of decision that goes to the jury not only invites but requires it to make a "subjective judg-ment call" about the wrongdoer's deserts and character. Other ostensibly factual *mens rea* elements—premeditation and awareness—remain tightly tethered to such subjective judgment calls through both interpretive con-struction and the open-ended malleability of the substantive legal tests. And according to a Model Penal Code Comment, even the most factual or "descriptive" *mens rea* tests—knowledge and purpose—are morally rooted in the same depravities of heart or extreme indifference that make some unintentional killings murder.

> In a prosecution for murder, however, the Code calls for the further judgment whether the actor's conscious disregard of the risk, under the circumstances, manifests extreme indifference to the value of human life. The significance of purpose or knowledge as a standard of culpability is that, cases of provocation or other mitigation apart, purposeful or knowing homicide demonstrates precisely such indif-ference to the value of human life.[231]

Where there is ambiguity in the interpretation or application of even knowledge and purpose, there is room for judgments about the wrongdo-er's character and deserts to determine whether factfinders find the *mens rea* for guilt, and thus room for racially biased attributions, findings, and verdicts. Enough room to fill all our prisons to bursting with black bodies.

◆

Although Cardozo's warning about the dangers of character evidence are forceful and accurate, his claim that "character is never an issue in a criminal prosecution unless the defendant chooses to make it one" is misleading. If the prosecution cannot prove that the accused had bad character or criminal propensity in order to prove that he was more likely to have committed the charged criminal act, bad character can be inferred from a wrongful act. The jury can also infer from a criminal act that the wrongdoer has a depraved heart, insufficient care and concern for others, or other bad character traits for which he deserves blame and punishment. Character evidence also, according to Federal Rules of Evidence, "may be admissible for another purpose, such as proving motive, opportunity, intent, preparation, plan, knowledge, identity, absence of mistake, or lack of accident."[232]

Investigators who compare punishments meted out to Blacks and Whites for the same crimes can either completely miss or grossly underestimate such bias. Since race-based attribution bias infects jury findings about *mens rea,* much racial discrimination cannot be captured by seemingly neutral statistics about race and sentencing. That is, even if the sentences meted out to Blacks and Whites *convicted* of, say, murder or manslaughter were the same, it would not prove that white and black defendants are treated equally in the adjudication process. Rather, the real discrimination may very well have been swept under the rug of jury findings about the presence or absence of the *mens rea*—malice—for murder. These differential diagnoses of wrongdoing as a function of the wrongdoer's race result in racial differences in blame and punishment that are easily hidden from empirical examinations of racial biases in criminal justice. Comparing sentences meted out to Whites and Blacks convicted of the same crime would not capture it, because race-neutrality in sentencing at the back end of criminal adjudication can conceal profound racial discrimination in moral judgments by jurors and factfinders about black wrongdoers at earlier stages.

Despite the mistaken claims of some criminal scholars and commentators, each and every liability or grading threshold—from ordinary negligence to criminal negligence, from criminal negligence to ordinary recklessness, from ordinary recklessness (for manslaughter) to "extreme" or depraved heart recklessness (for murder), or from voluntary manslaughter to second degree murder—requires a direct moral judgment of the wrongdoer. The racial bias can remain hidden in jury characterizations, as the differences between these characterizations turn entirely on differences in the moral appraisals of wrongdoers by jurors, who are *directed* to morally appraise a wrongdoer before finding him guilty of any of these grades of criminal homicide.

All this casts serious doubt on the reliability, rationality, and trustworthiness of criminal conviction as a test for identifying morally-blameworthy Blacks who, according to some commentators, deserve our moral contempt and social ostracism for these convictions. And although criminal courtrooms are major construction sites for the biased social construction of morally blameworthy Blacks, other busy construction sites abound, for the same bias that infects moral judgments of Blacks by jurors infects moral judgments of blacks by ordinary people. Every time the moral turpitude of black wrongdoers becomes the topic of the moment on talk radio, in coffee shops, and around water coolers, another potential site for the biased social construction of black criminals becomes active, and this feeds back into legal decision-making. Cognitive and social psychology tell us that whether we are official or unofficial factfinders, given our inability to avoid most unconscious bias against certain stereotyped groups, we should approach our moral judgments of members of such groups with grave doubts about our objectivity and impartiality—in a word, with great "epistemic humility." This epistemic humility should temper our contempt toward black wrongdoers inside and outside the courtroom. We cannot solve the problem of racialized mass incarceration, we cannot stop the "niggerization" of our fellow citizens, we cannot build true solidarity, and we cannot make a more just society until it does.

CHAPTER **FOUR**

THE MIDWIFERY PROPERTIES OF THE N-WORD

Words are acts with consequences.
—Toni Morrison, Nobel Prize Lecture (1993)

Word work is the bread and butter of lawyers and the beating heart of the law. But is the legal lexicon, as some legal scholars contend,[233] so full of words with fixed and frozen meanings that its heart is languishing, or perhaps not beating at all? And more broadly: can *any* word or symbol in everyday public discourse be used to produce change, or, as some insist, do many carry fixed meanings that can only promote and protect the status quo? The beating heart of language is agency—the ability to bring about change—but words and symbols with fixed meanings remain prisoners of their past and lack the agency to mint new meanings and midwife new worlds. We must be the agents of that change and there must be agency in the word work we wield.

Two current debates—one over the meaning of the Confederate battle flag ignited by the Emanuel Nine murders, the other over the meaning of the N-word in popular culture and public discourse—shed light on this discussion about fixed meanings in legal discourse and political communication. Some battle flag and N-word opponents contend that both forms of symbolic communication must be banned from public discourse because they carry certain indelible meanings, because they are necessarily fraught with the danger of reproducing old, outmoded, oppressive worldviews. Such is the NAACP's position on the N-word and it is the attitude of some legal scholars and law students toward the legal lexicon.

Viewing words and symbols as simple reflections of "ideas" in people's heads leads some to regard them as mere tokens of consciousness that belong to the realm of ideology. This view relegates language to a minor role in social action: that of a passive conduit through which creative energies flow, but which is not itself a source of creative social change any more than a typewriter or word processor is a source of creative narratives in fiction writing. But whereas a typewriter cannot create a plot twist in an unfolding drama, a choice word can.

Nigga Theory affirms the radical agency of language, agency that creates us at the very moment it is being created. Meanings are prizes in a pitched battle among social actors seeking to establish and maintain their social identities and promote their social interests. We make history by making, contesting, and transforming the meaning of words and symbols. Since people form and transform communities and establish individual and social identities through social struggles over the meaning of words and symbols, a language with fixed and frozen meanings lacks the agency to generate new worlds: the heart of such language is no longer beating. But that is not the case with much legal or lay language, which remains contested and alive.

Even the vilest forms of symbolic communication lack fixed meanings and hence can be put to novel political (and artistic) uses. During its 2007 annual convention, the NAACP sought to purge popular culture and public discourse of the N-word by holding a public burial for it on Freedom Plaza in Detroit, Michigan. The ceremony included a march by delegates from across the country through downtown Detroit, led by two Percheron horses pulling a pine box adorned with fake black roses and bearing the remains of the racial slur. NAACP National Board Chairman Julian Bond, Detroit Mayor Kwame Kilpatrick, and the young delegates who organized the funeral were cheered by hundreds of onlookers. "We gather burying all the things that go with the N-word. We have to bury the 'pimps' and the 'hos' that go with it," said Mayor Kirkpatrick. The Rev. Otis Moss III, assistant pastor at Trinity United Church of Christ in Chicago, said in his eulogy of the word, "This was the greatest child that racism ever birthed."

The following obituary for the N-Word, written by Victoria Lanier, Erica McLaughlin, and Arielle Palmer, was read aloud at the funeral in Freedom Plaza on July 9, 2007 and usefully illustrates the approach to language frequently adopted by those who reject *all* uses of any form of the N-word:

> Born in America over 400 years ago, birthed to the unlikely couple Language and Hate, Nigger entered society to carry out his odium of black-skinned people. Christened by colonial settlers, Nigger packed his bags to find a comfortable, permanent home in America's Deep South. Although still in his early years, Nigger obtained widespread success in portraying ignorance, incompetence, and buffoonery as a direct relation to having dark skin. Nigger redefined what it meant to be black. A nigger could act and sing but could not speak properly or effectively. He could smoke and dance but he could not read and be educated. Nigger developed a whole line of products to market to those who practice in the profession of racial hatred. He coined the following terms: Niggerlover—one who was sensitive in any way to blacks. Niggerlipping—to wet the end of a cigarette while smoking, Nigger Milk—as advertised in a 1916 advertisement which showed a black baby drinking from a bottle of ink. Nigger produced these and countless other inventions which proved favorable among those who wished to maintain their supremacy by demeaning blacks in America.
>
> Finally, a group of intelligent and outspoken dark-skinned brothers and sisters decided to rebel against Nigger's dominance. As they formed the Civil Rights Movement, they fought against Nigger and his army of white supporters to reform society. Although he was almost killed during this time period, Nigger survived. Realizing it was inappropriate to blatantly continue his past message of white supremacy, "Nigger" changed his name to "Nigga" and assumed a new persona. Nigga, now disguised as an ally to black youth, could go undercover and position himself as a "link" to black unity. In the 1980s, Nigga was introduced to some new powerful partners with the rise of Hip-Hop, and he gained popularity in the media, among comedians, rappers and other entertainers convincing black people that despite his hateful roots, to be the "Nigga" was to be "down for the cause," to be "cool" and was about "keeping it real." "Nigga" made it hard for young NAACP activists to fight the battle for freedom while remaining a part of the hip-hop generation.

Although now in disguise, "Nigga" was recognized by those who remember his menacing consumption of the souls of their people. Nigga began to separate black youth from their proud history, and successfully encouraged youth of other races to join his campaign for the resurgence in demeaning the African-American race. Nigger sought to secure his place forever becoming synonymous with black people, even in the dictionary. The NAACP was triumphant in prevailing over Nigger's attempt to define himself as Nigger—a black person. However, Merriam-Webster's Dictionary today says that the word's usage among blacks is quote "not always intended or taken as offensive," and Dictionary.com says that Nigger is "sometimes used among African-Americans in a neutral or familiar way." Young black people claimed "Nigga" as their own, while many proud racists, once responsible for the word's popularity, and who are now banned from usage of the word, revel in the resurrection of their beloved friend.

Today, we will lay the word nigger to rest. We will no longer make "nigger" familiar or a part of our family. We will bury its offensive usage among people of all races, including African Americans. We will bury "nigger" next to his cousins, "jigaboo," "coon," "darkie," "pickanniny," "savage," "sambo," "mammy," "buckwheat," "boy," and "nappy-headed ho." We promise to be more creative in our rap lyrics, more respectful to our ancestors, more diligent in our fight for freedom. As we bury the word nigger, we are inspired by 2nd Corinthians Chapter 4 which says: We are troubled on every side, yet not distressed; we are perplexed, but not in despair; persecuted, but not forsaken; cast down, but not destroyed. Therefore, we do not lose heart, though outwardly we are wasting away, inwardly we are being renewed day by day. Nigger has terrorized us, but he has not beaten us, we have overcome him and we celebrate the end of his existence in our community. We officially declare him DEAD! We will not revive, resurrect, or recover him! We will rebuke, resist, and revoke him in the name of pride and progress. Ashes to Ashes Dust to Dust If God won't have him The Devil Must.[234]

This is an eloquent send-off, but it turns out reports of Nigga's demise were premature. Countless times a day the N-word rises like Lazarus to walk among us in popular culture, public discourse, and casual banter. Historically, both the Confederate battle flag and the racial epithet have been used to express anti-black beliefs and attitudes, but although no critical mass of black artists have inverted the historical meaning of the battle flag and used it to bond with other Blacks, the N-word has been widely appropriated by black artists such as The Last Poets, N.W.A Ice Cube, Saul Williams, Tupac Shakur, dead prez, Nas, Jay-Z, and Kendrick Lamar to also signal sympathy and political solidarity with other Blacks. My use of the N-word in my Critical Race Theory work is inspired by these masters of N-word-laden oppositional discourse.

But N-word abolitionists like the NAACP reject N-word-laden commentaries by rappers and law professors on the "common sense" ground that the N-word has fixed or "inherent meaning." For them, a racially oppressive "ideology" or "consciousness" or "mentality" accompanies all its utterances. These linguistic fundamentalists start with the undeniable premise that the N-word has virulently racist roots and draw the mistaken conclusion that *all* current uses and applications are tainted fruit of a poisonous etymological tree.

◆

Studies show that ordinary people without any technical expertise have theories—called *folk theories* or *folk models*—about everything important to them, from how the physical world works to "how we use words to refer to things in the world." A "folk theory," as George Lakoff points out, "defines common sense itself"; in his words, "we are all folk philosophers of language in that we have folk theories of reference." Paul Kay has shown that ordinary speakers of English hold the following folk theory of how we use words to refer to things: "words can fit the world by virtue of their inherent meaning." Put differently, it is common sense to think that words have "inherent meanings"—that is, meanings that competent speakers of a language know and make use of—and that words refer to things and *kinds* of things by way of those meanings. The word *duck* correctly refers to the *kind* of creature in the world that corresponds to the word's established "inherent meaning," namely, a bird with a broad, flat bill, short legs, and webbed feet. All members of the category designated by the word "duck" share those characteristics.[235]

This folk model of meaning neatly fits the NAACP's take on the N-word. For N-word eulogists, its inherent meaning derives from its historical use as a racial slur against Blacks. Because of its history, the word inherently signifies odious and contemptible black people, exhibiting the ignorance, incompetence, and buffoonery invoked in the eulogy. For convenience, let's say that the word simply means "Odious Black." But if the N-word's inherent meaning is "Odious Black," under our folk theory of reference, the word only correctly refers to persons in the world of *that* kind, to persons who belong to *that* category, who correspond to *that* meaning, who satisfy *that* definition—to persons whose properties include being odious and black. This provides the structure of Chris Rock's bit. The N-word cannot *correctly* be used to refer to, say, "black friends and neighbors and loved ones" because such persons, as objects of care and concern rather than odium and contempt, do not correspond to the inherent or true meaning of the word; they lack properties essential for membership in the N-word category. Accordingly, any effort by artists, academics, or activists to extend the range of application of the N-word to include "black friends and neighbors and loved ones" is doomed from the "common sense" or folk theory of reference expressed by the NAACP.

Philosophical theories that view meanings as ideas in the mind of the word-user add further support to N-word abolitionists. John Locke was an early supporter of this common "ideational theory of meaning,"[236] maintaining in *An Essay Concerning Human Understanding* that "words, in their primary or immediate signification, stand for nothing but the ideas in the mind of him that uses them."[237] Hobbes was another early supporter, declaring in *Leviathan* that "the general use of speech, is to transfer our mental discourse, into verbal; or the train of our thoughts, into a train of words." From this perspective, meanings are in our heads; they are mental happenings within the individual which become speech and understanding. For instance, let's assume that someone explains or introduces the N-word to someone else "by ostension," that is, by pointing to the kind of person for which the word stands. Many words in everyday language are taught and learned in just this way—one person explains or introduces a word to another by pointing to an entity or process (a chair, table, fire, fight) and uttering the word. Accordingly, someone introduces or explains the N-word to another by pointing to an "Odious Black" and uttering it.

How does any later application of the word flow from this act of naming? According to supporters of the mental image approach to meaning, whenever the word comes up again, it will necessarily call up an image or picture of the "Odious Black" in the mind. "Having the image is what understanding the word amounts to."[238] The same holds for future applications of the word: the image determines its future uses. The image dictates the use of the word and the use of the word flows from the mental image. From this standpoint, people only really understand what we say if they manage to construct a picture in their heads like ours. Eminent philosophers and psychologists like Bertrand Russell and E. B. Titchener have supported this image theory of meaning. Under this approach, "meaning is a mental activity" and in the absence of an image or other mental happening within the individual, "words are mere counters, capable of meaning, but not at that moment possessing it."[239]

If the meaning of the N-word lies in the mental image of odiousness, then it can be argued that an oppressive mentality or consciousness always accompanies certain words, and does so in ways that make them useless or counterproductive as tools for producing real change. Viewed in this light, a speaker or writer does not merely utter the N-word, he or she is uttered by it, for the word's inherent meaning colors the consciousness of all who use it.

◆

These "common sense" and philosophical theories of how words work cause some of my law students to worry about being "indoctrinated," "brainwashed," or "body snatched" in the process of learning to talk and think like a lawyer. (In the science fiction classic, *Invasion of the Body Snatchers*, townspeople are turned into their emotionless, characterless doubles by aliens whenever they fall asleep.) My students learn early that proper initiation into the law does not occur when they have memorized a raft of rules and legal principles, because the law evolves, and creative courts frequently overturn old rules and principles and create new ones. Instead, they know they have been properly initiated when they can translate their experience and that of their client into the legal vocabulary, into the current lexicon of the law. But, if the linguistic fundamentalists are right, then learning to talk and think like a lawyer may mean taking on an alien consciousness or worlview, one at odds with the values, loyalties, and commitments the student embraced before the first day of class.

Statistics may seem to support their fears, for while roughly 25% of incoming law students express an interest in doing public interest law upon graduation, less than 2% of graduates actually do. There are many explanations for this dramatic difference between what students say they want to do before they learn to talk and think like a lawyer and what they actually do after they master the legal lexicon (crushing student loans, for instance), but still the suspicion lingers for some that learning to talk and think like a lawyer can cause a shift in social consciousness and personal convictions away from pubic interest concerns and toward those of corporate America and laissez-faire free enterprise.

Reinforcing such concerns can be popular depictions of legal education in which, for instance, a crusty first-year law professor with a name like "Kingsfield" tells new 1L initiates that his class will transform their brains from mush to an organ that can think like a lawyer. Some understandably worry, however: How much of that so-called 'mush' is me—my values, viewpoints, convictions, and passions? Along with my hat, coat, and other unnecessary things, how much of 'me' do I have to check with the attendant at the coat closet on my way to the classroom?

As a 1L, I shared similar misgivings about the language of the law. The incisive words of Audre Lorde—a thoughtful black feminist lesbian poet and social commentator—rang in my ears throughout my fist year: "The Master's Tools Will Never Dismantle the Master's House." Because legal terms are tools and the legal lexicon is nothing but a toolbox full of words like Due Process, Criminal Intent, and The Reasonable Person, I construed her warning to be about the inherent limits of the tools of our trade—the language of the law. "The Master's House" refers to American racist patriarchy, and the language of legal rights did, in fact, function for many years as a vital tool in the historical construction and maintenance of that house. The tools condoned rape (a husband had a right to force intercourse on an unwilling and resisting woman, for instance, as long as they were married), slavery (a slave owner had a right to sell and beat his chattel), and Jim Crow (until *Loving v. Virginia*, my mom and dad did not have the right to marry in certain states). Lorde asks, "What does it mean when the tools of a racist patriarchy are used to examine the fruits of that same patriarchy?" Her answer: "It means that only the most narrow perimeters of change are possible and allowable." She concludes that although the Master's tools "may allow us temporarily to beat him at his own game," "they will never allow us to bring about genuine change."[240] This warning about the inherent limits of the tools of our trade, our legal words and definitions, if true, is demoralizing to someone seeking to use the language of the law to challenge unwarranted privilege backed by precedent and tradition.

The claim that we can be trapped in a certain way of thinking about and looking at the world by our words and their inherent meanings can seem commonsensical. Take the words used by economists, psychologists, and sociologists to explain the poverty and crime in South Central, Los Angeles, for instance—*supply and demand, marginal productivity, Pareto efficiency, utility function, and rational utility-maximizing egoist; id, ego, superego, projection, repression, psychological trauma, Oedipal complex; social structure, structural differentiation, socioeconomic stratification, role, and norm.* Clearly the very "ideas" policymakers can form about poverty and crime will be heavily influenced by their language, the words choosing the "ideas" the policymaker can form rather than the policymaker first forming the "ideas" and then searching for the right words to express them. These words seem to speak the policymaker (that is, direct her attention, channel her perceptions, and shape her ideas, consciousness, and outlook) as much as the policymaker speaks the words (that is, uses the words to express ideas or represent external reality). By the same token, some law students worry that an indelibly corporatist or liberal or conservative consciousness may accompany talking and thinking like a lawyer. The legal lexicon brims with old words like "rights" and "duties" and "privileges." Are these ancient legal words and concepts indissolubly wedded to a certain way of looking at the world? Is legal discourse a lingual trap that cannot bring about lasting change?

This is the position taken by Leslie Bender in "A Lawyer's Primer of Feminist Theory," where she argues that mainstream legal discourse—that is, "rights-talk"—in tort law is intrinsically connected to an egoistic male perspective and to male values. In her words:

> Tort law should begin with a premise of responsibility rather than *rights,* or interconnectedness rather than separation, and a priority of safety rather than profit or efficiency. The masculine voice of *rights,* autonomy, and abstraction has led to a standard that protects efficiency and profit; the feminine voice [of caring, context, and interconnectedness] can design a tort system that encourages behavior that is caring about others' safety and responsive to others' needs or hurts, and that attends to human context and consequence.[241]

Bender's claim that a certain voice, set of values, and viewpoint always accompany the word "rights" exactly parallels the claim that the N-word has an inherent meaning. Professor Bender's critique of rights-talk dates back to Karl Marx's attack on what the French Declaration of 1793 had taken as the fundamental rights of man, namely, the rights of liberty, property, security, and equality. As Marx put it:

None of the supposed *rights of man*...go beyond the egotistic man... that is, an individual separated from the community, withdrawn into himself, wholly preoccupied with his private interest and acting according to his private caprice.[242]

For Marx, rights-talk expresses bourgeois ideology, that is, such talk reflects the wish of the capitalist entrepreneur to be free from social limitations and social accountability—free from any duties of care and concern for the well-being of people he exploits. For Marx, both *in content* and *in form* "rights" merely promote and protect the selfish interests of acquisitive individuals, and rights-talk merely reproduces an atomistic and egoistic worldview.

In content, the right of liberty, defined as the right to do anything that does not harm others, is a right rooted in separation from (rather than solidarity with) others. My right of liberty gives me a fenced-off area of freedom from which I can exclude all others and within which I am privileged to invade the interests of others without doing anything the law will call a "harm" or "wrong." Through the atomizing lenses of my right to liberty, I look at others not as brothers or sisters or friends or neighbors but as limitations on my freedom, and viewing others as limitations leads me to feel hostility and resentment toward them. "The right of man to freedom," says Marx, "is not based on the union of man with man, but on the separation of man from man."[243] Property rights also erect a fence around each individual: "The right of man to property is the right to enjoy his possessions and dispose of the same arbitrarily without regard for other men, independent of society, the right of selfishness." The right to equality merely assures that each individual enjoys these anti-social rights of personal liberty and private property without discrimination, "that each man shall without discrimination be treated as a self-sufficient monad."[244] Finally, the right of security backs up these other self-regarding, atomistic, and asocial rights with guns and badges and "the concept of the police"—it puts the force of the state behind social relations and institutions rooted in egoism and so merely provides "the assurance of egoism."

In form, rights reflect and reinforce an individualistic ideology by assuming that the members of a society are perpetually ready to set at one another's throats and need state-backed (ultimately police-backed) personal rights to repel one another (one wields rights as one would a sword and shield to fend off or eject trespassers and potential trespassers, those who will incessantly seek to encroach upon one's fenced off area of personal freedom and private property). Finally, the abstract *form* of rights as neutral rules that treat everyone alike hides from view the dominance of haves over have-nots and the powerful over the weak. For instance, legal analyses of the rights and duties of people who make promises (the law of contracts) and people who injure others (the law of torts) pay no attention to underlying unequal distributions of wealth and power. Rather, as Richard Abel notes in his Marxist critique of Anglo-American tort law, the rightness of those unequal distributions is taken for granted and attention focused only on the changes in the status quo ante brought about by the accident or broken promise.[245] So, the abstract *form* and the bourgeois *content* of rights-talk conspire to make such talk the indelible expression of bourgeois individualism. Rights, in a word, always mean *bourgeois* rights—their form and content rob them of the power to promote unity over hostility, community over egoism, and solidarity over separation. Accordingly, rights-talk (and by extension, legal language) cannot bring about real progressive social change. It can only reflect and reinforce bourgeois ideology—bourgeois visions, voices, and values.

Feminists and Marxists reject rights-talk on the same fixed-meaning grounds that NAACP critics reject the N-word. Like critics of rights discourse, critics of N-word-laden rap or spoken word performances contend that both in *form* and *content* these profane racial utterances, these groupings of rule-governed racial epithets, reflect racist beliefs, and reinforce a racist worldview. In *content*, critics assume that N-word-laden performances have an inherently racist "meaning"—such talk is a reflection, however indirect and removed, of an underlying anti-black point of view. And they suppose that the profane, abusive, vulgar, and irreverent *form* of such talk echoes and reinforces the disrespect for black personhood in the content. So, critics conclude that the profane *form* and the racist *content* of N-word-heavy discourse conspire to make such talk the indelible expression of racist beliefs and attitudes. Its form and content, too, rob it of the power to promote unity over hostility, community over animosity, and solidarity over separation. Accordingly, neither rights-talk nor N-word-laden discourse can contribute to progressive political discourse.

Fortunately for those of us professionally or personally committed to producing social change through words, symbols, and discourses (including hoary old lexicons with sickeningly sexist, racist, homophobic histories), Lorde, Marx, Bender, and the NAACP are right in focusing our attention on language as an instrument through which power is exercised. But they are wrong in saying that certain words and discourses are inherently oppressive or self-abnegating or atomizing or socially marginalizing and can only reflect and reinforce the status quo. They are right that there are many lethal discourses of domination and exclusion that thwart empathy, stall conscience, and preserve privilege, but words don't just link established or "fixed" meanings and corresponding references. Rather, social actors contest the meanings, references, and "correct" applications of words in the process of constituting their social identity and vindicating their social existence. What was an "incorrect" reference for a word yesterday can, abruptly or by degrees, turn into a "correct" reference today as social actors rally in support of a new application. Simply put, any words and symbols can be deployed as political tools for any cause; in the realm of political communication and public discourse, there are no fixed meanings. Look at the career of "queer" as a word, for instance. Once a hateful epithet, it now figures in a field of critical theory called Queer Theory that emerged in the early 1990s out of the fields of queer studies and women's studies and includes queer readings of texts and critical reflections on "queerness" itself. Viewing words and symbols and discourses as volatile political tools highlights their capacity to be detached from their roots and used subversively to generate new meanings, create new alliances, and produce profound change.

◆

The commonsense, fixed meaning, folk theory of how we use words to refer to things in the world highlights the way words can be great devices for transmitting factual information. But in his famous paper, "The Meaning of a Word," J.L. Austin asks, "Why do we call different [kinds of] things by the same name?"[246] Why do people use the same word for very different "senses?" For instance, why do we use the word "mother" to refer to kinds of mothers—including birth mothers, donor mother, surrogate mothers, adoptive mothers, foster mothers, and step mothers (and mother of invention, mother of vinegar, and den mother)—or the word "game" to refer to many different kinds of games, some competitive, others not, some that are all luck, others that are all skill? A commonsense, but mistaken explanation would be that the kinds of things named by the same word are similar in some way, that they share something in common—they form a "classical category" on the basis of what they all have in common and the name applies to this category.

Austin torpedoed this commonsense view by pointing out that the different senses of a word like "mother" or "game" frequently do not have properties in common.[247] For instance, there is no common set of properties shared by all the following kinds of mothers: those who give birth, those who donate an egg, those who give birth but did not donate the egg, those who lack any genetic or birth connection but who are legal guardian and nurturer, those who lack any genetic or birth connection but who are paid by the state to nurture, those who lack any genetic or birth connection but who are current wives of the fathers. As Lakoff says, "The concept mother is not clearly defined, once and for all, in terms of common necessary and sufficient conditions." Thus, the word "mother" has noncentral *extended senses*—birth, donor, surrogate, adoptive, foster, step—and a central *prototypical* sense, namely:

> **A person who is and always has been female and given birth to the child, supplied her half of the child's genes, nurtured the child, is married to the father, is one generation older than the child, and is the child's legal guardian.[248]**

In this case there are a variety of "principles of extension" from the central or prototypical sense to noncentral extended senses—some based on giving birth, some on genetics, some on social, cultural, and legal factors. [249]In the end, the mother category, like most other categories in ordinary public discourse, is one whose contours and membership depend on social conventions rather than shared properties. And as I say, then there is metaphorical speech, the mother of all ambiguities and much invention.

Lakoff calls categories like "mother" *radial*, as opposed to classical, categories. In his words, "[a] radial structure is one where there is a central case and conventionalized variations on it which cannot be predicted by general rules." A key characteristic of a radial category like mother is that the prototype or central case does not and cannot determine which subcategories (for instance, which candidates for the "mothers" designation) can properly or correctly belong to the category. As Lakoff notes, there is "no general rule for generating kinds of mothers."[250] By the same token, there is no general rule for generating kinds of people to whom the N-word can refer. Because the extended senses of the N-word need not share anything in common with the prototypical sense of the word, the senses do not form a classical category—based on what they all have in common—to which the word applies. Rather, the senses of the N-word are simply culturally and politically determined and have to be learned rather than logically deduced. In a word, the N-word category is *radially structured*. The boundaries of radial categories can be extended by social actors in imaginative, creative, and unpredictable ways. The career of a word in political communication and public discourse, its developmental arc over time, cannot be logically deduced from its origins. Just as, in the words of Oliver Wendell Holmes, "the life of the law has not been logic; it has been experience," we can say the life of ordinary language, too, has been not logic but experience.[251] And a major part of the experience that shapes the meaning of language, a major mechanism or principle of extension for senses and concepts, is a word's political usefulness in helping unify individuals and create social identities.

Wittgenstein emphatically declared that "nothing is more wrongheaded than calling meaning a mental activity." Instead, he located word meanings outside the heads of speakers—in the function that words have as "signals" passed back and forth between people in the course of purposeful and shared activity. Wittgenstein coined the term "language-game" to emphasize "the fact that the *speaking* of language is part of an activity or of a form of life."[252] One famous language-game he describes involves a builder, called A, communicating with his helper, B. The game nicely illustrates the different ways that words carry meaning or function in shared, purposeful activity; it also nicely shows how unnecessary it is to look for the meaning of language in "mental pictures" or "subjective thoughts, beliefs, intentions" or any other mental activity that accompanies talking and understanding. B's job is to pass A stones of various kinds—bricks, slabs, columns, etc.— When A shouts "brick" or "slab" or "column." Words like "red" and "blue" are given a role in the game, so A can shout "red slab," and B will pass slabs of a certain color. The game could be developed to have conventions about word order, so that if A said "slab, column, brick," this means that B is to bring them in a definite order, they can be given words or symbols that determine the number of slabs or columns or bricks. Words that act like proper names (that is, represent unique entities rather than kinds of entities) could be added to the game.

Each verbal signal has its own function. For instance, the words "slab" and "brick" function in their language-game very differently than the words "here" and "there" or "red" and "blue" or the numerical signs "a," "b," "c," and "d." As Wittgenstein puts it, "Think of the tools in a tool-box: there is a hammer, pliers, a saw, a screw-driver, a rule, a glue-pot, nails and screws. The functions of words are as diverse as the functions of these objects." Once we see clearly that different words function differently in mediating a shared activity like building something, we also see clearly that words can only be understood in terms of how they are woven into those patterns of shared activity. "Only in the stream of thought and life do words have meaning," says Wittgenstein.[253] The stream of life that pulses through a language-game—the shared and purposeful activity that the game makes possible—creates meanings or "uses" for the words in the game. "For a large class of cases—though not for all—in which we employ the word 'meaning,'" he says, "it can be defined thus: the meaning of a word is its use in the language."[254]

Thus, says Nigga Theory, the meaning of *Nigga* is its use in language, and since its uses are many, its meanings are many.

◆

One of the most potent uses of words in our collective stream of life is as "performatives," especially as a "political performatives," as discussed earlier. The N-word can be a political performative, the word "rights" can be a political performative, as I mentioned earlier, my hair is a political performative—indeed, any form of linguistic or nonlinguistic symbolic communication can be a political performative. When old words and symbols are used as political performatives, they can take on radical, even revolutionary, new meanings.

This brings us to the most important questions of this analysis: What makes a performative word or symbol "political," and what social action does such political communication perform? There are two common reductive conceptions of politics that obstruct a clear view of the creative role performatives play in politics. The first is that politics is something that occurs only in the state, that it is "the art or science of political government" (*American Heritage Dictionary of the English Language*, first entry for "politics"). Under this *state model of politics*, political activity in contemporary America can easily be equated with representative government and a representative political system.

The second views political activity as a contest over the power to make the rules of the game and to determine the distribution of goods and services and taxes and jobs—a contest over who gets what, when, and how. Call this the *spoils model of politics*.

But "Say it loud, I'm black and I'm proud" cannot qualify as a political slogan under the spoils model because it makes no claim on resources or decision-making authority. Nor can it qualify as political communication under the state model because it does not focus on "the affairs of a government or of the groups or parties within it." It is politically performative, but what is its politics?

◆

While power is the object of most political theory, power takes many forms. Anything that can produce or resist social change is a form of power, including money, social status, tradition, and the barrel of a gun. Yet in democratic nations, social change has been produced—power has been effectively wielded—by unarmed socially marginalized and poor people without tradition or weaponry on their side, so there is a kind of power in democracies that can prevail over guns, money, and entrenched privilege, and that is the power of numbers—of individuals working together as a collective social actor to achieve a common project. Workers movements, the civil rights movement, the women's movement, and a host of successful conservative social movements attest to the power of numbers in a democracy to produce (and resist) social change.

Numbers alone mean nothing. Numbers without unity, solidarity, and collective identity carry little weight in a democracy. In a democracy, political power consists critically in the formation of the "us" and the "them" which make collective social action possible. So the most basic political question in a democracy is: what forces create commitment, unity, and solidarity among individuals? What factors can unify and bond individuals in a democracy? What forms of communication constitute political forces just as much as guns and money and elective offices? Words and other communicative symbolism play a decisive role in the process of creating our political identities and our contests. Indeed, words and symbols and discourses play as big a role as a person's status as black person, woman, immigrant, worker, or business owner.

It is common to hear that people form social identities and bond together in collective action due to "common interests." A social structure that places one group of individuals dominant over another—White over Black, men over women, rich over poor, or any relationship between the dominant and the subordinate group—we can call a vertical relationship. This vertical relationship also defines the horizontal relationships among members of each group. Thus, Blacks, women, and the poor have "true" or "common interests" by dint of their common subordination to Whites, men, and the rich respectively.[255] In other words, the vertical structure of domination and subordination creates a corresponding horizontal structure of "common" or "objective" or "exogenous" or "true" interests among all those in the same social position. Under the "true" or "common interests" theory of unity among individuals, "common interests" give an alliance of individuals a collective identity and common consciousness, and, consequently, anyone who does not think and act in harmony with his or her "true" or "common interests" is self-abnegating and has "false consciousness."

The "common interests" model of bonding, solidarity, and politics is half right, since sharing a relation to a structure of social domination or privilege provides a vital basis for unity, and since common life experiences, especially the shared experience of a common oppression, subordination, or exploitation can be an important basis of much political bonding. But common life experiences are far from sufficient bases for bonding and solidarity within a group. The "common interests" model ignores the force of words and symbols in the formation and maintenance of people's social and political identities. Vertical and horizontal relationships do not necessarily thrust identities on people; men and women choose their individual and collective identities—a physically disabled, black, lesbian senior citizen who is a devout Muslim could choose any of seven horizontal relationships as the one most important to her personal and social identity. She could also talk about "intersectionality" and claim all seven identities, or she could decline the invitation to claim any of them, defining herself instead primarily as an environmentalist or animal rights advocate or robust individualist who refuses to define herself in terms of any social category or to engage in any unified social action. Whatever her choice of social identities and political projects, it will only very partially be dictated by the position she shares with others in the social structure.

Closer to home, take me: Like many people, I am in both dominant and subordinate groups. Vertically, I am in a dominant class and gender but subordinate race. Thus, in my dominant social positions I have horizontal relationships with people in high tax brackets and with men; in my subordinate social position, my horizontal relationships are with Blacks. I can easily multiply my vertical and horizontal relationships: light skinned vs. dark skinned, straight vs. gay, Christian vs. Muslim, able-bodied vs. physically disabled, citizen vs. undocumented worker, English speaking vs. non-English speaking, mentally healthy vs. mentally ill, and so on. Include intersectionality as an additional irreducible form of domination and subordination and there are endless permutations, endless layers of horizontal structural relationships on which individuals could base their identity and political activity. What's more, once a collective social actor, an "us," comes into existence, there are many centripetal forces—the many internal divisions and conflicting perspectives based on these differences of gender, class, religion, and the rest—threatening its unity and cohesion and hence its power.

Thus a multiplicity of "us and them" divisions is possible in any society. Not every possible "interest group" is an "organized interest group" and not every organized interest group earns or keeps the loyalty and commitment of all its potential members. Thus, collective social actors, collective social identities, are the outcome of social struggles over identity and community, not the expression of social structures.

◆

Individuals use political performatives to create and transform communities and to establish individual and collective identities. Most simply, political performatives are words and symbols and discourses that perform the social action of bonding and unifying individuals into collective social actors, the ultimate source of power in a democracy. Political performatives are tools—linguistic and nonlinguistic forms of symbolic communication—people use to forge the unities that make collective action possible. Political performatives acquire their force through their ability to unite people in action.

Words like "I pledge allegiance" epitomize *linguistic* bonding performatives, which, in a democracy like ours may create multiple affiliations because individuals may pledge loyalty to multiple (sometimes even competing groups). The same words in the context of a cult of personality in totalitarian states would leave much less room for the creation of multiple political identities. The Confederate battle flag controversy ignited by the Emanuel Nine murders illustrates the performative role of flags in creating and transforming communities. The "us" the American flag originally stood for did not include Blacks, who, according to the Supreme Court's 1857 Dred Scott decision, could never become citizens of the United States and "had no rights which the white man was bound to respect."[256] The "us" and "them" constructed by the American flag before the Civil War was the same "us" and "them" of the original Confederate flag: no Confederate flag was necessary before that war because the Stars and Stripes already stood for an "us" of white American citizens and a "them" of black non-citizens and chattel slaves. It took 600,000 dead men in a cataclysmic race war to transform the American flag into an emblem that includes black folk in its "us."

It took another struggle—the civil rights movement—to make the "us" of the American flag still more racially inclusive. After *Plessy v. Ferguson*, the 1896 SCOTUS decision that made separate-but-equal the law of the land, the American flag stood for a racially segregated "us," especially for pro-Jim Crow Americans; the flag stood for an "us" of white first-class American citizens and a "them" of black second-class citizens. In the 1950s and 60s, many American citizens embraced the Confederate battle flag in order to unify and rally a segregationist "us" against an integrationist "them." Legislative decisions during those years to feature the battle flag in the redesign of state flags across the South were *at least partly* responses to SCOTUS desegregation decisions like *Brown v. Board of Education* (1954) and other federal pressures to desegregate. Just as before the Civil War there was no need for a separate Confederate flag to stand for slavery because the American flag itself already stood for that, before the civil rights movement there was no need for a separate Confederate flag to stand for segregation because Old Glory itself already stood for that. At two crucial turning points in the history of American race relations, as citizens and lawmakers sought to expand the "us" represented by the American flag to be more racially inclusive, other citizens and lawmakers rallied around some version of the Confederate flag in support of a narrower, more exclusive "us."

Many groups and individuals fly the American and Confederate battle flag together, as if they don't stand for competing conceptions of "us." One can contend that the two flags do not stand for contradictory conceptions of "us" if he or she can show that the battle flag can mean something other than support for segregation or white supremacy—something such as, say, Southern pride. A 2013 YouGov poll found that while more Americans overall saw the battle flag as a symbol of Southern pride than of racism, many more Democrats than Republicans and many more Blacks than Whites viewed it as a symbol of racism. Confederate battle flag critics use the symbol to isolate a "them" of segregationists and white supremacists and to mobilize a racially liberal and inclusive "us." Many battle flag supporters say they use the same symbol to distinguish an "us" of folk *with* Southern pride from a "them" of folk *without*. Some other battle flag supporters such as the KKK use the emblem to isolate a "them" of inferior blacks and to mobilize a racially illiberal and exclusionary "us." Because no words or symbols have indelible meanings, many different claims can be made about the battle flag's meaning. These conflicting claims set the stage for today's impassioned political struggle over the Confederate flag, whose meaning is not inherent or fixed and frozen but rather is a prize in a pitched conflict among groups attempting to describe their social reality, constitute their social identity, and vindicate their social existence.

So, rather than social groups being produced by their common interests, social actors produce *themselves* through their political performatives—their flags, pledges, anthems, monuments, books, plays, movies, marches, protests, and parades. Our political communication does not just *reflect* our interests, it *creates* our interests; it does not just reflect who we are, it creates "us." Races, ethnicities, genders, classes, ages, workers, and LGBTQ+ persons, as collective social actors with collective social identities, are produced by these forms of political communication. Our sense of common interests reflects the successful deployment of political performatives. That words like African Americans, Muslims, women, and LGBTQ+ can evoke a sense of community, loyalty, and commitment to a common purpose reflects generations of social conflict over words and meanings and discourses that identify a common understanding of a social structure.

Like a flag, the word "right" often functions as a political performative, a way of distinguishing between "us and them" and unifying "us" in social action. Rights discourse does not reflect an atomistic worldview or any other underlying intellectual edifice. While it cannot be denied that the discourse of rights has been (and is still being) used to legitimate social and economic inequality, major advancements for racial minorities, women, same-sex couples, and workers have come out of social struggles over rights. Calling a liberty or social interest a "right" enhances the ability of social actors to label illegitimate assertions of power and thereby to arraign a "them" and rally a democratic "us." Uttering the word "right" can serve the same purpose as unfurling a flag—it helps bond individuals and, by shining a light on unwarranted privilege, provides a framework for group demands. The discourse of rights is simply a mechanism for the formation of group action and its force lies entirely in its ability to unite people in action.

My dad, for instance, captured in the Warden's own law books the very verbal weapons he successfully wielded against the Governor and State of Ohio. After teaching himself the vocabularies of constitutional law and criminal procedure, he wielded "bourgeois" rights-talk—old words like *habeas corpus* and due process—against the State of Ohio, fiercely contesting the meaning of these words with prosecutors and Attorneys General in writs and oral arguments before state and federal tribunals until finally his conviction was overturned by the Sixth Circuit Court of Appeals in the case of *Fred Armour v. W. D. Salisbury*, Superintendent, 492 F. 2nd 1032 (6th Cir. 1974).

Thinking about rights or any other bit of language in terms of fixed inherent meanings asserted by legal theorists like Professor Bender trivializes the creative role words play in political communication and the creative power of *any* words to acquire and create new meanings. In political battles, just as the howitzers, cannons, missile launchers, and other artillery captured from the enemy in a revolutionary war can be among the most powerful weapons in the arsenal of freedom fighters, the words of oppressors can be among the most powerful weapons in the legal and political vocabulary of people resisting oppression. Because words lack fixed, essential, true, real, or inherent meanings, words are weapons that can be captured from and turned against adversaries. This logic applies to rights discourse as surely as it does to all words and symbols in ordinary language and political communication.

Which brings us at last to the word many view as the linguistic equivalent of the Confederate battle flag, namely, the N-word. Historically and still to this very day both the N-word and the battle flag did (and still do) in some settings perform the social action of distinguishing and distancing an inferior black "them" from a superior white "us"—and in this role it is one of the most violent and blood-soaked verbal acts in the English language. Blacks, too, sometimes deploy the N-word against other blacks as an act of "lateral denigration," as in Rock's "I love black people but I hate niggas" put-down. But unlike the Confederate battle flag, which generally has not been appropriated by the black community as part of their public discourse, the N-word—as the NAACP N-word eulogy pointed out—has been adopted by black writers, artists, entertainers, and ordinary citizens and put to a variety of positive uses. For instance, some politically engaged black rappers like Kendrick Lamar, Earl Sweatshirt, Tupac Shakur, Nas, Ice Cube, and Jay-Z use the N-word as a political performative to bond with the very same black criminals Rock used it to push away from. Other black poets (see, for instance, National Poetry Slam Champion Saul Williams' poem "Sha-Clack-Clack") and writers frequently use the N-word as a general term of solidarity and fellowship. And in my sphere of social activity, legal scholarship, I have used the N-word in catchphrases like *Call me a*

Nigga to distinguish between an "us" of blacks who stand in solidarity with black criminals while seeking to promote reconciliation, restoration, and redemption in criminal matters and a "them" of people who are chary of sympathy for black criminals and who seek to "otherize" them in matters of blame and punishment.[257] Deploying the N-word in certain settings can serve the same purpose as unfurling a flag—it can help bond individuals and, by shining a light on unwarranted privilege or unjust subordination, provide a vehicle for social solidarity and framework for group demands. In its N-word eulogy, the NAACP found such positive applications of the word just as objectionable as the negative ones because of the word's negative and for them inherent meaning. Thanks to our earlier discussion, we can now plainly explain to NAACP N-word eulogists and lingual fundamentalists why their anti-N-word fixed-meaning argument, though steeped in "common sense" and supported by respected philosophers and progressive writers, misses the point. The meaning of the N-word is simply its different uses in overlapping spheres of social activity. They are right about the N-word, and so are we.

Whether the social and political utility of a given use or application of a word or symbol outweighs its social and political costs can always be debated for any word or symbol. I happen to think the N-word's political utility (especially in the hands of thoughtful black poets and writers and performers) outweighs its social disutility at this time, but in any case, the issue of whether one form of symbolic communication or another should be used in political communication can never be resolved simply by appeals to fixed or inherent meanings.

◆

The folk theory of fixed inherent meanings trivializes the creative role of words in political communication and the creative power of *any* words to acquire and create new meanings. Thomas Paine, whose impassioned words helped ignite the American Revolution and fan the flames of revolution, exemplifies this point. "These are the times that try men's souls," begins Paine's impassioned essay "The Crisis" in December 1776, following on his pamphlet *Common Sense*, a powerful piece of propaganda published in Philadelphia earlier that year and selling 150,000 copies nearly overnight. Although the flame of revolutionary resistance was already alive when Paines's pamphlets hit the streets of Philly, many historians contend that his word work "unified dissenting voices and persuaded patriots that the American Revolution was not only necessary, but an epochal step in world history." John Adams said: "Without the pen of Paine, the sword of Washington would have been wielded in vain."[258] As historian Eric Foner rightly notes, Paine's mastery of the political art forges political identities *through* transforming the meanings of words:

> One of the keys to social change is change in the nature of language itself, both in the emergence of new words and in old words taking on new meanings. ...[Thomas] Paine helped to transform the meaning of the key words of political discourse...[Paine helped] to promote revolution by changing the very terms in which people thought about politics and society.[259]

Words are weapons that can be captured from and turned against adversaries. This logic applies to the word Nigga as surely as to every other word in ordinary language and political communication.

Words like "Nigga" are detachable tools that can be modified and reapplied to produce social change by bonding people in unified opposition against a common foe.[260] Just as the words "Say It Loud I'm Black and I'm Proud" and "Black is Beautiful" bonded Blacks in the oppositional political discourse of the 1960s, "Call *me* a Nigga" can bond black criminals and non-criminals in matters of blame and punishment in the oppositional political discourse of today. In a word, nigga-talk can make the frozen circumstances dance by playing to them their own melody.

CHAPTER **FIVE**

METAPHYSICAL THEATRE AND NIGGA THEORY
IN NINE ACTS

S tatements like "With this ring, I thee wed" and "I pledge allegiance" and "Women Unite, Take Back the Night" are not the only forms of symbolic communication that can forcefully bond people; as I used my hair to illustrate earlier, nonlinguistic forms of symbolic communication like hair, clothes[261] architecture, dances, melodies, rituals, and ceremonies can just as forcefully bond people. In a word, discourses go beyond words. As Clifford Geertz observes in his study of the 19th-century Balinese state:

> The Balinese, not only in court rituals but generally, cast their most comprehensive ideas of the way things ultimately are, and the way that men should therefore act, into immediately apprehended sensuous symbols—into a lexicon of carvings, flowers, dances, melodies, gestures, chants, ornaments, temples, postures, and masks—rather than into a discursively apprehended, ordered set of explicit "beliefs."[262]

Whether the communication takes the form of words or "sensuous symbols," the point of discourses through which individuals are bonded is to create and maintain a certain social reality, not merely to reflect it. Geertz's analysis of Bali captures this point elegantly:

> Statecraft is a thespian art. But there is more to it than this, because the pageants were not mere aesthetic embellishments, celebrations of a domination independently existing: they were the thing itself ... The state ceremonials of classical Bali were metaphysical theatre: theatre designed to express a view of the ultimate nature of reality and, at the same time, to shape the existing conditions of life to be consonant with that reality: that is, theatre to present an ontology and by presenting it, to make it happen—make it actual.[263]

Nigga Theory includes just such linguistic and nonlinguistic political per-formatives, words, phrases, and symbols designed to bond lucky non-crim-inals and unlucky criminals in the interest of unified social action on behalf of reviled black criminals.

◆

As mentioned in the introduction, I deployed the N-word in this spirit in 2007 in Bovard Auditorium at the University of Southern California as part of the Provost's Visions and Voices Series. *Race, Rap, and Redemption,* a piece of metaphysical theater I wrote and co-produced with Ron Garet, with Jo-anne Morris as executive producer. In it I tried to do what anthropologist Clifford Geertz suggests political theater does for its culture: it expressed my view of "the ultimate nature of reality" and was simultaneously meant to "shape the existing conditions of life to be consonant with that reality."[264] The piece expressed a certain moral ontology, a substantive position on the nature of moral reality—that there is no moral difference between blameworthy and blameless Blacks. More precisely, my position was that our condemnations of black criminals are irrational, illegitimate, and unreliable, and that not only are so-called niggas worthy of our sympathetic identification and social sol-idarity, *Nigga* is a word that performs that solidarity. Through interwoven artistic performances and critical reflections, *Race, Rap, and Redemption* sought to bond black criminals and law-abiding audience members, to get members of the audience to view black criminals as "us" rather than "them."

The proofs and arguments presented consisted of words, performanc-es, and "sensuous symbols"—including a marching band, anthems, ritual, dance, short film, dramatic monologue, sermon, a raft of melodies, spoken word, and gansta rap—that invited the audience, sitting as factfinders charged with morally assessing an egregious violent black wrongdoer, to sympathetically identify with that particularly unsympathetic wrongdoer, and hence through him, *all* black criminals. The black wrongdoer on whom we focused was Stanley "Tookie" Williams, Crips co-founder and convicted murderer, who was executed by the State of California after then Governor Arnold Schwarzenegger, in a carefully worded letter, refused to grant clemency on the ground that Mr. Williams had not achieved "personal redemption" in his 24 years on death row.[265] The goal of *Race, Rap, and Redemption* was to initiate the audience into the linguistic and nonlinguistic discourses that would bond them into a collective "us," defined by our shared understanding of the humanity of violent black wrongdoers and our refusal to monsterize them. As Geertz observed, community building "is a thespian art," designed to "present an ontology"—a view of our collective social identity—"and by presenting it, to make it happen—make it actual." [266]

James Boyd White asks us to consider what happens when a person opposed to racism is told a successful racist joke; as White observes, "he laughs and hates himself for laughing; he feels degraded, and properly so, because the object of the joke is to degrade."[267] The reason we feel uneasy in our laughter at a racist or sexist joke is because we realize that to laugh at such a joke is to—at that instant—become a certain kind of person, to constitute ourselves as racists or sexists. The joke, like any other text (including scholarly books, poems, legal opinions, and musical performances) is an *invitation* to distinguish between a respectable "us" and a laughable (often inferior and alien) "them" and to constitute oneself as one of "us."

Rock's refrain, "I love Black People but I hate niggas," wears its "us–them" invitation on its sleeve: "them" niggas are the butts of the joke "us" Black People are laughing at. In precisely the same vein, popular white political comedian Bill Maher delivered the following joke on his show *Real Time* while holding up a pill dispenser:

> If you think there's a pill for everything in this country, look at some of the ones they have in the pipeline ... ahhh, this is good, it 'Fights the infections picked up from crack prostitutes, Campho-Shaniqua, Reliable Pain Relief, Trusted by Crack Whores Everywhere, Easy to Swallow Liquid Formula.

The audience and three special guests (two white women, one white man) burst into laughter. Black girls and young ladies named Shaniqua, sitting in front of their TV sets as defenseless as open ears, had to swallow the indignity of this pointed punch line followed by sharp-edged shrieks of laughter from the panelists and studio audience. The most important *meaning* of a word, text, joke, or performance—which means, as we have seen, the use of a joke—often "is to be found in the community that it establishes with its audience."[268] Maher's joke invited its audience, Blacks and Whites alike, to see themselves as part of a respectable and upright "us" laughing down at morally deficient black women. Maher could count on guffaws from many Good Negroes—especially Good View Park Negroes who give their girls names like Madison, Chelsea, Courtney, and Taylor and are happy to accept an invitation to heap derision on the disproportionately poor black women who the punchline singles out. Or, again, Bill Cosby: "the lower economic and lower middle economic people are not holding their end in this deal." These jokes are part of the political theater that, day by day, creates, recreates, and reinforces a racist American ontology.

As White points out, part of the relationship between a reader (or an audience) and a writer (or speaker/performer) is "a kind of negotiation in which the reader constantly asks himself what this text is asking him to assent to and to become" and whether he accepts or rejects those invitations to become that person. In White's words:

> The reader's engagement with the text is thus by its nature tentative: while responding to the text he is always asking how he is responding, who he is becoming, and checking that against the other things he is. Sometimes he is fooled, as by the racist joke, when he becomes a momentary and chagrined racist ...; but sometimes—and this is the central point—he is educated, for reading is a process in which the reader himself, through a process of assimilation and rejection, response and judgment, becomes more fully one set of things that it is possible for him to be.

White then concludes these observations with a ringing insight: "Reading works by a perpetual interchange between the person that a text asks you to become and the other things you are." The educator in me wanted each member of the audience for *Race, Rap, and Redemption* to continuously ask how he or she was responding to these invitations to bond with black criminals, who he or she was becoming, and checking that against the other things that he or she was; the advocate in me hoped each would accept the invitation and include black criminals in "us." By the same token, as an educator I expect each reader to interrogate her responses to this text, to accept or reject the person it invites her to become, and through these acts of assent and repudiation to become more fully one set of things that it is possible for him to be; as an advocate I hope each opts to become a *Nigger Lover*.

◆

Race, Rap, and Redemption opened with a nonlinguistic performative utterance by the USC Marching Band, a recognizable and forceful form of symbolic bonding. Like Geertz's pageants of classical Bali, marching bands both express and *create* solidarity among collective social actors; these "sensuous symbols" are forceful "us"/"them" performatives commonly uttered in institutions of higher learning (Fight On Trojans!) and showcased in 4th of July events that celebrate and create "us" as an alliance of loyal and committed individuals who call ourselves Americans.

In Act II, I asked the audience: "Should 'we' pour liquor for Tookie?" That is, should those of "us" in that auditorium full of members of the "Trojan family" (whose South Central setting produce many descriptions in the Daily Trojan of generically black and brown assailants) participate in a ritual—the pouring of liquor or "libations"—that symbolically expresses and creates a bond between the people pouring the libations and the people to whom the libations are addressed. If "we" poured liquor for Tookie, we disproportionately lucky and privileged, law-abiding Trojans would performatively bond with a condemned black gangbanging murderer, and, on a deeper level, with disproportionately unlucky and underprivileged black and Latinx criminals in the surrounding South Central neighborhood. The audience was asked, *Should we law-abiding and crime-conscious Trojans, through this libations ritual, bond with criminals, even murderers?*

Act III answered "yes" to this query in the form of a libation song, titled "Just a Moment," by rappers Nas and K'waan, which contained lyrics such as:

"Can we please have a moment of silence?
That's for my Niggaz doin' years of confinement ...
And can we have another moment of silence?
For brothers who died from black-on-black violence"

Nas is commonly characterized as a "gangsta rapper," meaning that his lyrics purport to describe the reality of inner-city life—sometimes in words that wound and offend—for impoverished black youth growing up poor and black and outside the law. Critics reproach him for romanticizing gangs and criminal life, but it is worth asking whose artistic expression has more powerfully romanticized gangster life—on the one hand, Oscar-winners Francis Ford Coppola (the *Godfather* trilogy), Martin Scorsese (*Goodfellas* and *Casino*), and Oliver Stone (*Scarface*), or, on the other, rappers Tupac Shakur (*All Eyes On Me*), Nas (*Illmatic* and *Stillmatic*), Jay-Z (*American Gangster*), and Ice Cube (*AmeriKKKa's Most Wanted*, *Death Certificate*, *Predator*, and *Laugh Now, Cry Later*), N.W.A (*Straight Outta Compton*), dead prez (*RBG: Revolutionary but Gangsta*). It is beyond the scope of this work to probe old debates about whether gansta rap should exist, except to note that rumors of its death have been wildly exaggerated for many years and that Jay-Z released his 11th consecutive number one album in 2017, eclipsing every other act in musical history except the Beatles. Our more narrow questions in *Rap, Race, and Redemption*, as well as in *Nigga Theory* more broadly, are these: Can gansta rap songs and performances, these linguistic and nonlinguistic utterances, perform the social action of bonding black criminals and non-criminals? Can the profane words and narratives and other forms of symbolic communication in gangsta rap function like national anthems, flags, bumper stickers, and Geertz's "metaphysical theatre" in creating (rather than merely reflecting) unity with other individuals—in this case, with other individuals who are black, disproportionately poor, and guilty of criminal wrongdoing? Can the transgressive art form be an "us" *and* "them" political performative that bonds morally lucky haves with morally unlucky have-nots? In short, can gangsta rappers, many of whom acknowledge criminal pasts that would qualify them as "niggas" according to Chris Rock, penetrate pop culture with their own Nigga narratives and in the process transform some attentive and thoughtful listeners into Nigger Lovers? I think the success of hip-hop as a defining genre of our time, with gangsta rappers like Pac, Nas, and Hov among its most commercially successful and critically acclaimed icons, says yes.

Act IV consisted of Macy Gray's Orchestra of 12-18-year-olds performing, first traditionally and then in the musical vernacular of hip-hop, a beloved and forceful unifying performative that I've participated in hundreds of times at black gatherings, celebrations, and formal ceremonies—The Negro National Anthem: "Lift Every Voice and Sing." National anthems are prototypical songs of solidarity, their function as political performatives sitting in plain view, and the live performance showed that shifting to hip-hop can enhance the anthem's bonding force.

Act V applied the insight of Act IV about hip-hop in general (namely, that its songs can function as songs of solidarity) to so-called gangsta rap. It was a continuation of my collaborations over the years on art and social justice projects with Tupac Shakur's first manager, Leila Steinberg, and it wedded Pac's linguistic performative utterances to nonlinguistic dance movements for the purpose of bonding black criminals and non-criminals. The Lula Washington Dance Company performed an interpretive dance to Tupac's classic rap narrative "Brenda's Got A Baby." The song opens with Pac lamenting that a 12-year-old black girl named Brenda's had a baby, to which his interlocutor responds, "That's not our problem, that's up to Brenda's family." Pac's interlocutor attempts to distinguish and distance Brenda and her kind from the rest of "us." Pac then spins a "disadvantaged social background" narrative from Brenda's perspective, a narrative of abuse and neglect that leads her to toss her newborn into a trash bin, until, wracked by guilt, she retrieves him, then turns to crime (selling crack and prostitution) for subsistence—her story culminating in the frozen epitaph "prostitute found slain/And Brenda's her name/she's got a baby." This narrative is a bonding performative that invites us to make impoverished criminal outcasts like Brenda one of "us," deserving of our sympathy, solidarity, and understanding.

As Toni Morrison puts it, "Narrative is radical, creating *us* at the very moment it is being created."[269] We constitute ourselves as collective social actors through the narratives we recount and those we discount. Prosecutors know well that vividly recounting the *victim's* narratives can stir contempt and indignation in jurors toward wrongdoers and forcefully drive a social wedge between the factfinders and the accused—paving the path to a guilty verdict. Conversely, advocates for wrongdoers know that recounting the *wrongdoer's* narrative can stir sympathy and understanding in jurors toward wrongdoers and forcefully forge a social bond between the two—paving the path to acquittal. More generally, one's choice of "narrative perspective" itself can be an important nonlinguistic form of symbolic communication, something that creates or disowns social ties between wrongdoers and the rest of us by inviting an audience to become *a certain kind of people*—either the compassionate-and-understanding-toward-human-frailty kind or the-compassionate-toward-innocent-victims-and-contemptuous-of-those-who-harm-them kind. Not surprisingly, then, narrative perspective itself (i.e., whether we view criminal wrongdoing from the standpoint of victims and their suffering or wrongdoers and their extenuating circumstances) is often the object of social struggle. Good Negro Theory (in keeping with the "victims' rights movement") generally views matters of blame and punishment from the perspective of victims; in contrast, Nigga Theory, while mindful of the trauma of victims and in full support of restoration efforts aimed at mitigating their pain and suffering, generally approaches matters of blame and punishment from the perspective (and through the personal narratives) of the wrongdoers; it recognizes that "hurt people hurt people," that victimizers from one perspective are often victims from another, and makes individualized justice to criminal defendants (the value at the heart of the presumption of innocence, "that bedrock 'axiomatic and elementary' principle whose 'enforcement lies at the foundation of the administration of our criminal law'"[270]) categorically more important than "serving the greater good" or maximizing social welfare. As part of an oppositional discourse, Tupac's lyrics paint a nuanced picture of someone who is both a law-breaker and a victim and deploy the narrative perspective of the law-breaker—an impoverished crack-dealing prostitute named Brenda—in a song of solidarity. In sum, Act V was a black-lawbreaker bonding performative rendered in rap and interpretive dance.

Act VI opened with a query: what if the baby Brenda left behind was passed through the foster care system, suffering severe child abuse before becoming the officially irredeemable Stanley Tookie Williams? As Bob Herbert wrote, many such victims tend to be from twisted, violent families, their lives full of "unrelieved torment," and in telling versions of this story, gangsta rap can be viewed as the voice of the Niggas, by the Niggas, for the Niggas. It is its capacity to be the voice of voiceless black criminals in social and political discourse that makes gangsta rap relevant to the concerns of Nigga Theory.

Acts VII featured a spoken word performance by Saul Williams. I will confess a prejudice in favor of word work without musical accompaniment or other complementary elements, word work unplugged, if you will, for as a lawyer I know word work best and consider linguistic bonding performatives—say, the searing words of Thomas Paine's *Common Sense* or Lincoln's "Gettysburg Address"—to be uniquely forceful "us"–"them" tools and weapons. (In his eulogy on the slain president, Senator Charles Sumner observed that "the battle [for Gettysburg] itself was less important than the speech.") Paine's and Lincoln's words of solidarity do much more than merely describe, report on, or passively transmit information about the world. Rather, their words were deeds—they were social acts that created, established, and maintained communities. Linguistic bonding performatives like Paine's "These are the times that try men's souls" and Lincoln's "...our fathers brought forth on this continent, a new nation, conceived in Liberty, and dedicated to the proposition that all men are created equal" powerfully illustrate the agency of words. People produce and transform themselves through their struggles over the meaning of these same linguistic acts. Against this background, Saul William's intoned in Sha-Clack-Clack:

> I am as I was and will be because I am and always will be
> that nigga
> I am that nigga
> I am that nigga
> I am that timeless nigga that swings on pendulums like vines
> through mines of booby-trapped minds that are enslaved by time

Ron Garet, Carolyn Craig Franklin Chair in Law and Religion, opened Act VIII with a sermon on the mystery, meaning, and hope of redemption for even the most condemnable black criminal, told from the standpoint of Scripture. Kanye West's "Jesus Walks" helped frame his sermon. Ron trained for the clergy before choosing the contemplative life of the legal academy, and sermons are forceful bonding performatives couched in the language of morality and spiritual transcendence. We could not adequately consider the question of Tookie's personal redemption (a spiritual concept that Governor Schwarzenegger made a life-and-death legal test) without considering the power of the pulpit to deploy—through sermons—redemption, atonement, salvation, mercy, and forgiveness. What these spiritual verbal formulations *mean*—the "who" and "for what" of their application—can become the defining struggle in "who" we are as an alliance of loyal individuals; contests over their very meanings can form and transform the "us" and "them" of politics. Thus, Garet's utterances demonstrated the power of sermons to deploy political performatives like mercy, redemption, and forgiveness, and to forge social bonds with criminals.

Garet tells a version of the biblical story of the Good Samaritan, only it is set outside an urban gated community. The neighbors in Garet's story are a Latinx woman and Brenda, the 12-year-old subject of Tupac's "Brenda's Got a Baby." The neighbor is the one who heals, because she knows hurt, Garet said.

The neighbor is our redeemer, and though we do not see her face, hers is the face of the poor and the molested.... The neighbor is our redeemer, and though we do not see his face, his is the face of the enslaved and the lynched.

And as he offers the hope of redemption and a better future through solidarity and understanding, Garet invites listeners to assume their own roles.

We are the defendants, the prosecutors, the judge and the jury. We are the accuser and those who stand accused. Bring light to us tonight. Bring light to the lonely and dark places. Amen.

Act IX brought everything together in a live performance by gangsta rap icon, Ice Cube, of his "Fuck tha Police," the fittingly profane outcry against police brutality from the 1988 album *Straight Outta Compton*, which he recorded with the legendary group called N.W.A (Niggaz Wit Attitudes). These lyrics used coarse, crude, brutal words to describe a coarse, brutal social reality—the reality for black teenagers in Compton and South Central and many other poor black neighborhoods across the nation in those early days of the crack plague. Style and content meshed perfectly. The political animal in me recognized it immediately, when I first heard it while a law student, as an anthem for young black victims of police brutality, a verbal and musical bonding performative that, like the show it was now closing, invites listeners to include young black suspects and criminals in the collective "us" and corrupt, brutal police in the opposing "them."

Not only profanely eloquent and politically forceful, the words also proved tragically prophetic: the seething resentment, frustration, and rage at police brutality that they expressed culminated in the 1992 LA Riots, Uprisings, or Civil Disturbances (depending on the political perspective of the observer), triggered by the acquittal of police officers videotaped beating black motorist Rodney King at the end of a car chase. Nothing better foreshadowed those riots (or chronicled the festering frustrations behind them) than the lyrics of "The Nigga Ya Love to Hate" from Cube's 1989 album *AmeriKKKa's Most Wanted*:

I heard payback's a motherfucking nigga
That's why I'm sick of gettin treated like a goddamn stepchild
Fuck a punk cause I ain't him

You gotta deal with the nine-double-M
The damn scum that you all hate
Just think if niggas decide to retaliate

In *Straight Outta Compton* (1987), *AmeriKKKa's Most Wanted* (1989), *Death Certificate* (1991), and *Predator* (1992), Cube deftly deployed the discourse of Niggas in solidarity with black criminals (the first lines of which I quoted earlier):

Kicking shit called street knowledge
Why more niggas in the pen than in college?
Now cause of that line I might be your cellmate
That's from the nigga ya love to hate

Accordingly, he qualifies as a, if not *the*, leading early architect of the socio-political brand of gangsta rap that qualifies as "nigga-talk" under my earlier definition—namely, profane and N-word-laden oppositional discourse on behalf of disproportionately poor black criminals. He followed "Fuck tha Police," with more recent bonding performatives like "Guns and Drugs" and "Nigga Trap" from his 2007 LP *Laugh Now, Cry Later*. These pieces, too—constituent performatives of Nigga Theory—refuse to locate responsibility for wrongdoing solely or even primarily in the internal deficiencies and choices and subjective wickedness of impoverished wrongdoers rather than in external circumstances like hunger, fragmented families, biased law enforcement, dilapidated schools with hostile teachers and administrators, and hyper-segregated drug-infested crime-ridden slums, projects, and ghettoes. In their best songs, leading gangster or hardcore rappers like Cube, Nas, and Jay-Z focus on the accountability of society, on the social inequalities that breed criminal behavior rather than the subjective culpability of those committing prohibited acts, on the sociological and political rather than the moral determinants of wrongdoing.

Nigga Theory takes this sociological perspective on criminal wrongdoing to argue that moral luck renders moral assessments of wrongdoers irrational and illegitimate. Whenever social reasons masquerade as moral reasons, the moral claims reflect not objective truth, but competing social interests and social domination. Explanations for wrongdoing can either separate or bond criminals and non-criminals, and Nigga Theory encourages the latter. "Free will," "choice," "personal responsibility," and "moral depravity" are typically deployed to maintain a law-abiding "us" united in opposition to a criminal "them," while "savage social inequality" "structural violence," "racial oppression," and "predatory capitalism" typically are rallying cries for those who seek to create and reinforce a very different alliance of loyal and committed individuals. This is the deep insight of gangsta rap, an art form that at its best weds the profound to the profane. Rather than expressing the nihilism it has often been charged with, it is an eloquent plea for solidarity framed by a first-hand (street) knowledge of the racial injustice at the center of the American justice system. The goal of *Race, Rap, and Redemption* was to create an evening in which the Ivory Tower met the "boulevard" in a way that transformed both sides.

CHAPTER **SIX**

HOW RACE TRUMPED CLASS IN 2016

Racial animus has not had such a staunch and unapologetic champion on the national scene since George Wallace—who told the *National Review* in 1967 that he was a segregationist ("I believe in segregation all right") and denounced the Voting Rights Act of 1965 as well as other "so-called 'Civil Rights Acts'"—ran for president in 1968. Trump's history of otherizing black folk is long and sordid. In 1973 The US Department of Justice sued the Trump Management Corporation for violating the Fair Housing Act after finding evidence that Trump had, among other things, refused to rent to black tenants and lied to black applicants about whether apartments were available. In 1989, after four black and one Latino teenager—the Central Park Five—were accused of attacking and raping a jogger in New York City, Trump immediately ran an ad in local papers demanding, "BRING BACK THE DEATH PENALTY. BRING BACK OUR POLICE!" Despite the later DNA-based exoneration of the teens after they spent seven to 13 years in prison, and the city's $41 million settlement with them, he still maintains their guilt.

According to a book by John O'Donnell, former president of Trump Plaza Hotel and Casino in Atlantic City, Trump declared "Black guys counting my money! I hate it.... I think that the guy is lazy. And it's probably not his fault, because laziness is a trait in Blacks. It really is, I believe that. It's not anything they can control." In 1992 the Trump Plaza Hotel and Casino paid a $200,000 fine because it transferred black and women dealers off tables to accommodate the bigotry of big-time gamblers. In 2011 Trump zealously promoted false rumors that Barack Obama, America's first black president, was not born in this country. In 2011 he claimed Obama wasn't qualified to get into Columbia or Harvard Law School and demanded the release his university transcripts.

He has been repeatedly slow to disavow white supremacists who endorse him and often retweeted messages from white supremacists and neo-Nazis during his first 2016 presidential campaign. In the week after white supremacist protest in Charlottesville, Virginia, he said there were "some very fine people" among the white supremacists. In 2017 he repeatedly attacked NFL players who kneeled during the national anthem to protest police brutality and systemic racial oppression in America. In short, no presidential candidate in my lifetime has called me a nigga so often and in so many ways.

◆

One standard explanation for President Trump's victory in the 2016 election is that economic vulnerability and anxiety motivated his voters. Given his many racist statements over the years, the loud lower-class part of his base, and his own wealth, the election in 2016 has occasioned many analyses of the intersection of race and class in his rise to the office. The threshold question is: Does economic distress cause racism? Do precarious material conditions push racism to the forefront—that is, as the pie shrinks, are people more likely to go tribal to protect their share, and because the salient tribal identity in America is race, do people then turn into racists or at least become more virulently racist when their economic prospects dim? In "Stop Blaming Racism for Donald Trump's Rise" in *The Washington Post*, Jeff Guo answers this question in the affirmative: "Plenty of evidence suggests that economic anxiety can *cause* racism, by amplifying resentments and fostering suspicion of outsiders and racial minorities."[271] In support of this assertion he quotes a 2013 study published in *Political Science Quarterly* which reached the conclusion that "The effect of economic hardship is to activate prejudices that are latent, adding fuel to the fire of preexisting views."[272] The main evidence he offers for this proposition is from general opinion surveys, in which pessimism about overall economic conditions correlates with intolerant attitudes towards "others." Based on a 2016 study of the American National Election Survey, a poll that asked people detailed questions about their personal lives and political views, he found that "racial resentment and anti-immigration sentiments" correlate with views on the economy:

> Those who think that the nation's economic performance is worse or getting worse also tend to think that immigration is generally bad for the nation, and that black people are just "not trying hard enough" to get ahead.[273]

People who believed that the economy was doing "much better" than a year ago had below-average levels of racial resentment, while most who believed that the economy was doing "much worse" were extremely racially resentful—far more so than the average American. More often than not, he asserts, racist "ideas connect to deeper economic concerns." In these conclusions, he is in harmony with many other leftists and liberals. The lesson he draws from the data is that "the best strategy to ease the racial resentments among Trump's supporters is to address their economic concerns."

This betrays a deep misunderstanding of the relationship between economic concerns and racial attitudes. Guo goes so far as to contend that not only do economic and racial anxiety act through one other, they actually amount to the same feeling:

> When pundits credit the Trump campaign's success to the "resentful views of people upset about declining white privilege," doesn't that sound a lot like economic anxiety? Isn't economic status the essence of [white] privilege?

Guo is far from alone in making this argument, which assumes that the correlation between economic anxiety and racial resentment proves that the former caused the latter, that economic anxiety is the pregnant chicken and racial resentment, the resultant egg. But of course, perceptions of the economy are often biased and shaped by subjective attitudes, and people see empirical information about objective reality through the lens of their preexisting beliefs and attitudes. Psychological research suggests that people's positions on public policy matters are resistant to change, even in the face of strong evidence to the contrary. In "Cultural Cognition and Public Policy," Dan Kahan

163

and Donald Braman point out that such "cultural cognition" explains why individuals often do not alter their view when confronted with contradictory facts, but rather opt to reject such information instead.[274] If cultural lenses strongly influence how people view empirical reality, then rather than negative perceptions of the economy driving racial resentment, racial resentment might be driving negative perceptions of the economy.

In *Post-Racial or Most-Racial*, Professor Michael Tesler shows that, just as a large body of research shows that party identification strongly influences people's beliefs about the state of the economy (both Democrats and Republicans think economic conditions are better when one of their own is president), racial attitudes often drive subjective perceptions of external economic conditions. Based on survey data in one study from 2012, he found that, after four years of Obama in the White House had primed racial attitudes, people who expressed greater racial resentment were less likely to perceive the objective economic truth at that time, namely, that the unemployment rate had improved. In another survey of the same individuals before and after Obama first became president, he found that racial resentment strongly predicted economic perceptions—the greater a person's level of racial resentment, the gloomier their economic perceptions. [275]

Other studies show that perceptions of the economy did not cause people to increase or decrease their underlying levels of racial resentment. To the contrary, several studies, using a variety of different surveys, found very little change in overall levels of racial resentment as a consequence of the 2008 Great Recession, with some data even suggesting a slight reduction in racial prejudice during the bleakest days of that economic crash. "The evidence is pretty clear, then, that economic concerns are not driving racial resentment in the Obama Era," Tesler concludes. [276]

Inquiry into the causal connection between economic woes and racism yields two valuable insights. First, in many cases, racism seems to be making people anxious about the economy rather than vice versa. Second, the reason for this is that subjective perceptions of objective facts (like economic conditions) often depend on people's political leanings and cultural cognitions. Our minds' apprehension of the world, our perceptions of objective reality, are mediated by political and cultural beliefs; we see the world through ideological and cultural lenses.

The "left behind" thesis, characterizing the white working class as disenfranchised victims of capitalism's cruelties, served as an indictment (again, by both liberals and conservatives) of social justice advocates who focus "too much" on religious and ethnic minorities, on a narrow "us," rather than on an economically inclusive class-based "us" that includes poor and working-class whites. At the same time this narrative keeps alive the liberal hope that such voters can be reached by a more left-leaning, redistributionist economic policy.

This explanation also confers innocence on all whites from every class: poor and working-class whites can't really be blamed for succumbing to racist rhetoric in view of their economic distress, while middle- and upper-class whites can't be blamed for Trump because he was foisted upon the nation, not by them, but by those at the bottom, the poor and working-class voters from whose furious frustration and anxiety-ridden precarity he rose. Finally, the "left behind" thesis also confers innocence on the Democratic Party itself, making the irrationality of easily-manipulated poor and working-class whites the cause of their election loss rather than, say, the failure of Obama, Clinton, and others at the top of the Party to deliver on promises of a truly alternative and transformative politics, resulting in a less enthusiastic turnout for Democrats in the election, with many of those who had turned out for Democrats in the previous two national elections staying at home.

So, in keeping with the "left behind" thesis, on November 9th, the day after the 2016 election, *The New York Times* front-page article on Trump's triumph called it "a decisive demonstration of power by a largely overlooked coalition of mostly blue-collar white and working-class voters." But this convenient account does not square with the American National Election Study, the longest-running election survey in the United States, which revealed that, among "people who said they voted for Trump in the general election, 35% had household incomes under $50,000 per year (the figure was also 35% among non-Hispanic Whites), almost exactly the percentage in NBC's March 2016 survey," which showed that, as Nicholas Carnes and Noam Lupu wrote in the *Washington Post*, "only a third of Trump supporters had household incomes at or below the national median of about $50,000. Another third made $50,000 to $100,000, and another third made $100,000 or more, and that was true even when we limited the analysis to only non-Hispanic whites."[277] In the general election, like the primary, two thirds of Trump voters were in the top half of the economy. So if one assumes that being working class means being at the lower end of the economic spectrum, then one has to conclude that the vast majority of Trump supporters in the 2016 election were simply not working class. Better-off and well-off whites were anything but immune to his appeal.

Intent on stereotyping and scapegoating working-class Whites, these pundits defined "working class" as those without college degrees and then pointed to the jaw-dropping fact that Mr. Trump won 71% of the two-party vote among Whites without a college degree, which far exceeded the performance of any Republican going back to at least 1980. Although Trump won by only a four-point margin over Clinton among whites with a college degree, he enjoyed a nearly 40-point advantage among non-college educated whites. His support from this group was especially important in Wisconsin, Michigan, and Pennsylvania, the three states on which the election ultimately hinged. Whites in those three states without a college degree made up between 40 and 47% of the electorate and Trump won each state by about 30 points over Clinton.[278]

Observers used this education gap or "diploma divide" to conjure images of economically distressed and angry working-class whites "left behind" during the economic recovery that took place under the Obama Administration and to whom Trump's populist economic message spoke forcefully: economic distress, they agreed despite the evidence, drove white working-class Americans into the welcoming arms of a nakedly racist demagogue.

One problem with this explanation of the diploma divide is that many Trump voters without diplomas were relatively affluent. Carnes and Lupu note that, "among white people without college degrees who voted for Trump, nearly 60% were in the top half of the income distribution." "In fact," they observe, "one in five white Trump voters without a college degree had a household income over $100,000." So using education to measure the white working class can lead to false conclusions about the nature and scope of Trump's appeal. Contrary to the contention that Trump owed his victory to a "coalition of mostly blue-collar white and working-class voters," the American National Election Study reveals that white non-Hispanic voters without diplomas making below the median household income made up only 25% of Trump voters. Most of his voters had *not* been chewed up and spit out by a bad economy.[279]

A much deeper problem with the "left behind" explanation is its implicit assertion that people are drawn to racist rhetoric and anti-immigrant rhetoric because they are looking for a scapegoat for their own economic disenfranchisement. In other words, economic suffering robs people of moral agency, or at least undermines it, thereby impelling such racially illiberal choices—economic distress makes poor and working-class folk uniquely susceptible to ethno-nationalist demagoguery, in fact makes them racially illiberal. This claim, as demonstrated in a recent study published by the Democracy Fund's Voter Study Group (VSG) and co-authored by George Washington University political scientists John Sides and Robert Griffin, is fake news.[280]

Conventional measures of economic "anxiety" use an individual's broad-based economic perceptions, and as mentioned, those often merely reflect that person's political leanings. The VSG study instead used a much tighter, more detailed measure of "economic distress," defined by an individual's response to a number of detailed questions about their own direct experiences with financial instability or hardship. The report found that black and Latinx people report experiencing more economic distress than do white folk; that is, they are more likely than Whites to report difficulty making housing, loan, or credit card payments and to report insufficient savings. It also found that working-class white people are not especially distressed in relation to other groups. In fact, whites without a college diploma reported a *lower* level of distress than college-educated black and Latinx Americans. At every income level, non-white people reported more economic distress. In the words of the researchers:

> Contrary to the popular narrative, VOTER Survey results show that economic distress is not distinctively prevalent among the white working class. It is much more a fact of life for people of color. In part because of this, Trump voters in 2016 do not report more economic distress than do Clinton voters. If anything, the opposite is true.

That last finding bears repeating: Clinton voters reported more economic distress than Trump voters—economic distress is more strongly linked to support for liberal, not conservative, economic policies! That finding chimes with a 2017 study by the Public Religion Research Institute and *The Atlantic* which found that "White working-class voters who reported that someone in their household was dealing with a health issue—such as drug addiction, alcohol abuse, or depression—were actually less likely to express support for Trump's candidacy," while white working-class voters who had lost of social and economic standing were no more likely to favor Trump. White working-class Americans who bear the brunt of early death from drugs, alcohol, and suicide—dubbed "deaths of despair" by Princeton economists Anne Case and Angus Deaton in their landmark 2015 paper "Rising Morbidity and Mortality in Midlife among White Non-Hispanic Americans in the 21st Century"—were actually less likely to support Trump. Besides, economic distress simply was not distinctively prevalent among the white working class in 2016. As Sides and Griffin found, "in surveys conducted both before and after the election, Trump voters did not report higher levels of distress than did Clinton supporters." They conclude, in sum, that "economic distress was not the central cleavage in the American electorate in 2016."[281]

If economic distress standing alone had been a strong driver of support for Trump, black and Latinx voters should have surged toward the Republican column: these communities were disproportionately devastated by the Great Recession, precipitated by predatory lending practices that targeted people of color. But these most economically vulnerable Americans instead supported Clinton overwhelmingly. Economic distress alone does not dictate a voter's choice. Mediating the relationship between someone's economic misfortunes and their choice of any candidate are their values, beliefs, attitudes, interpretations of the world, assumptions about the way it works, and motivations. Hence black voters, whom the Great Recession left much more vulnerable than white ones, were not, just because of their economic distress, driven to take out their anger and frustration on the incumbent party by voting for Trump.

Three University of Massachusetts political scientists—Brian F. Schaffner, Matthew MacWilliams, and Tatishe Nteta—analyzed data from two nationally representative surveys; first, a pre-election poll of 2,000 American adults and second, a Cooperative Congressional Election Study (CCES) of 3,500 individuals. Their dependent variable, the effect whose cause they sought, was a vote for Trump or Clinton. Their independent variables, the factors that might explain why people voted as they did, were economic dissatisfaction, racism, and sexism. If, for instance, increased levels of economic dissatisfaction are associated with increases in the likelihood of a Trump vote, even after taking into consideration and making allowances for other factors that might explain voters' choices, such as partisanship (most people simply vote for their party's candidate) and ideology, then we can attribute at least some of his support to voters' economic concerns, depending on the strength of the association.

To measure prejudiced attitudes toward women, they created a "hostile sexism scale" based on the levels of respondents' agreement or disagreement with the following four statements:

1. Women are too easily offended.
2. Many women are actually seeking special favors, such as hiring policies that favor them over men, under the guise of asking for "equality."
3. Women seek to gain power by getting control over men.
4. When women lose to men in a fair competition, they typically complain about being discriminated against.

To measure racial attitudes, they created a "denial of racism scale" based on the intensity of respondents' agreement or disagreement with the following three statements:

1. White people in the US have certain advantages because of the color of their skin.
2. Racial problems in the US are rare, isolated situations.
3. I am angry that racism exists.

These items capture the extent to which individuals deny or acknowledge the existence of racism and feel empathetic about its costs. Finally, to measure economic dissatisfaction, one survey included an item asking, "All things considered, how satisfied are you with your overall economic situation?" accompanied by five options ranging from "extremely satisfied" to "not satisfied at all," while the other survey asked whether their household income had increased, decreased, or stayed about the same over the four years preceding the election.

The researchers found small coefficients for economic dissatisfaction but "the coefficients for the denial of racism and hostile sexism scales" were "quite large," with the "coefficient for denial of racism exceeded only by partisanship in terms of its strength of association with support for Trump."[282] So, a person who was otherwise average in all other variables—the classic "average man or woman"—but who registered the most sexist attitudes on the hostile sexism scale had a .66 probability of voting for Trump. A person would have only a .34 predicted probability of voting for Trump if she registered the least sexist attitudes. Thus, moving from one end of the sexism scale to the other was associated with more than a 30-point increase in support for Trump among the average likely voter. The relationship for the denial of racism scale was nearly identical—moving from the highest levels of acknowledgment and empathy for racism to the lowest levels was associated with about a 30-point increase in support for Trump. And while the coefficient for hostile sexism was not as strong in the CCES survey, the association with racism denial was even stronger—moving from the most acknowledging of racism to the most denying of racism was associated with a 60-point increase in support for Trump. Simply put, Schaffner et al. found "large changes in the probability of voting for Trump as one moves from low to high levels of racism or sexism."

So, what caused whites without college degrees to vote for Donald Trump more readily than whites with college degrees? In the words of Schaffner et al., it wasn't primarily economic concerns:

> We find that racism and sexism attitudes were strongly associated with vote choice in 2016, even after accounting for partisanship, ideology, and other standard factors.... Indeed, attitudes toward racism and sexism account for about two-thirds of the education gap in vote choices in 2016.

Other researchers reached similar conclusion, with Michael Tesler, for instance, finding the negative effects of education on white support for Trump vanishing after accounting for attitudes toward blacks and immigrants. Specifically, he found that "after controlling for both racial and immigrant resentment ... less educated whites were no more likely to support Donald Trump than their better educated counterparts."[283] The diploma divide in white support for Trump is primarily a racial attitude divide. Most simply, the education gap was not about education, it was about race—it was a racial attitude gap disguised as an education gap.

◆

Nevertheless, one major argument against the conclusion that Mr. Trump's campaign succeeded by tapping into the racism of white Americans is that between 6.7 and 9.2 million voters switched from voting for Barack Obama in 2012 to Donald Trump in 2016; given the closeness of the election, these Obama-Trump switchers were one key reason Trump prevailed. *The New York Times's* Nate Cohn wrote on the night of the election, for instance, that "Clinton suffered her biggest losses in the places where Obama was strongest among white voters. It's not a simple racism story."[284] *Morning Joe's* eponymous Joe Scarborough cited Cohn in his gleeful dismissal of the suggestion that racism motivated Trump voters, declaring:

People who live by the data should die by data, and the data, according to Nate Cohn of the *New York Times* says this, and let those who have ears to hear, hear: The very people who helped elect Barack Obama president of the United States twice just elected in Wisconsin, in Michigan, in Ohio and Pennsylvania Donald J. Trump. It's the data.[285]

And on the same show filmmaker Michael Moore responded to the contention that Trump's victory was rooted in racial animus with the sarcastic quip, "They're not racist...They twice voted for a man whose middle name is Hussein."[286] These remarks rest on a misguided white redemption narrative in which by voting for Obama, "white America" exorcised its racist demons and received the absolution it craves. But not only did Obama lose the white vote by 12 points in 2008 and 20 points in 2012, more to the point, voting for a black president once or even twice does not mean that someone is beyond anti-black bias. It's possible to support Obama in particular while remaining prejudiced against Blacks as a group. It's not uncommon for a successful, "deserving" black person to get the following backhanded compliment and clumsy bouquet from well-meaning whites: "I don't think of you as black." In the words of Evelyn Lewis, the first black woman to make partner in a major San Francisco law firm, "[W]hat you do well will reflect well on you, but only as an individual. And what you do poorly—well, that's when what you do will be dumped on the whole race." So voters who viewed Obama as an exception to their negative stereotype about Blacks nevertheless could have harbored deep-going bias toward Blacks as a group. What's more, voters' racial biases, though real and significant, may have been temporarily overridden by other concerns like the Iraq War or Great Recession. Trump's racially inflammatory rhetoric and Clinton's positioning of herself as a racial justice advocate on issues like police violence and immigration may have turned the election into a referendum on race relations in America in a way that it wasn't in 2008 or 2012 when Obama steeped himself in post-racial rhetoric. Whatever the truth, good data should reveal it.

After analyzing in-depth survey data about voters who switched from Obama in 2012 to Trump in 2016, Diana C. Mutz, a University of Pennsylvania political science professor, published an article in the *Proceedings of the National Academy of Sciences* which adds to a now compelling body of evidence that the Trump election was about racial rather than economic anxiety. She based her analysis on a nationally representative *panel* survey, which includes identical questions asked of roughly the same 1,200 voters in both October 2012 and 2016.

Panel data and fixed effects panel analyses are widely recognized as providing the most rigorous test of causality possible with observational data. By tracking the same voters in 2012 and 2016, she could observe which voters switched from Obama in 2012 to Trump in 2016 and then investigate why.

To test the "left behind" thesis, she looked at change over time in family income, whether respondents were looking for work, and their subjective perceptions of family finances. To the extent that Trump gained support from former Obama voters who felt left behind, those experiencing either personal economic decline or increases that do not keep pace with the nation as a whole should have been more likely to punish the incumbent party for their economic worry and misfortune by shifting in the Republican direction in 2016. Mutz found no evidence that those with stagnant or declining income were more likely to support Trump. Losing a job or income between 2012 and 2016 did not make a person any more likely to switch to Trump, nor did the mere perception that respondent's financial situation had worsened, nor that person's opinion on how trade affected personal finances, nor unemployment. To the contrary, she found that "living in an area with a high median income positively predicted Republican vote choice to a greater extent in 2016," which is "precisely the opposite of what one would expect based on the left behind thesis."[287]

The strongest predictor of a Trump vote was a sense of racial or global threat. Those who felt a rising sense of threat to the dominant group's status were particularly likely to shift from voting for Obama to voting for Trump. Put differently, when a person's desire for group dominance increased from 2012 to 2016, so did the probability of defecting to Trump. Three other scholars—UCLA's Tyler Reny, UCR's Loren Collingwood, and Princeton's Ali Valenzuela—used another panel survey (they draw on a database with information on more than 64,000 American voters) to take a statistical look at a large sample of white Obama-Trump switchers and, using different measures of attitudes towards racial minorities, hostility to mass immigration, and economic stress than Mutz, reached conclusions perfectly in harmony with hers. Specifically, they found that 1) "racial and immigration attitudes were strongly associated with vote switching in the 2016 election"—the more racially resentful an Obama or third-party voter was, the more likely they were to switch to Trump, 2) class was largely irrelevant in switching to Trump, when keeping racial attitudes constant, and 3) correlations between measures of economic stress and switching from Obama in 2012 to Trump in 2016 were weak or absent. "We find a much stronger association between symbolic racial and immigration attitudes and switching for Trump and Clinton than between economic marginality or local economic dislocation and vote switching," they write. "In fact, we find marginally small or no associations between any of our economic indicators and vote switching in either direction." Further, "we find little evidence that working-class whites were significantly more motivated by racial and immigration attitudes to switch than non-working-class whites."[288]

To corroborate the findings of her panel survey, Mutz also analyzed a separate cross-sectional survey, conducted in October 2016 by the National Opinion Research Center (NORC) at the University of Chicago. Three questions explicitly asked respondents about their concern over future expenses, but such concern did not predict greater support for Trump—anxieties about retirement, education, and medical bills had little impact on whether a person supported Mr. Trump. But her cross-sectional data confirmed the status threat thesis. For instance, respondents were asked to what extent various groups in America were discriminated against, including Christians, Muslims, men, women, Whites, Blacks, and Hispanics. If threat to dominant group status helps explain Trump support, people who perceive dominant social groups like men, Christians, and whites as discriminated against more than lower status groups—despite mountains of evidence that, for example, Whites as a group still earn more, live longer, and feel overall happier than Blacks—should be more likely to vote for Trump. She found that perceived discrimination against high-status groups did substantially increase the likelihood of supporting Trump. In other words, a sense of racial, gender, and religious status threat consistently predicted support for Trump.

Just in case the economic anxiety "Zombie idea" is still twitching after the foregoing studies, here are a few more nails in its coffin. Sean McElwee and Jason McDaniel at *The Nation* examined the relative importance of racism and economic anxiety to voting in 2016 on the basis of another cross-sectional survey, the comprehensive 2016 American National Election Studies (ANES) pre- and post-election survey of over 4,000 respondents. Using questions from the ANES 2016 survey, they looked for links between 1) respondents' racial attitudes and a vote for Trump or Clinton and 2) their perceptions of economic anxiety and a vote for Trump or Clinton. To test the relative impact of individual economic anxiety and racial animus in the form of either "racial resentment" or "black influence animosity,"[289] researchers asked what predicts votes for Trump? They found that "[b]oth racial resentment and black influence animosity are significant predictors of Trump support among white respondents, independent of partisanship, ideology, education levels, and the other factors included in the model." In their words,

> The results indicate a probability of Trump support higher than 60% for an otherwise typical white voter who scores at the highest levels on either anti-black racial resentment or anti-black influence animosity. This compares to less than 30% chance for a typical white voter with below average scores on either of the two measures of anti-black attitudes. There is approximately a 10% probability of a Trump vote for an otherwise typical white voter at the lowest levels of racial resentment.[290]

They also found that economic anxiety was not a significant predictor of voting for Trump. The Sides and Griffin study discussed earlier came to the same conclusion, finding that "economic anxiety was actually decreasing, not increasing" in the run-up to the presidential election; "attitudes about race and ethnicity" were "more strongly related to how people voted."[291]

In May 2017, *The Atlantic* and Public Religion Research Institute, or PRRI, published the results of a joint analysis of post-election survey data, specifically focused on white, working-class voters, whom they defined as people without college degrees or salaried jobs. They found that 64% of these voters had chosen Trump, while only 32% chose Clinton. Contrary to the "left behind" thesis, however, indicators of economic anxiety were not linked to support for Trump; consistent with the "race trumps class" thesis, a strong independent predictor of how white working-class people would vote, controlling for other demographic variables, was anxiety about cultural change. Some 68% of white working-class voters said the American way of life needs to be protected from foreign influence. And nearly half agreed with the statement, "things have changed so much that I often feel like a stranger in my own country." Together, these variables strongly predicted support for Trump, with 79% of white working-class voters who had these anxieties choosing Trump, while only 43% of white working-class voters who did not share one or both of these fears casting their ballot the same way.

White working-class voters who say they often feel like a stranger in their own land and who believe the US needs protecting against foreign influence were 3.5 times more likely to favor Trump than those who did not share these concerns.[292]

After partisan affiliation, it was cultural anxiety—feeling like a stranger in America, supporting the deportation of immigrants, and hesitating about educational investment—that best predicted support for Trump.

◆

As a proponent of Nigga Theory, I find the fact that Trump floated to victory on the raft of racism not at all surprising. As I said, he finds a way to call me a nigga every day. And he does so with symbols as well as words. His famous wall is a political performative. Nobody really thinks it will do anything to change the flow of desperate migrants, nobody thinks it makes anyone safer or more secure, nobody thinks it really matters, except as a symbol. It is the anti-Statue of Liberty, the insult to her welcome. And as a political performative it has been very effective at building solidarity, just as the "lock her up!" chants did. The one performative *means* that racism is okay, the other that sexism is okay. In a sense, the Trump campaign was entirely performative—he offered no specific proposals, no economic plan, no foreign policy, no plan for health care, none for infrastructure. And in his serial destruction of agreements, regulations, government agencies and departments, alliances, and treaties, he has seemed to remove the "creative" from "creative disruption." What he has accomplished is to take the 40% of the country that feels its privilege threatened and turned them into a solid voting bloc, and he did so by saying yes to them, yes, you are right, women are a threat to your dominance, black people are a threat to your dominance, brown people are a threat to your dominance, gay people are a threat, Iranians are a threat, Muslims are a threat, Mexicans are a threat— stick with me, and we will stay on top forever.

And they will if we cannot forge an even wider solidarity. Call me a nigga, Donald Trump—I will use it to help build a more perfect union.

CHAPTER **SEVEN**

CONDEMNING "NIGGAS"

Harvard philosophy professor Tommie Shelby refers to truly disadvantaged black neighborhoods as "dark ghettos" and to their residents as "ghetto denizens," and this may strike a sour note with some readers. Even though "ghetto" is defined as "a quarter of a city in which members of a minority group live especially because of social, legal, or economic pressure," it is also often used as a derogatory adjective—"That's so ghetto" to mean something unrefined, low-class, cheap, and inferior, or "He/She is ghetto" to mean someone unrefined, low-class, cheap, and inferior. This pernicious sense of ghetto inspired a book entitled *150 Ways To Tell If You're Ghetto* (1997), by Shawn Wayans, Suli McCullogh, and Chris Spencer, which is full of one-liners such as: "You know you're ghetto if you've ever snuck a 40-ouncer into church" or "...if you're hooked on Ebonics." Although the word originated in Europe to describe Jewish quarters in cities, in the context of US history its meaning has mutated to refer primarily (though not exclusively) to disadvantaged urban enclaves that are majority black and to behaviors that are stereotypically associated with the residents of such inner-city neighborhoods.

At a recent USC symposium, Shelby addressed his provocative nomenclature, pointing out that he follows distinguished black theorists like Kenneth B. Clark in deploying the sometime epithet as a term of art. His bold and incisive *Dark Ghettos: Injustice, Dissent, and Reform* reframes the racial justice debate roiling America today and effectively captures the moral tensions, nuances, and paradoxes of race, place, and class in America's most maligned and marginalized neighborhoods. As proponent of Nigga Theory, I applaud and respect Shelby's thoughtful, critical use of the edgy, loaded, to some even offensive term, and see his argument as complementary to my own theoretical and historical work. Like *Nigga*, "ghetto" can be troublesome in some respects but unique-ly effective in others: both words can be razor-wired epithets that cut and wound, but, when used with care and precision, both can also forge unique connections and provoke special insights. So it is fitting that the last chapter of Shelby's book centers on Nas, an artist who deftly wields the N-word in his politically charged gangster rap, just as Shelby deploys the G-word with surgical dexterity in reframing the debate about truly disadvantaged blacks.

Shelby reframes the debate by foregrounding issues of basic justice usually submerged in these discussions. Poor and oppressed blacks are not hapless victims of impersonal forces in Shelby's work, not people in need of help or rescue by complicity-free Good Samaritans, but instead fellow citizens disadvantaged by an unjust social system we all participate in. From this systemic perspective, the duty to address the plight of poor Blacks is not about charity, pity, or mercy, it's about justice, and discharg-ing that duty of justice may require those advantaged by our unjust social structure to relinquish their advantages.

Shelby criticizes many commentators, policymakers, and ordinary cit-izens who disregard these basic issues of fairness, instead viewing dark ghettos as social problems to be solved rather than as consequences of injustices we must collectively own up to. To be more specific, he points out three critical issues buried by the popular but narrow "medical" focus on "what ails poor Blacks":

1. The narrow focus on alleviating the burdens of poor Blacks takes for granted gross racial inequalities in the distribution of wealth and power in society.
2. That narrow focus leads social observers to mistake resistance, re-bellion, and dissent (e.g., refusing to do menial, low-wage, dead-end work or conform to certain dress codes and rules of decorum) for pathology or dysfunction.

3. The narrow focus on poor black victims diverts attention from those of us who have been unjustly enriched by our inequitable social structure.

To foreground these issues of basic justice and hold them in bold relief, Shelby's book views dark ghettos through a "systemic-injustice" framework that focuses on the fairness of social structures. It was moral philosopher John Rawls who made the overall justice of social arrangements the focus of his 1971 book *A Theory of Justice* (a work my USC colleague Marshall Cohen rightly heralded as "magisterial" in 1972 in *The New York Times Book Review*).[293] Rawls arrived at three normative tests for judging a social scheme's overall justice: equal liberty, fair equality of opportunity, and the difference principle. Injustice, from this standpoint, is the failure of social institutions to satisfy these tests and hence live up to justice's demand. But when serious injustices—major deviations from the ideal principles—are identified, we need a Theory of Injustice, what Rawls refers to as "a *nonideal theory* which specifies and justifies the principles that should guide our responses to injustices." In essence, *Dark Ghettos* gives us a theory of injustice for truly disadvantaged Blacks.

◆

Injustices—deviations from the ideal principles of justice—can be small or great, minor or serious. Some injustices may be tolerable while others (slavery and Jim Crow, for instance) may be clearly intolerable. In obvious cases of intolerable injustice, John Rawls and Tommie Shelby are of one mind: we do not have obligations to submit to institutions that exceed the limits of tolerable injustice. In the words of Rawls: "Unjust social arrangements are themselves a kind of extortion, even violence, and consent to them does not bind." By this logic, Skid Row in downtown LA, with one of the nation's largest populations of unhoused residents (75% of whom are black), is one of America's starkest expressions of structural and institutional violence. And prison cells brimming with black bodies may also express structural and institutional violence—though we'll soon see how hotly contested this claim can be.

The gestalt shift that Shelby's systemic-injustice perspective invites and supports, like that of Nigga Theory, constitutes a frontal assault on "personal responsibility" and "politics of respectability" approaches to the plight of poor blacks, according to which problems that disproportionately afflict blacks (such as crime and racialized mass incarceration) are attributed to their bad choices, lack of personal responsibility, and moral deficiencies rather than to social oppression. And no one better symbolized the sanctimonious spirit animating such respectability politics than disgraced moral scold Bill Cosby, Dr. Huxtable himself, in his infamous NAACP speech. Cosby ridiculed the notion that black criminals should be viewed through political lenses as victims of social oppression rather than through moral lenses as victims of their own character flaws and authors of their own predicaments:

> Looking at the incarcerated, these are not political criminals. These are people going around stealing Coca-Cola. People getting shot in the back of the head over a piece of pound cake! And then we all run out and are outraged, "The cops shouldn't have shot him." What the hell was he doing with the pound cake in his hand? I wanted a piece of pound cake just as bad as anybody else, and I looked at it and I had no money. And something called parenting said, "If you get caught with it, you're going to embarrass your mother." Not "You're going to get your butt kicked." No. "You're going to embarrass your family."

Lest anyone believe that Cosby's attitude is a relic of a benighted bygone era, Denzel Washington, when asked about the prison-industrial complex while he was promoting his 2017 film, *Roman J. Israel, Esq.*, about a brilliant but flawed black lawyer who cares for the poor and dispossessed, answered, "It starts at the home.... It starts with how you raise your children.... So you know I can't blame the system.... It's unfortunate that we make such easy work for them."

Dark Ghettos drives a stake through the heart of this wrongheaded zombie perspective on black criminals. Shelby deploys the techniques of analytic philosophy to frame his theory of injustice, the goal of which is solidarity with black criminals, welfare recipients, single mothers, and others viewed as "bad Negroes" by condescending critics. He lays out the moral limits for policy, including state antipoverty and anticrime interventions. And he develops a "political ethics of the oppressed" that defines what the unjustly disadvantaged themselves are morally required and permitted to do in response to unjust social arrangements—that is, when does someone oppressed by an unjust society have a civic duty to obey the law? When do they have a natural duty to obey? And when do they have no such duty at all?

◆

A central claim of the theory of injustice Shelby articulates is that the very "existence of dark ghettos" in America "is simply incompatible with any meaningful form of reciprocity among free and equal citizens"—that is, that the existence of ghettos is "a consequence of injustice." This core claim forces him to take a controversial stand on one of the most hotly contested questions in law and conventional social morality—namely, the issue of causation. Shelby says that one of the main objectives of his book is to "specify what it is about the social structure of the United States that justifies the claim that ghettos are a product and reliable sign of systemic injustice."

He claims that, "as a philosopher writing about ghetto poverty, my role is not to identify the causes of ghettos" (a claim he repeated at our symposium), but he organizes the book as a set of reflections on just that: on the "widely endorsed," empirically-supported "central factors in explaining ghetto poverty," not just general issues of racial and economic injustice, but specific ones like racial profiling. Crime, he writes, is a response to the "ghetto plight." He discusses the implications of "[t]he fact that ghetto poverty has been caused by racial and economic injustice." Later, he says, "The frustration of dealing with racial discrimination by employers probably leads more blacks into the criminal underground than would otherwise end up there." After describing the ghetto neighborhoods (lacking jobs, decent schools, and safe streets) to which many Blacks are relegated by forces beyond their control, he points out that some who are stuck in these unjust circumstances choose illegal means to generate needed income. He makes many other implicit and explicit causal claims throughout the book about the relationship between structural and institutional injustice and decisions by dark ghetto residents to break laws and cause harm to their neighbors, and he does so without shame or shaming. Shelby's ghetto theory is a Nigga Theory.

No matter how much we may wish to avoid them, controversies over causation haunt all legal and moral discussions of poverty, crime, and mass incarceration. Do poverty and crime result from external factors beyond the control of "dark ghetto denizens"? Or are they caused by the bad choices of immoral and irresponsible wrongdoers? Shelby fully recognizes this causation concern: "Many people, including some black people, believe that the ghetto poor are responsible for perpetuating their own poverty, and for this reason they don't view ghettos as unjust or a sign of injustice."

Shelby never adequately addresses the causation conundrum, however, this recurrent conflict between structure and agency, institutional constraint and individual choice, macro-level social factors and voluntary criminal wrongdoing.

As discussed above, substantive criminal law often does not treat subsequent human action, action that follows from some other actor's conduct as being *caused* by that initial actor, even when the subsequent human action (i.e., the second person's action) is abundantly foreseeable. The law assumes that antecedent events do not cause a person to act in the same way they cause things to happen. Hence, the results that follow from the second person's actions are viewed as being caused by him or her alone.

Of course, just because, in criminal law, an actor's choice to commit a crime generally (though not invariably) breaks the causal chain between his wrongdoing and whatever factors set the stage for or enabled such criminal conduct, it does not follow that we must approach causation that way in political morality or in other domains where "explanations" of criminal conduct are developed. As Shelby acknowledges at the outset, for ghettos to be viewed as unjust or as a sign of intolerable injustice, these causation questions must be confronted. Causation is a messy and complicated concept that raises perennial questions about subjective culpability in criminal law, but how we think about causation jibes in important ways with how we think about a wrongdoer's moral blameworthiness or *mens rea*.

Unpacking these connections and relationships could go a long way toward helping citizens and policymakers see how state-sanctioned segregation (traditional Jim Crow) can plausibly be viewed as morally equivalent to racialized mass incarceration (the New Jim Crow), how self-destruction can plausibly be viewed as morally equivalent to social oppression, and how macro-level injustices can *cause* criminal wrongdoing. It could go a long way toward helping people view black criminals not as evil, but as signs and symptoms of intolerable injustices for which we as a society are collectively responsible.

◆

Regardless of how one resolves the causation issue, the justice question with which Shelby opens his chapter on crime remains apt: "Do the ghetto poor have an obligation to respect and abide by the law?" Viewing matters from a Rawls-inspired systemic-injustice framework, Shelby asks whether poor blacks who perpetrate crimes thereby violate their civic responsibilities. Shelby concludes that they do not, that blacks who commit public welfare offenses such as prostitution and selling drugs do not violate civic responsibilities nor do they deserve public condemnation or state-imposed punishment. He does say, however, state-imposed punishment is deserved for serious crimes that are inherently wrong, such as murder and rape, so long as the state at least provides them with fair trials and unbiased verdicts.

The core insight here is that a truly disadvantaged black person who commits a crime does not owe a debt to society in the way someone more privileged does. For a person only owes such a debt if there is mutual benefit for everyone participating in the overall social scheme. If everyone is benefiting from a fair system of social cooperation, then anyone who fails to exercise self-control and obey the law gains an unfair advantage over those who have chosen to lawfully control themselves. To restore fairness, this advantage must be taken away from her; she deserves punishment in the sense that she owes payment for the benefits. The Latin *Retribuo*—the root of "retribution," a primary justification for punishment—literally means "I pay back." But as Jeffrie Murphy points out, this "gentlemen's club" picture of the relation between citizens and society does not describe the actual relationship between the residents of dark ghettos and the larger social system; indeed, these individuals would be hard-pressed to name the benefits for which they are supposed to reciprocate through their lawful obedience.[294] Do they owe a debt for the cynical deindustrialization of inner cities in the 1960s, 1970s, and 1980s that left them marooned in dying rustbelt metropolises without jobs? For the crumbling schools, substandard housing, inadequate health care, less-than-subsistence welfare payments, police brutality, biased courtrooms, and exclusion from the political process? Debt for what?

Drawing out the implications of this core justice-as-fairness insight, Shelby argues that if social institutions exceed the limits of tolerable injustice, then the ghetto poor do not violate or shirk civic obligations when they refuse to respect the authority of the law (qua law). Following Kant and Rawls, Shelby argues that the individual's civic obligations are rooted in reciprocity. Because the basic structure of American society fails to embody the value of reciprocity (in his words, "the existence of the dark ghetto ... is simply incompatible with any meaningful form of reciprocity among free and equal citizens"), when the ghetto poor refuse to respect the authority of the law (qua law), "they do not thereby violate the principle of reciprocity or shirk valid civic obligations." He adds: "Not all crimes perpe-trated by the ghetto poor are wrong, and ... condemning criminal transgres-sions as a violation of civic responsibility is misplaced."

◆

Even in a fundamentally unjust society that exceeds the limits of tolerable injustice, however, Shelby argues that the ghetto poor have *natural duties* to one another (and to others) not defined by civic reciprocity and thus not negated by intolerable injustice. Natural duties hold between all persons regardless of whether they are fellow citizens: "one has civic obligations qua citizen and natural duties qua moral person." These duties include a duty not to be cruel or cause unnecessary suffering, for instance. "Yet fulfilling one's natural duties to others may nevertheless be compatible with a num-ber of unlawful actions"; for instance:

> Taking the possessions of others, especially when these others are reasonably well off, may be permissible.... Mugging someone at gun-point is not permissible but shoplifting and other forms of theft might be permissible.... Participating in gangs may be a defensible and effective means to secure needed income. Something similar can be said in favor of prostitution, welfare fraud, tax evasion, selling sto-len goods....

In an unjust state that has not maintained an equitable distribution of bur-dens and benefits in the cooperative scheme, when the oppressed violate the law, they do not take unfair advantage of the compliance of others and thus their acts cannot be condemned for lacking civic reciprocity. So the state may lack the moral standing to condemn or punish mere social welfare (*mala prohibita*) crimes.

◆

But can a seriously unjust state at least condemn *mala in se* crimes—i.e., acts that are seriously wrong in themselves, that often disproportionately afflict other truly disadvantaged Blacks in the form of so-called "black on black" vi-olence? What if, for instance, the state is complicit in the crimes it would con-demn—for instance, what if there were demonstrable state complicity in the crack plague (through the CIA-Contra connections revealed by journalists like Gary Webb, by formal US Senate hearings, and by internal investigations of the CIA itself)? Does a state have the right to condemn its own accomplices for their foreseeable violent crimes in furtherance of drug trafficking? No, says Shelby: "When a state is complicit in the wrongs it punishes ... it lacks the moral standing to [publicly] condemn these wrongs and is therefore rightly criticized for these unjustified expressive acts of condemnation.... And this loss of [moral] standing might extend beyond condemning legal defiance to condemning the wrongs themselves."

And according to the theory of "penal expressivism," if a state lacks the moral standing to condemn a crime, then it also lacks the right to hold the wrongdoer accountable for it, and if it can't hold him accountable, it can't permissibly punish him either. From this standpoint, a state in an unjust society is stuck on the horns of a dilemma: "It can punish those it has no right to punish or it can fail to protect those it has treated unjustly," like law-abiding but vulnerable dark ghetto residents.

Shelby avoids this dilemma by arguing that a state's right to *punish* a wrongdoer does not depend on its right to *condemn* him or her. To support this claim, he first points out that the state can punish people it cannot morally condemn. (As I teach my criminal law students, the state certainly does punish people whom it cannot morally condemn in areas such as strict liability public welfare offense, mistake of law doctrine, and refusals to individualize the Reasonable Person test, to name a few.) The justification for the state's right to punish violent crime and other *mala in se* offenses is not reciprocity or its moral standing to condemn but rather the need to protect the vulnerable from unjustified harm by deterring wrongdoers. For Shelby, the state's enforcement legitimacy (its right to penalize actions that are "seriously wrong in themselves") rests on something like a right of self-defense and a right to defend others (what he calls a right to intervene to prevent an unjust attack). To deter would-be aggressors before they have a chance to victimize others, a state that lacks legitimate authority can still threaten and penalize persons who engage in *mala in se* offenses as long as there are adequate due process protections and adjudications of crimes are fair and unbiased. In Shelby's words, "These penal sanctions don't express condemnation, and may be applied simply as a crime control measure" to incentivize actors to obey laws against *mala in se* crimes. His approach to punishment is not utilitarian, but it is forward-looking and focused on deterrence.

◆

The strongest objection to Shelby's rigorous, original, cogent thesis that I can imagine a critic making is that, if many occupants of "dark ghettos" come to view criminal laws as either not expressing moral condemnation or lacking legitimacy, then more residents will suffer serious harm at the hands of criminals. Criminal laws designed to protect the vulnerable from a host of unjustified harms by deterring wrongdoers though the threat of punishment, studies suggest, do not work. People obey the law (including laws designed to protect vulnerable people from harm) not principally because of the threat of punishment, but because they fear the disapproval of their social group if they violate the law, and because they generally see themselves as moral beings who want to do the right thing as they perceive it. In short, social group disapproval and internalized norms keep people from breaking laws that protect vulnerable residents more than the deterrent threat of punishment itself.

Nevertheless, the criminal law can play a significant role in protecting vulnerable citizens by nurturing norms against certain kinds of wrongdoing. For example, when it comes to the norm against nonconsensual sex, progressive jurisdictions have eliminated the force requirement and defined consent as granted only by an affirmative expression of willingness. Criminalizing certain behaviors can sometime nurture a prohibitory norm, as arguably it has in the areas of drunk driving, domestic violence, and sexual harassment. (By contrast, criminalization failed miserably to nurture the prohibitory norm behind the national prohibition of alcohol in the 1920s and early 1930s.) By the same token, the act of decriminalization functioned to dilute existing norms against same-sex intimacy (see *Lawrence v. Texas*), fornication, and adultery.

Many people are inclined to accept the law—including laws that protect vulnerable citizens against serious *mala in se* crimes—as a source of moral authority that they themselves should take seriously. In this way, criminal laws that protect vulnerable dark ghetto residents can play a role in the moral thinking and internalized moral standards of people tempted to commit serious crimes. Studies suggest that the level of commitment to obey the law is proportional to what one scholar calls the law's "perceived legitimacy."[295] More specifically, if one regards the law as a legitimate source of rules—if the law has "moral credibility"—then actors should be more likely to regard its judgments about right and wrong actions as a relevant factor in their own moral thinking and hence they will be more likely to obey laws that prohibit *mala in se* crimes. If the criminal law does not have a reputation as an institution focused on morally condemnable conduct, it may have no hope of helping shape the moral thinking of actors in ways that protect potential victims. And so the objection to Shelby's thesis is that, given the criminal law's power to nurture norms that protect dark ghetto residents is directly proportional to its perceived legitimacy and moral credibility, then undermining the law's legitimacy could expose residents of dark ghettos to more crime.

At our USC symposium, Professor Shelby gave two responses to this objection. First, he pointed out that the criminal law does not currently enjoy a high level of moral credibility and legitimacy among truly disadvantaged inner-city residents, so his or anyone else's theories about its lack of legitimacy are not likely to make things much worse. I'm not convinced this is true, as many law-abiding dark ghetto residents don't hustle and do hold the criminal law in high regard. The widespread sense of injustice that followed the acquittal of the four police officers videotaped beating Rodney King 25 years ago occasioned a massive loss of legitimacy and triggered one of the most violent and damaging urban uprisings in American history. The 1992 L.A. uprising did not erupt when the images of King's beating first saturated the airwaves, and this undermines the claim that rioters were merely hooligans looking for any excuse to go off. Rather, ghetto residents waited for justice, waited for the criminal justice system to honor its promise of neutrality, and they took to the streets only when that promise seemed so shamelessly flouted. If poor urban Blacks embrace Shelby's theory of injustice, the criminal law's loss of moral credibility might even turn dark ghettos into powder kegs.

Shelby countered that, even if revealing or broadcasting these truths about the law's lack of legitimacy did result in an increase in serious crimes against dark ghetto residents in the way social science suggests, what's the alternative? Not telling the truth, not telling it like it is? I am personally willing to pay a high price to vindicate certain values, including truth, sincerity, and authenticity. But I also know many proponents of personal responsibility in criminal matters who would readily if not eagerly trade truth for safety, sincerity for security, and honesty for respectability in the eyes of whites.

Condemning niggas, given the lack of true justice for residents of the dark ghetto, is wrong. Undermining the legitimacy of the law is also wrong.

Nigga Theory weds analysis of the sort Shelby is undertaking—analysis of criminal procedure, blameworthiness, injustice, systemic oppression, racism—with solidarity and hope. We need to fix the law. We need to bring light to the dark ghetto. We need to fight injustice. We need a full and active empathy. *Call me a Nigga*, I say, and I will answer the call.

CHAPTER **EIGHT**

NIGGA THEORY AND PRAXIS: WHERE THE RUBBER MEETS THE ROAD

Praxis is the process of using a theory in a practical way, and this book has tried to provide a moral, legal, and political theory for radically progressive praxis in matters of blame and punishment by law enforcement, lawmakers, judges, jurors, writers, artists, and ordinary concerned citizens. Within this framework, one very practical policy matter at the core of our criminal justice system, one issue that any theory of justice must address, is the death penalty.

Philadelphia's "top cop," District Attorney Larry Krasner, did what a radically progressive prosecutor does when he asked the Pennsylvania Supreme Court in July 2019 to declare capital punishment an unconstitutional violation of "the state Constitution's ban on cruel punishments" because it is racially biased, arbitrary, and discriminates against the poor. He cited a study, conducted by his office, that revealed a jaw-dropping 72% of Philadelphia death sentences were overturned during post-conviction review between 1978 and 2017, often due to inadequate legal representation. And although "less than 45% of Philadelphia's population is black, 82% of the Philadelphians on death row are black." Hence "the vast majority of the condemned were indigent members of a racial minority group, who were represented by 'woefully' under-funded court-appointed attorneys."[296] Put differently, poor black males (women comprise less than 2% of inmates on death row) are most likely to be deemed deathworthy in adjudications of just deserts. It is rare for prosecutors to argue in favor of leniency for condemned murderers, and rarer still to argue against the inclusion of capital punishment in the mix of criminal justice policies government ought to pursue. But Krasner joined a small group of prosecutors who have called for their states to end this practice, a practice the brunt of which is borne by poor blacks. To illustrate the application of Nigga Theory to a concrete and specific criminal justice policymaking matter, let's take a hard look at capital punishment through its radically progressive lenses.

Executions resumed in the United States in 1977, and by 2016 about 1,437 had taken place. The rate of executions reached its peak in 1999, when 98 people were put to death, but it dipped significantly in later years, with just 28 people executed in 2015. The rate of death *sentences* peaked at 317 in 1996 but declined to 73 in 2014 and 49 in 2015, echoing the drop off in execution rates over the same time frame. Nevertheless, capital punishment enjoys a lot of public support, which ranged from a low of 42% in support in 1966 to a high of 80% in support in 1994. Although grassroots opposition to the death penalty has grown with increasing evidence of wrongful convictions and of innocent people sentenced to death, over 60% of Americans still support it, with its level of support dropping to roughly 50% when the question is framed as a choice between capital punishment and life imprisonment without the possibility of parole. Yet, despite its substantial public support, in the last 15 years multiple states have abolished the death penalty (either by legislative repeal or court decision) or introduced bills proposing moratoria, suspending executions to prevent the execution of innocent people, accompanied by a willingness to resume executions when the risk of false convictions is reduced or eliminated through things like better lab procedures, improving the reliability of forensic testimony, and better legal representation.

As pointed out in the Introduction, DNA exonerations—the possibility of executing the innocent—have played a big role in the decline in public support for the death penalty over the last 20 years, with erstwhile supporters of capital punishment like Republican Governor George Ryan of Illinois granting clemency to all 171 inmates on death row after 13 inmates on death row in Illinois were exonerated, some just hours before their scheduled executions.

Because Nigga Theory centers on wrongdoers who have actually committed violent crimes, including violent capital offenses, it focuses on wrongdoers on death row whose guilt is not in doubt. Accordingly, its opposition to the death penalty does not center on "saving innocent lives," that is, the risk of wrongful convictions and executions notwithstanding. Nigga Theory centers on the "truly guilty" rather than the truly innocent because advocating for the truly innocent in death penalty cases is like advocating for low-level nonviolent offenders in drug cases: doing so can be done comfortably within the confines of conventional morality, but it doesn't address the fundamental problem. No radical overhaul in moral, legal, and political practices is necessary to humanize low-level nonviolent offenders or the factually innocent. But because Nigga Theory recognizes the greatest driver of mass incarceration and threat to racial justice in criminal matters as the disproportionate blame and punishment of guilty black people who have committed serious or violent offenses, its rejection of capital punishment does not rest on the fact or frequencies of false convictions. The determination that someone is deathworthy is a "general" *mens rea* issue, calling for a frontal moral judgment of the subjective culpability of the defendant to determine whether he is one of the "worst of the worst." After a jury finds a defendant guilty of first-degree murder, there is a sentencing phase in which the sentencer determines whether, based on specified aggravating and mitigating factors, the wrongdoer is guilty of "super" first-degree murder, if you will—an even more blameworthy "grade" of murder than ordinary first-degree murder standing alone.

At its core, the determination (by a judge, jury, or legal precedent) that someone is or is not deathworthy requires a proportionality judgment, a judgment that the wrongdoer's level of subjective culpability justifies the ultimate punishment. That is, that the punishment must fit the blame—not that it "fit the harm" but "fit the *blame*," the subjective culpability. Without unduly minimizing the grave injustice of false convictions in capital cases, the excessive blame and punishment of violent black offenders, those who most stoke the urge for retaliation and revenge, is a much more widespread and destructive problem, and an infinitely bigger driver of racialized mass incarceration, than the problem of wrongful convictions or executions of innocent blacks.

Another problem with framing opposition to the death penalty in terms of "saving innocent lives" is that this same logic and rhetoric gets deployed so often *in support of* the death penalty by its proponents. Professors Cass

Sunstein and Adrian Vermeule, for instance, argue that if the death penalty were known to deter, then the government would be obligated to use it to save innocent lives. Assuming that capital punishment were known to deter, in their words, "[the] legal regime whose package of crime-control instruments happens not to include capital punishment [is] a policy that inevitably and predictably opts for more murders rather than fewer."[297] For them, government is just as responsible for the murders it fails to adequately deter as it is for the killers it executes. From this perspective, the state's choice to cause the death of convicted killers through lethal injections is morally equivalent to its choice to cause the deaths of innocent victims at the hands of killers left undeterred due to its anti-death penalty policy. Since the state can deter private murders and save innocent lives by taking guilty ones, it should include capital punishment in its policy mix, according to this logic.

All such deterrence-driven defenses of the death penalty (or any other criminal sanction, for that matter) seek to justify punishment on the basis of the positive purposes it serves—here, saving innocent lives—rather than on the one and only just basis for punishment from the standpoint of Nigga Theory, namely, a wrongdoer's own personal moral fault, including excuses, explanations, justifications, and mitigating circumstances. Nigga Theory rejects all deterrence-driven, utilitarian, cost-benefit, consequentialist, instrumentalist justifications for punishment because such frameworks permit the state to shift the focus of attention from the subjective culpability of the accused to the harm he or she has caused. Such forward-facing justifications allow the state to intentionally inflict suffering on individuals whenever doing so would make others in society better off, irrespective of the just deserts of the individuals being made to suffer. But the presumption of innocence, which the Supreme Court recognizes as "that bedrock 'axiomatic and elementary' principle whose enforcement lies at the foundation of the administration of our criminal justice," requires strict and unwavering attention to the just deserts of alleged wrongdoers, even when the social benefits of disregarding the deserts of an alleged wrongdoer include saving innocent lives. Thus, the criminal law's proof beyond a reasonable doubt requirement, which "provides concrete substance for the presumption of innocence" and is the law's "prime instrument for reducing the risk of convictions resting on factual error," has roots running back to William Blackstone's oft-repeated adage that it is "better that ten guilty persons escape, than that one innocent suffer."[298] Some jurists and commentators have supported even higher ratios, such as 100 to one, or more. If the standard of proof for a criminal trial were merely a preponderance of the evidence (i.e., just slightly more likely than not) rather than proof beyond a reasonable doubt, yes, there would be more false convictions, but also there would be fewer false acquittals (factual errors that result in freeing guilty persons). Empirical research confirms that jurors are more likely to convict when instructed under a more-likely-than-not standard than when instructed under a reasonable-doubt one.[299]

But why is the risk of false convictions "far worse" than the risk of false acquittals? Why is it more important under our constitution to minimize the risk of convicting the innocent than to minimize the risk of acquitting the guilty? From a deterrence-driven, utilitarian, cost-benefit perspective, it may cost many more innocent lives to falsely acquit and release 10 (or 100, or more) suspected serial killers who are guilty than to falsely convict one suspected serial killer who is innocent. Why give the benefit of the doubt to suspected wrongdoers at the expense of foreseeable innocent victims of this higher standard of proof? If our overriding concern in criminal matters were simply protecting innocent lives from inadequately deterred murders, the criminal law could significantly reduce the false acquittals of dangerous wrongdoers and thereby arguably save many more innocent lives *overall* if it got rid of the presumption of innocence and made it sufficient for criminal conviction for a jury to believe it to be more likely than not that the alleged perpetrator was at fault in a violent crime.

Suppose that it would minimize the loss of innocent lives and maximize overall social welfare to require a lower standard of proof in criminal trials, including capital cases, such as a 50% plus a feather standard. Significantly more innocent people suffer capital punishment under this lower standard, but suppose that those numbers pale in comparison to the number of innocent lives this diluted standard of proof could save by reducing false acquittals and deterring private murders. Would such circumstances justify the state in punishing citizens under this lower preponderance test? Only if we convince ourselves that it is acceptable in our criminal justice system—and social system more generally—for the state to deliberately inflict death or serious stigma and suffering on its people, irrespective of their level of subjective moral culpability, for the sake of promoting the greater good. Only if we convince ourselves, in other words, that it would be acceptable in our social system to, say, round up all redheads and make them lifelong slaves, irrespective of their fault or just deserts, so long as doing so produces more overall satisfaction than frustration, more social benefit than social cost.

Redheads and their allies, however, could decisively counter such claims by using a non-utilitarian, non-consequentialist, non-instrumentalist moral framework to assert that even if it could be somehow demonstrated that the social benefit of their underserved suffering outweighed its social burden, the balance of societal gains and losses is irrelevant to the rightness or wrongness of the stigma and suffering the state can deliberately inflict on its citizens. They would assert that the state is only justified in deliberately imposing serious stigma and suffering on citizens who deserve it. And in criminal matters, *desert*, the extent to which a person *deserves* punishment, depends entirely on that individual's subjective moral culpability—with punishment graded in proportion to desert so that the punishment always fits the blame. This non-consequentialist justification of punishment is commonly called "retributivism," and under it individuals should never be punished simply to promote the safety or wellbeing of others or to further any other social goal, for the social consequences of punishment are irrelevant to the question of its fundamental fairness to the individual.

Instead, retributivists believe people should only be punished if and to the extent that they deserve it, and they only deserve it if they commit a prohibited act with subjective culpability or *mens rea*. From a retributivist standpoint, in other words, the presumption of innocence gives every individual a fundamental *right* not to suffer punishment in the absence of proof beyond a reasonable doubt of moral culpability, even if maintaining such a high standard of proof results in the loss of many innocent lives due to false acquittals and inadequately deterred private murders. The rights of individuals, as John Rawls and Ronald Dworkin and others point out, cannot be reduced to cost-benefit calculations or the "serpent-windings of utilitarianism." The promise of individualized justice, rooted in the right of each individual to equal dignity, concern, and respect—that is, the right of each not to be sacrificed on the altar of the greater good or making others better off—can be extremely costly, but such is the price of our constitutional commitment to the "bedrock and axiomatic" presumption of innocence.

This is why Nigga Theory adopts a rights-based rather than cost-benefit or consequentialist moral framework in criminal justice matters. From a retributive perspective rooted in individual rights, whether the death penalty saves innocent lives through its deterrent effect is irrelevant to its legitimacy. The only possible legitimacy for the death penalty depends entirely on whether a given violent wrongdoer deserves death, that is, whether he or she acted with sufficient subjective culpability to qualify as deathworthy.

This move limits the scope of the death penalty by placing major limitations on the kinds of arguments and range of justifications proponents can logically advance in support of capital punishment. By embracing classic retributivism, Nigga Theory rules out the constant attempts by pro-death penalty proponents to shift the focus in a capital case from the wrongdoer's subjective moral blameworthiness to the harm he actually caused (the justification for punishment under theories of retaliation and revenge) or the social purposes his execution can serve (the justification for punishment under utilitarian, "expressive," and social cohesion theories of punishment).

Theories of retaliation and revenge tie (capital) punishment it to the revulsion, resentment, anger, righteous indignation, outrage, and hatred produced by the death and suffering of the victims. Under eye-for-an-eye notions of retaliation, "if you steal from another, you steal from yourself; if you strike another, you strike yourself; if you kill another, you kill yourself"—those who do harm to others should be harmed in return, regardless of their personal excuses or explanations. And under theories of revenge, in the words of James Fitzjames Stephen, it is "highly desirable that criminals should be hated, [and] that the punishments inflicted upon them should be so contrived as to give expression to that hatred.... The doctrine that hatred and vengeance are wicked in themselves," he continues, "appears to me to contradict plain facts."[300]

Horrendous accidents, for instance, often generate calls for punishment rooted in retaliation and revenge, irrespective of the harmdoer's moral culpability. Thus, as a publicity stunt in 2003, a tour manager for the heavy metal band Great White ignited fireworks on stage at a Rhode Island night club, which lit flammable soundproofing foam, setting off a fire in the crowded wooden building that killed 100 people and injured more than 200. The manager pleaded guilty to 100 counts of involuntary manslaughter as part of a plea bargain authorizing the judge to impose a maximum 10-year sentence. The prosecutor sought the maximum, but the judge sentenced him to a 4-year prison term, with parole eligibility after serving one-third of his sentence. The judge pointed to the accidental nature of the deaths and the manager's strong likelihood of rehabilitation in view of his willingness to accept responsibility and remorse.

The sentence struck the relatives of some of the victims as outrageously lenient. One parent, whose son was killed and daughter injured, commented: "One year for every 25 people that died—it's crazy." This kind of statement links a wrongdoer's desert, how much punishment he deserves, to the harm caused by his offense rather than to his subjective culpability. For example, suppose a negligently distracted driver runs a stop sign while glancing at her cell phone and broadsides another car killing its single occupant a fiery crash. Further suppose that the jurisdiction's typical criminal sentence for careless vehicular manslaughter is three years. Does she deserve more punishment for the exact same act of inadvertence if the fiery crash took the lives of multiple occupants in the other car? Does she deserve still more punishment if the fiery crash involved a packed school bus and the death of all its occupants? By hypothesis, her subjective culpability, her blame, is the same in all three situations, so increasing her punishment in any of the last two cannot be justified on classic retributive grounds. Punishing her more for more deaths, moving from "the punishment must fit the blame" as a just principle of proportionality to "the punishment must fit the harm," is a fundamental change from retribution to retaliation. And this is what some of the victims' families wanted to see.

Others did not view the punishment as "an insult to the memory of the victims" or too lenient. A mother who lost her son said, "I think it's a fair and just reaction. He didn't set out to kill anybody. It was a horrendous accident." The father of an 18-year-old victim of the fire testified that his son would have wanted the family to accept the wrongdoer's apology. Theories of retaliation are often confused with those of retribution, but classic retributivism keeps punishment wedded to a wrongdoer's subjective culpability, whatever the revulsion, hatred, outrage, and moral indignation those harms produce in the minds and emotions of ordinary decent human beings.

Victim-impact statements in death penalty cases provide another illustration of how often our punishment of wrongdoers is tied to retaliation and revenge rather than subjective blameworthiness. In state and federal sentencing proceedings courts now routinely take into account statements from victims and family members detailing the damaging aftermath of the crime. Such statements often describe the suffering of victims and their families, including the sometimes devastating physical, emotional, and financial consequences of the crime. Sometimes such statements also express the punishment preferences of the victims or family members, which judges may give substantial weight to, rather than, in the alternative, strive to be more neutral and detached in the exercise of their sentencing authority. Studies suggest that, as we might suspect, the inclusion of victim evidence increases the likelihood that jurors will return a death sentence.[301]

Thoughtful judges recognize that victim-impact statements again shift the focus of a punishment proceeding from the proper measure of a wrong-doer's desert. As one California appellate case aptly put it:

> A defendant's level of culpability depends ... on circumstances over which he has control. A defendant may choose, or decline, to premed-itate, to act callously, to attack a vulnerable victim, to commit a crime while on probation, or to amass a record of offenses.... In contrast, the fact that a victim's family is irredeemably bereaved can be attributed to no act of the will of the defendant other than his commission of homicide in the first place. Such bereavement is relevant to damages in a civil action, but it has no relationship to the proper purposes of sentencing in a criminal case.[302]

In *Booth v. Maryland* (1987), SCOTUS followed this same sound logic and by a 5-4 majority found the use of victim-impact statements in cap-ital sentencing to assess the defendant's subjective culpability and hence deathworthiness to be unconstitutional. But it flip-flopped a few years later in *Payne v. Tennessee* (1991), where a majority held that, in arguing for the death penalty, victim-impact testimony and the prosecution's argu-ments based on it were relevant to the central factor in the determination of the defendant's deathworthiness, namely, somehow, his subjective moral blameworthiness:

> [A] state may properly conclude that for the jury to assess mean-ingfully the defendant's moral culpability and blameworthiness, it should have before it at the sentencing phase evidence of the specific harm caused by the defendant. "[T]he state has a legitimate interest in counteracting the mitigating evidence which the defendant is en-titled to put in, by reminding the sentencer that just as the murderer should be considered as an individual, so too the victim is an individ-ual whose death represents a unique loss to society and in particular to his family.[303]

To clearly see the irrationality of victim-impact statements in assessing the subjective moral culpability of a wrongdoer, imagine two drivers who run the same stop sign under identical circumstances. Each kills the single occupant of a different car. From the standpoint of retributive justice, the subjective moral culpability of both drivers was the same, so the punishment should be the same, too. But suppose that the victim of the first driver was a mother survived by a large and close-knit family, including a three-year-old son, Nicholas, as it was in *Payne*. The state presents the following testimony of Nicholas' grandmother about his reaction to the loss of his mother:

> He cries for his mom. He doesn't seem to understand why she doesn't come home. He comes to me many times during the week and asks me, Grandmama, do you miss my mommy? And I tell him yes. He says, "I'm worried about my mommy."[304]

The victim of the second, however, was survived by few friends and no family. Despite being no more blameworthy, the first now faces much stiffer punishment in sentencing proceedings, tied not to her subjective moral culpability, but to retaliation and revenge—tying her negligence, in other words, to the revulsion, hatred, and outrage produced in most of us by the wrongdoing rather than to her own individual just deserts. Following this same logic, courts have held that testimony that a victim's aunt suffered a lethal heart attack after hearing of her nephew's murder and that a victim's father gave up his career after hearing of his daughter's murder is admissible on the question of how much punishment the wrongdoers should get, allowing retaliation and revenge to drive the sentencing decision. The temptation is always strong to switch from making the punishment fit the blame to making it fit the outrage, which in many cases means inflicting extra and undeserved suffering on an offender, in excess of that called for by his subjective culpability.[305]

This is why debates about *theory* (here, different justifications for punishment) matter, and why this book is titled Nigga *Theory*, for different theories and justifications are often at war with each other, creating a constant need to choose between them in criminal justice matters. The same factors—e.g., a mental disorder or addiction—that might support less punishment under a retributive, subjective culpability theory might support *more* punishment under a deterrence-driven or utilitarian theory that focuses on "saving innocent lives" (through incapacitation or by maximizing penal disincentives). Nigga Theory sides with classic retributivism because it provides a principled upper limit on punishment based on an individual wrongdoer's subjective culpability and requires proportionality between the level of culpability and the severity of punishment.

The other justifications (retaliation, revenge, deterrence) lack principled upper limits: for instance, neither eye-for-an-eye retaliation nor revenge rule out torturing a wrongdoer who tortured his victim, and just as in some cases the threat of the death penalty arguably better deters certain wrongdoers than the threat of life without parole, the threat of a being executed through protracted torture may better deter certain wrongdoers than the threat of death by a lethal injection protocol ostensibly designed to be painless (numerous recent botched executions and gruesome spectacles to the contrary notwithstanding). In contrast, Immanuel Kant, a foundational retributivist, rejects torture (even as he champions capital punishment for killers on *lex talionis* or eye for an eye grounds). He warns that the execution of a condemned murderer "must be kept free from all maltreatment that would make the humanity suffering in his person loathsome or abominable."[306]

Retributivism's proportionality principle figures centrally in SCOTUS's decision to recognize an upper limit on the severity of punishment. In *Furman v. Georgia*[307] (1972), a 5-4 majority of the Court held that the death penalty, as then administered, violated the Eighth Amendment's prohibition of "cruel and unusual punishments." Four years later the Court reinstated the death penalty in *Gregg v. Georgia*, where the Court lays out its analytic framework in death penalty cases, the same framework it later uses to limit the kinds of people who can be found sufficiently wicked to deserve state execution.

In *Gregg*, Georgia state courts upheld a jury's decision to impose the death penalty for two counts of murder, and SCOTUS granted review. At the outset of the opinion, Justice Stewart, writing for the majority, talks about the nature of the words in the Eighth Amendment—the meaning of language like "cruel and unusual" and "excessive"—that fits hand in glove with Nigga Theory's core claim about words and concepts: their meanings are not fixed and frozen but rather mutable, malleable, contestable, and evolving. "[T]he Eighth Amendment has not been regarded as a static concept," Stewart points out. "The Amendment must draw its meaning from the evolving standards of decency that mark the progress of a maturing society." Like the N-word, the words of the Eighth Amendment refuse to be nailed down to inherent meanings or shackled to original intents. Their meaning mutates as contemporary values evolve; so regard for changes in public perceptions of decency concerning the infliction of punishment must infuse interpretations of the Eighth Amendment.

Stewart recognizes that popular perceptions of standards of decency cannot be the last word on what punishments it is fair to inflict, because such perceptions may not "comport with the basic concept of human dignity at the core of the Amendment." To comport with human dignity, he reasons, the punishment must not be "excessive," which means it must not be "cruelly inhuman" or "grossly out of proportion to the severity of the crime." Prevailing standards of decency had not yet evolved to the point where capital punishment no longer could be tolerated, he found, and so the death penalty comports with basic human dignity because it expresses society's moral outrage at the killing and helps satisfy "[t]he instinct for retribution" in ways that are not "grossly disproportionate" to the crime of murder in all cases. Evidence of whether the death penalty deters capital crimes was inconclusive, so the general justification is retributively proportionate punishment and an expression of society's moral outrage. He then turned to the arbitrariness and racial bias that plague capital punishment and asserted that they can be reined in and kept at tolerable levels with procedures and standards that cabin the discretion of sentencers. These discretion-channeling procedures and standards consist of a bifurcated trial that separates the determination of guilt stage of the trial from a later sentencing stage, and clear standards that guide and limit the sentencers' determination of deathworthiness during the sentencing stage.

And yet as we have seen, discretion is where arbitrariness and bias lurk, live, flourish, and operate in the substantive criminal law and the adjudication of just deserts. Whenever and wherever the letter of the law reposes discretion in a judge or jury, conscious and unconscious bias, including racial bias, thrives. It might seem that the most straightforward way to wring excessive sentencing discretion and its racial bias out of death penalty cases would be simply to mandate the automatic imposition of a capital sentence upon conviction of certain kinds of murders. Replace nebulous standards with bright line rules. Take away discretion, take away room for arbitrary and biased decision making. If "equal justice for all under the law" means neutrality and evenhandedness in the distribution of punishment and administration of justice, it might seem that surely this is the best way to achieve it. For instance, automatically put everyone convicted of first-degree murder to death. Full stop.

Our discussion of the social construction of black murderers exposed the practical doctrinal problem with a mandatory approach, however: we saw how easily a "bright line" legal requirement, like the "premeditation" requirement in first-degree murder, can be manipulated by jurors, consciously or unconsciously, to give expression to their underlying moral intuitions, visceral reactions, and racial biases. We saw that the more a wrongdoer or the crime she committed inflames jurors' retributive urge or retaliatory impulses, the more likely jurors are to "find" the required aware mental state through, for instance, their interpretive construction of the facts, even if evidence of premeditation is weak at best. Consistent with our analysis, in striking down a North Carolina statute mandating automatic death for all first-degree murders, the *Woodson v. North Carolina* plurality observed that past experience with such sentencing suggested that juries would simply refuse to convict of capital murder when they felt that the punishment of death was too severe, that is, did not fit the blame. If automatic death follows from a finding of premeditation, a jury that does not think the wrongdoer deserves death can bend over backward not to find premeditation on the facts. So mandatory schemes often don't guide discretion so much as relocate the opportunity to exercise it to an earlier point in the proceedings, an earlier point in the adjudication of the wrongdoer's just deserts. For that reason the *Woodson* plurality pointed out that the "mandatory statutes enacted in response to Furman have simply papered over the problem of unguided and unchecked jury discretion."[308]

The problem of unguided and unchecked jury discretion and flexible legal standards—e.g., Reasonable Person, in the situation, gross deviation, depraved heart, "outrageously or wantonly vile"—run through every nook and cranny of the substantive criminal law.[309] Such open-ended nondescriptive standards also "simply paper over the problem of unguided and unchecked jury discretion" and the racial bias that inevitably accompany it.[310]

Yet, despite their many shortcomings, bright line, mandatory rules undeniably do reduce discretion more than flexible standards. So, again, if lawmakers were really serious about neutral, evenhanded, unbiased distributions of death in capital cases, then, as North Carolina law makers tried to do in *Woodson*, they could make some headway by replacing amorphous standards with bright line rules mandating an automatic death sentence for certain kinds of murder, such as those in the first degree. Which brings us to the Court's core objection to mandatory death statutes, one that would hold even if such statutes completely stamped out unguided discretion, bias, and arbitrariness in sentencing, for *Woodson*'s core objection to mandatory punishments is that they show insufficient respect for the fundamental value of individual dignity at the heart of the Eighth Amendment, which requires, according to *Woodson*:

> The particularized consideration of relevant aspects of the character and record of each convicted defendant before the imposition upon him of a sentence of death.... A process that [fails to provide such consideration] ... treats all persons convicted of a designated offense not as uniquely individual human beings, but as members of a faceless, undifferentiated mass to be subjected to the blind infliction of the penalty of death.

In stressing the overriding importance of individual dignity and individualized justice (indeed, the importance of individualized justice *to* individual dignity), this very non-consequentialist, non-utilitarian way of talking and thinking about the Eighth Amendment is very congenial to the retributivism that underlies Nigga Theory. The Court fully recognizes that wringing arbitrariness and racial bias from the criminal justice system are vital pursuits, crucial to the legitimacy of any system of punishment, but it also recognizes that those concerns do not trump the wrongdoer's right (rooted in respect for his person and recognition of his individual dignity) to a fully individualized assessment of his subjective culpability and just deserts. In *State v. Forrest*, for instance, the defendant took a handgun with him on a visit to his hospitalized, terminally ill dad and, tearful, weeping, and desperate, killed him with a single shot to the head. The North Carolina Supreme Court upheld his conviction for first-degree murder. Subjecting someone like Forrest to mandatory execution irrespective of his own individual level of moral culpability, punishing him the same as a terrorist who shoots up a church, sacrifices Forrest's individual dignity for the sake of evenhandedness, neutrality. Evenhandedness and neutrality are two requirements that must be met for a criminal justice system to maintain its legitimacy, but, by the same token, the legitimacy and moral credibility of the criminal justice system also suffers a severe blow when the state inflicts underserved punishment on individuals by disregarding their personal, individualized, subjective culpability. "Equal justice under law" must entitle defendants to both an impartial and an individualized judgment of their moral culpability.

This same logic of "individualized justice for all under law" even led the Court to strike down capital statutes that were not completely mandatory but merely limited the kinds of excuses, explanations, and mitigating factors that a sentencer could consider. In *Lockett v. Ohio*, for instance, the Court held it constitutionally impermissible for a capital statute to keep a sentencing judge from considering a wrongdoer's youth, her minor role in the offense, lack of serious criminal record, or likelihood of rehabilitation.[311] And in *Eddings v. Oklahoma* it held that it was also impermissible for the sentencing judge not to consider that the 16-year-old offender had a history of beatings by a harsh father and serious emotional disturbance. The Court reasoned that "a consistency produced by ignoring individual differences is a false consistency"—seeking to wring arbitrariness and bias out of death penalty proceedings by ignoring individual differences in subjective culpability (desert) is simply unjust.[312] In capital cases, the state should not prevent arbitrariness and bias by treating even the most violent wrongdoers as "members of a faceless, undifferentiated mass to be subjected to the blind infliction of the penalty of death."[313]

So whereas *Furman* and *Gregg* seek to confine, limit, and guide the sentencer's discretion in the name of consistency and nondiscrimination, *Woodson* and *Lockett* seek to maximize the sentencer's discretion in the name of individualized justice and making the punishment fit the blame. This tension—or antinomy—between these two principles and lines of cases in the Supreme Court's Eighth Amendment Jurisprudence cannot be resolved or reconciled, and so for supporters of the death penalty it requires a stark choice in capital cases: either abandon the hope of unbiased and consistent punishment or abandon concern for individualized justice and the individual dignity of the condemned. Justice Antonin Scalia compared the tension between guided discretion and individualization in capital cases to the "tension between the Allies and the Axis Powers in World War II" and supported tossing out the requirement of individualized sentencing (*Woodson* and *Lockett*) because he could not find concern for this form of individualized justice in the text of the Eighth Amendment. While it is beyond the scope of this book to debunk originalism, this objection falls under the category of Zombie ideas of fixed and frozen meanings.

Justice Blackmun shared Scalia's take on the irreconcilable war between the requirements of individualized sentencing and guided discretion (reducing bias and arbitrariness by limiting discretion as to blameworthiness) in Eighth Amendment law, but unlike Scalia, and consistent with the retributivist, rights-based legal framework of Nigga Theory, he refuses to sacrifice individualized justice and individual dignity to address other problems and concerns. And he also balks at the idea of unchecked discretion and its attendant bias and arbitrariness. Accordingly, he takes the most principled and coherent position and rejects capital punishment altogether:

Experience has taught us that the constitutional goal of eliminating arbitrariness and discrimination from the administration of death can never be achieved without compromising an equally essential component of fundamental fairness—individualized sentencing.

It is tempting, when faced with conflicting constitutional commands, to sacrifice one for the other or to assume that an acceptable balance between them has already been struck. In the context of the death penalty, however, such jurisprudential maneuvers are wholly inappropriate. The death penalty must be imposed "fairly, and with reasonable consistency, or not at all."

From this day forward, I no longer shall tinker with the machinery of death. For more than 20 years I have endeavored—indeed, I have struggled—along with a majority of this Court, to develop procedural and substantive rules that would lend more than the mere appearance of fairness to the death penalty endeavor. Rather than continue to coddle the Court's delusion that the desired level of fairness has been achieved ... I feel morally and intellectually obligated simply to concede that the death penalty experiment has failed.

The theory underlying ... *Lockett* is that an appropriate balance can be struck between the *Furman* promise of consistency and the *Lockett* requirement of individualized sentencing.... While one might hope that providing the sentencer with as much relevant mitigating evidence as possible will lead to more rational and consistent sentences, experience has taught otherwise. It seems that the decision whether a human being should live or die is so inherently subjective—rife with all of life's understandings, experiences, prejudices, and passions— that it inevitably defies the rationality and consistency required by the Constitution.

These two contradictory principles and lines of cases—*Woodson* and *Lockett* versus *Furman* and *Gregg*—continue to coexist in our Eighth Amendment jurisprudence in part to help our court system coddle the delusion that intolerable levels of bias and arbitrariness have been wrung from this nation's deliberate distribution of death, when in fact they have not. The death penalty simply cannot be administered in a fair and unbiased way in modern America. The only possible fair application is no application: it needs to be abolished.

◆

We need to move, in other words, from tinkering with the machinery of death to scrapping the machine.

Racial bias plagues capital punishment and robs it of legitimacy, but the problem with the death penalty runs deeper than just bias. Suppose we were able to wring every ounce of racial bias about a wrongdoer's deathworthiness from the judgments of judges and jurors? Suppose, in other words, that we found a way to completely de-bias sentencers so that they provided neutral, evenhanded evaluations of the blameworthiness of wrongdoers in the sense that similarly situated black and white ones were judged just the same. Even these completely colorblind moral judgments of sentencers about the subjective culpability and just deserts of violent wrongdoers may still impose punishments on them that are draconian and excessive, that is, disproportionate to their subjective culpability.

Indeed, as Hyman Gross points out in *A Theory of Criminal Justice*, the proportionality requirement rests on the same principle that forbids punishment of the innocent, "for any punishment in excess of what is deserved for the criminal conduct is punishment without guilt."[314] The requirement that punishment be proportional to the seriousness of the offense is a central limit dictated by the Eighth Amendment, and because Nigga Theory seeks to harness the power of the principle of proportionality to limit "excessive" sentences, we need to first reject all utilitarian concerns such as crime control and prevention. When Jeremy Bentham wrote his massively influential utilitarian theory of punishment in 1789, England punished all felonies with death. He reacted to those grossly excessive sanctions by advocating for "rules of proportion between crimes and punishments," maintaining that "all punishment in itself is evil" and "ought only to be admitted in as far as it promises to exclude some greater evil"—that is, only in as far as its social benefits outweigh its social costs.[315]

Despite the progressive, reformist spirit that animated its origins, utilitarianism, by making the greater good rather than respect for the individual its focus, provides no real protection for personal innocence or against severe sanctions for even minor offenses. We saw its disregard for personal innocence earlier in this chapter where, from a pure cost-benefit perspective, it may be cheaper to convict the innocent than acquit the guilty. And if you define proportionality in utilitarian terms, then an extremely severe punishment may not be "excessive" as long as it's necessary to deter wrong-doing that is more costly *overall* or in the aggregate. For instance, while it might seem obvious to some that the cost of locking people up for minor offenses exceeds the benefit, for others the math may look quite different: suppose that a subway system loses many millions of dollars every year as a result of customers jumping turnstiles without paying, and despite security cameras and other precautions, they can catch only a tiny fraction of offenders. Because under utilitarianism the severity of the punishment can be ratcheted way up to make up for a low risk of detection or apprehension, it could be cost-justified to mete out a 25-year sentence to an 18-year-old turnstile jumper!

Precisely this utilitarian way of thinking about the proportionality grounds the Court's grim conclusion in *Ewing v. California* (2003): that the Eight Amendment's proportionality requirement does not prohibit the state of California from sentencing a repeat offender—who walked into a pro shop of the El Segundo Golf Course and limped out with three golf clubs, priced at $399 apiece, concealed in his pants leg—to a prison term of 25 years to life under its "Three Strikes and You're Out" law.[316] Writing for a plurality of the Court, Justice Sandra Day O'Connor reasoned that, when a defendant claims only that his own personal noncapital sentence is disproportionate under the unique facts of his own case, the prospect of big utilitarian benefits in deterrence and incapacitation can be enough to satisfy the "narrow proportionality principle" implicit in the Eighth Amendment's prohibition of cruel and unusual punishment and so pass constitutional muster. Under this "narrow proportionality principle," the Eighth Amendment does not forbid merely disproportionate sentences; "[r]ather, it forbids only extreme sentences that are 'grossly disproportionate' to the crime."[317] Because O'Connor roots this high threshold requirement of "gross disproportionality" in the utilitarian concerns of deterrence and incapacitation, the "gross proportionality" test provides very little protection against shockingly severe punishment. Even Justice Scalia, himself no friend of the proportionality principle in Eighth Amendment jurisprudence, rightly pointed out in his Ewing concurrence that "Proportionality—the notion that punishment should fit the crime—is inherently a concept tied to the penological goal of retribution." After noting that Justice O'Connor's plurality opinion "in all fairness, does not convincingly establish that 25-years-to-life is a 'proportionate' punishment for stealing three golf clubs," he accurately observed: "It becomes difficult to even speak intelligently of 'proportionality,'" once "the State's public-safety interest in incapacitating and deterring recidivist felons" are given significant weight. Why such utilitarian factors have "anything to do with the principle of proportionality is a mystery," he rightly concludes.

In another case decided with *Ewing*, *Lockyer v. Andrade*, Andrade stole videotapes from a Kmart on two occasions, the first time taking videotapes worth $84.70, the second, $68.84. Both offenses were classified as petty thefts—normally a misdemeanor—because both amounts were under $200. But the three-strikes statute was applied to his case because of his previous convictions: two counts of transporting marijuana, two misdemeanor thefts, and three counts of residential burglary. Consequently, for each of the petty thefts, he got 25 to life, each sentence to run consecutively. 50-year minimum for two petty thefts!? Writing for a five-member majority, Justice O'Connor refused to overturn the sentence on proportionality grounds, prompting Justice Souter, writing for four dissenters, to say that "[i]f Andrade's sentence is not grossly disproportionate, the principle has no meaning."[318] If the demands of deterrence and incapacitation, these "serpent-windings of utilitarianism," can render an extremely severe punishment permissible for a trivial offense, then there's no reason to think a Court following Justice O'Connor's approach would not uphold a 25-year (or even life) sentence for our hypothetical turnstile jumper. For classic retributivists, such utilitarian cost-benefit thinking would be irrelevant to the *wrongness* of sentencing a young person to life behind bars after her, say, fifth conviction for turnstile jumping. In other words, many will object to the punishment on grounds of fairness, not utility. However much such a punishment promotes or protects the greater good or other interests, proponents of fairness in sentencing will insist, such severe punishments are simply so out of sync with her personal culpability that they are for that reason alone "grossly disproportionate."

For those whose moral intuitions balk at "25-years-to-life for stealing three golf clubs," or a 50-year minimum for two petty thefts, or life imprisonment for turnstile jumping, or a sentence of 200 years without possibility of parole (consecutive 10-year sentences on each of 20 counts) for a first-time offender for possession of 20 images of child pornography (that he had downloaded from the internet[319]), or a life sentence with the possibility of parole for a defendant who obtained $120.75 by false pretenses and whose two prior offenses were felony convictions for "fraudulent use of a credit card to obtain $80 worth of goods or services" and for "a forged check in the amount of $28.36,"[320] we do not find them "grossly disproportionate" merely because we believe or intuit that there are less costly alternatives to such severe sentences that would deter just as effectively. Many of us would continue to find these punishments unconscionably disproportionate even if we were totally convinced that less costly alternatives do not have the same deterrent effect, because at bottom our intuitions about proportionate punishment are rooted in fairness rather than social utility: we object to the unfairness of imposing more punishment on a wrongdoer than he deserves. Our respect for the individual dignity of each person makes us uncomfortable when we deal with them merely as a tool of social policy or instrument of social engineering, a thing, which we do when we punish people more than they in fairness deserve in order to promote and protect other interests. As these cases illustrate, considerations of deterrence and incapacitation often support much more severe sentences than those of retribution. Not always, in every case, of course—sometimes utilitarian factors may point to a punishment substantially less severe than retributive ones because moral panics or political fearmongering or other emotional factors can push people to heap excessive moral blame on certain kinds of wrongdoers (e.g., sexual and drug offenders), leading lawmakers to have an exaggerated sense of the moral culpability of some wrongdoers and hence punish them more than would lawmakers focusing just on deterrence and incapacitation. But as we shall see, the retributive approach to the proportionality requirement provides courts with the most principled way to both establish upper limits on sentences for violent or serious crimes and remain true to the individualized justice imperative.[321]

To its credit, SCOTUS has begun to deploy a broader interpretation of the Eighth Amendment's proportionality principle in death penalty cases to provide constitutional protection against capital punishment for whole categories of guilty murderers who, from a retributive standpoint, often lack sufficient subjective culpability to qualify as the "worst of the worst," even though the harm they caused generates great outrage, resentment, revulsion, anger, hatred, and contempt in ordinary people. The Court has started to hold that certain categories of killers cannot be sentenced to death even if the gory and gruesome details of the crime, or victim-impact testimony, are so gut-wrenching that many sentencers would find the killer deathworthy.

The Court's first bold step in this direction came in the 2002 case of *Atkins v. Virginia*, where the defendant and another man abducted the victim at gunpoint, robbed him of the money he was carrying, drove him to an automated bank machine in his truck where cameras recorded their withdrawal of more cash, then took him to a secluded area where they killed him with eight shots. In the sentencing phase of the trial, the defense's expert witness, a forensic psychologist who had evaluated Atkins before trial, concluded that he had an IQ of 59 (the mean score of the test is 100, with 1-3% of the population having an IQ between 70 and 75 or lower). The *Woodson/Lockett* commitment to individualized justice and unguided mitigation meant that the jury heard about his cognitive and volitional deficiencies in the penalty phase. Nevertheless, the jury decided that the aggravating factors (which in capital crimes, recall, can include evidence irrelevant to the personal subjective culpability of the wrongdoer, such as victim-impact statements) outweighed the mitigating ones and sentenced Atkins to death. Just because jurors, without a trace of racial bias or any other social prejudice, take a wrongdoer's mitigating circumstances or attributes into consideration in assessing his or her deathworthiness does not mean they will give them adequate weight or keep the inquiry into his or her desert focused on blame rather than harm, on the actor rather than the consequences of his act, on retribution rather than retaliation and revenge. Racially neutral, fully individualized moral judgments of wrongdoers are not the same as substantively fair moral judgments of them. In other words, the Court has begun to recognize that all-too-human sentencers cannot be trusted to strike a fair and measured balance between aggravating and mitigating factors in many capital murder cases, because, in the words of the Court, the crime "in many cases will overwhelm a decent person's judgment."[322]

Noting at the outset that the standards used to determine whether a punishment violates the Eighth Amendment's prohibition of "excessive" sanctions are those evolving ones that prevail today rather than those in effect when the Bill of Rights was adopted, the *Atkins* Court proceeds to formulate a two-step process for assessing the "proportionality" of a capital sentence (as opposed to non-capital sentences like those involved in *Ewing* and *Andrade*): first, determine the content of today's evolving standards and whether there is an emerging societal *consensus* against capital punishment for certain kinds of wrongdoers, and second, the Court's own independent assessment of the core penological justifications—retribution, deterrence, incapacitation[323]—for the punishment. Note that in capital cases, the Court uses a "broader" test of proportionality than the "narrow proportionality principle" it uses in individual non-capital sentences where the Court must first find as a threshold matter that a sentence is "grossly disproportionate," a nearly impossibly high threshold hurdle, as we saw in *Ewing* and *Andrade*. In capital cases, in contrast, the Court has found a number of death sentences disproportionate. When execution rather than Life Without Possibility of Parole (LWOP) hangs in the balance, the Court immediately looks at how other jurisdictions treat the crime at issue and how the same jurisdiction treats other crimes—essentially an inquiry into present public judgment or evolving standards of decency.[324]

As the first step in its two-step process, the *Atkins* Court found evidence of an emerging societal consensus against executing such wrongdoers in the consistent direction of legislative changes in many states, with more and more states enacting statutes that exempt intellectually disabled the from the death penalty. (The Court identifies a clearly retributive reason for this emerging societal consensus on the impermissibility of executing intellectually disabled offenders, namely, because, due to their deficiencies in areas of reasoning, judgment, and control of their impulses, "they do not act with the level of moral culpability that characterizes the most serious adult criminal conduct.") Such consensus information—what most people and their representatives believe and do—sometimes may be helpful in determining the boundaries of morally acceptable beliefs and practices, but the popularity of beliefs and practices is not knockdown proof of their moral acceptability. Because most Germans held anti-Semitic beliefs and attitudes in the run up to WWII does not mean anti-Semitism was morally acceptable anywhere or anytime, however popular at a given place and time. This same problem arises in the area of self-defense, where reasonable beliefs are defined as typical (or popular) beliefs; therefore widespread anti-black beliefs and fears are viewed as understandable and reasonable. Prevailing beliefs and practices may reflect social prejudices that do not deserve judicial deference from judges seeking to make principled decisions.

In the second step of its two-step assessment of the death penalty (which from the principle-centered approach of Nigga Theory should be the Court's first and only step in its methodology), the *Atkins* Court exercised its own independent judgment on whether the penological goals of retribution, deterrence, and incapacitation support an exemption from the death penalty for this entire category of offenders. From a retributive standpoint, the Court finds that disabilities in areas of reasoning, judgment, and impulse control make the intellectually disabled *categorically* less morally culpable: "If the culpability of the average murderer is insufficient to justify the most extreme sanction available to the State, the lesser culpability of the intellectually disabled offender surely does not merit that form of retribution." When the Court turns to the utilitarian justifications for punishing the intellectually disabled, on the other hand, they offset one another; the same cognitive and volitional disabilities that make the intellectually disabled less like to be deterred also make them more dangerous (because of said lack of control) and so more in need of incapacitation.[325] So in *Atkins*, the retributive theory pulls the laboring oar in putting an upper limit on punishment, narrowing the permissible scope of the death penalty.

Three years after *Atkins*, the Court again deployed its broader interpretation of the Eighth Amendment's proportionality principle to provide constitutional protection against capital punishment for another whole category of guilty murderers, holding in *Roper v. Simmons* (2005) that the death penalty is a disproportionate punishment for offenders who were juveniles at the time of their crimes. Following its *Atkins* methodology, it found an emerging societal consensus against the execution of juvenile wrongdoers in a substantial number of states, an infrequent use of the juvenile death penalty where it remained on the books, and a consistent trend toward its elimination. Then the Court invoked common experience—what "any parent knows"—and "scientific and sociological studies" to show that "juvenile offenders cannot, with reliability, be classified among the worst offenders." The Court also recognized "the comparative immaturity and irresponsibility of juveniles," that juveniles "are more vulnerable or susceptible to negative influences and outside pressures," and that the personality traits of juveniles are "more transitory, less fixed." Then it concluded that once "the diminished culpability of juveniles is recognized; it is evident that the penological justifications for the death penalty apply to them with lesser force than to adults."[326]

◆

The Supreme Court's conclusion that whole categories of violent wrongdoers (the intellectually disabled and juveniles) should be exempted from the death penalty—based on mismatches between the subjective culpability of a class of offenders and the severity of their punishment—fits hand in glove with a core thesis of this book, namely, that both legal decision-makers and laypersons alike should practice profound epistemic humility in their moral condemnations of wrongdoers, especially but not exclusively black ones. The Supreme Court recognized in *Atkins* and *Simmons* that the inference from a bad act to a bad actor, from a violent and vicious crime to the most morally odious and hence deathworthy criminal, is too noisy, cloudy, and unreliable when wrongdoers have the cognitive and volitional limitations of juveniles and the intellectually disabled. It recognized that the moral judgments of factfinders can't be trusted when it comes to these kinds of wrongdoers, because the gravity of the crime can "overwhelm a decent person's judgment." As we have said, the temptation is too strong in many cases of violent homicide to shift the focus from the blameworthiness of the wrongdoers to the gravity of the harm—from retribution and just deserts to retaliation and revenge.

But once we acknowledge that the inferences of ordinary people about the moral culpability of certain categories of wrongdoers are too noisy and unreliable to make the basis of our most severe punishment, the obvious next question becomes why we do not, in fairness and consistency, recognize that ordinary people are just as prone to make noisy and unreliable inferences about anyone? Because up to 70% of death row inmates are estimated to suffer some form of mental illness, categorically exempting this class of offenders from the death penalty could make deep cuts in capital punishment.[327] Just as insanity destroys, undermines, or diminishes a person's capacity to reject what is wrong and conform to what is right, so do many forms of mental illness.

By the same token, so does child abuse. Given the desperate plight of battered children, a compassionate and consistent Court should consider a categorical exemption from the death penalty for such wrongdoers. Such a Court should also consider a categorical exemption from execution for wrongdoers from truly disadvantaged backgrounds. Judge David Bazelon proposed just such a defense, first in a separate court opinion and then in a law review article.[328] Bazelon's proposal grew out of his assessment that a number of defendants suffered the same kinds of cognitive and volitional defects that constitute excuses in cases where mental illness is found, but that they could not meet some of the technical requirements of the definition of legal insanity. Upon further reflection, Judge Bazelon realized that the mental impairments afflicting these defendants were the product of social, economic, and cultural deprivations or of racial discrimination, rather than of a clinically defined mental illness. Accordingly, he proposed a jury instruction that would permit acquittal where the crime was caused by the defendant's disadvantaged background. Specifically, he would instruct the jury to acquit (whereas I'm merely proposing that the offenders be spared execution) if it found that, at the time of the offense, the truly disadvantaged defendant's "mental or emotional processes or behavior controls were impaired to such an extent that he cannot justly be held responsible for his act."

Although Judge Bazelon did not expect that his new instruction would generate a flood of new acquittals, he hoped the instruction would force jurors to confront the causes of criminal behavior and thus compel the community to own up to its responsibility for the crime and for the plight of the accused. His position squares perfectly with Nigga Theory's arguments in support of our collective accountability for the foreseeable criminal consequences of our criminogenic social conditions and unjust basis social structure. My hope is that a categorical exemption from the death penalty for severely disadvantaged wrongdoers would force us as a society to confront our criminogenic social inequality and compel us to own up to our own responsibility for violent crime. In Judge Bazelon's words, "It's simply unjust to place people in dehumanizing social conditions, to do nothing about those conditions, and then to command those who suffer, 'Behave—or else!'"

And finally, once we acknowledge that the inferences of ordinary people are too noisy and unreliable to make the basis of our most severe punishments, we must also ask why we do not, in fairness and consistency, exempt all black wrongdoers from capital punishment on the ground that, because of empirically demonstrable biases such as attribution bias and ingroup empathy bias, ordinary people on juries are just as prone to make noisy and unreliable inferences about the subjective culpability and just deserts of black wrongdoers.

For instance, in a *Psychological Science* article titled "Looking Deathworthy: Perceived Stereotypicality of Black Defendants Predicts Capital-Sentencing Outcomes," researchers examined whether the likelihood of being sentenced to death is influenced by the degree to which a black defendant is perceived to have a stereotypically black appearance. Controlling for a wide array of factors, they found that in cases involving a white victim, the more stereotypically black a defendant is perceived to be, the more likely that person is to be sentenced to death.[329] For the same crime, ordinary people not only judge black hearts and minds more harshly than white ones, but the more stereotypically black a person's heart or mind, the more severe his or her moral condemnation. Hence, due to the kind of anti-black racial bias buried in the cognitive unconscious of millions of Americans, inferences that black wrongdoers are the "worst of the worst" are simply too noisy and unreliable to base executions on. Hence, consistent with the logic of *Atkins* and *Simmons*, no black wrongdoers should be subject to the death penalty for the foreseeable future.

◆

My analysis of the ubiquitous and undeniable phenomenon of moral luck raises serious doubts about the rationality, legitimacy, and reliability of our moral condemnations not just of black wrongdoers, but of *all* wrongdoers. Morally, we are *all* at the mercy of luck. The "self" of a wicked wrongdoer, like the "self" of a saint, is at bottom a tissue of contingencies. The upshot of that analysis was that we must practice epistemic humility in our moral condemnation of all criminal wrongdoers; why wouldn't we exempt *all* wrongdoers from capital punishment on the ground of the counterintuitive and undeniable phenomenon of moral luck? An ordinary middle-class white man or woman who commits a violent offense can also be at the mercy of factors beyond his or her control in the form of resultant, circumstantial, or constitutive luck. It takes epistemic hubris rather than humility to insist that our inferences about the moral culpability of even the most privileged wrongdoers are so rational, legitimate, and reliable that we can execute them in the name of retributive justice. Nigga Theory embraces retributive justice because retribution concerns itself only with the personal moral culpability of a wrongdoer. And since we know that moral luck and unconscious bias expose our moral judgments of culpability as irrational, illegitimate, and unreliable, eye-for-an-eye retributionists can no longer coherently or convincingly defend their demands for the most severe sentences. At minimum, the epistemic humility about our capacity to rationally and reliably condemn wrongdoers should compel principled retributivists to reject the death penalty.

CONCLUSION | CODA

Once principled retributionists fully reckon with their deep and abiding human fallibility in making moral judgments of others, including criminally violent others, they should temper the hard edge of their retributive urge with compassion and understanding for the human frailty of *all* wrongdoers they must evaluate. The rights and interests of victims of course must be recognized and vindicated, but that vindication need not take the form of the most punitive response possible. Too often, those of us who care about victims from socially marginalized groups (such as Blacks, women, LGBTQ+ folk) take the position that the only way to show sufficient care and concern for crime victims from those groups is to punish their victimizers as severely as possible. Proponents of such a position may be referred to as "carceral progressives," "carceral feminists," or "carceral advocates for the socially marginalized." Even activists who generally oppose mass incarceration and advocate for deep cuts in our prison population too often adopt punitive and carceral attitudes when a violent crime has been committed against a member of a marginalized group, especially if the offender belongs to a socially dominant one.

Take the case of Amber Guyger, the white police officer with the Dallas Police Department who entered the apartment of Botham Jean, a 26-year-old black man who was sitting in his living room eating ice cream and watching television. Ignoring several indications that she was on the wrong floor and about to enter the wrong apartment, Guyger mistook Jean's apartment for her own; hearing someone inside at a time when she was safely situated outside the apartment, she ignored her training, did not call for backup, barged in, mistook him for an assailant, and shot him dead. The entire encounter, including the shooting, happened within seconds. Although Guyger testified at trial that she drew her gun and commanded the dark figure walking quickly toward her to present his hands, medical testimony contradicted her, indicating that Jean was crouched at the time he was shot based on the trajectory of the bullet. Despite persistently (and alarmingly) low conviction rates for police-involved shootings, a jury convicted Guyger of murder. Prosecutors asked for a 28-year minimum prison sentence but she ultimately received 10.

Some of Jean's family members extended compassion and forgiveness to Guyger, but many observers viewed her 10-year sentence as unwarranted leniency—a slap on the wrist. One core complaint in social media was that white wrongdoers in general and police officers who commit crimes in particular are more often beneficiaries of compassion for human frailty than black wrongdoers. Some pointed to Crystal Mason, for instance, a black Texas woman who mistakenly cast an illegal ballot in 2016 and was given a five-year prison sentence, even with her probation officer testifying that he did not notify her that she could not vote. For all the reasons I discuss on where bias lives in the substantive criminal law and adjudication of just deserts, draconian and disproportionate sentences for black offenders are a feature of our criminal justice system, not a bug, quirk, or anomaly.

Nevertheless, I was deeply ambivalent about the murder verdict for Amber Guyger. The jury could have convicted her of murder, manslaughter, or acquitted her. The racial justice advocate in me ached for police accountability in the form of a criminal conviction. From a traditional, carceral perspective, a conviction for murder, with its potential 99-year maximum sentence in Texas, would send the strongest deterrence signal to other members of law enforcement whose trigger fingers get extra itchy or twitchy around ambiguous black men. Moreover, from the perspective of the expressive function of criminal law, a murder conviction could serve as an authoritative, public expression, in the form of punishment, of moral condemnation of officer-involved misconduct, as well as a "vindication" or affirmation of the dignity of innocent black people. But the decarceration advocate in me who fights against excessively punitive punishment, even for violent offenders like Guyger, and who recognizes that utilitarian and expressive approaches to criminal law that lean too heavily on deterrence fuel racialized mass incarceration—that part of me would have preferred a more lenient manslaughter conviction.

My kind of ambivalence doesn't seem to bother carceral feminist Michele Dauber, a law professor at Stanford who led a recall campaign against Aaron Persky, the California judge who drew national attention in 2016 when he sentenced a Stanford student, Brock Turner, to six months in jail for sexually assaulting an unconscious woman when he was 19 years old. A jury found him guilty of sexual penetration with a foreign object of an intoxicated person, sexual penetration with a foreign object of an unconscious person, and intent to commit rape. In addition to jail time, Turner also received three years of probation and was required to register as a sex offender. Stanford also expelled him and barred him from campus. Persky was the first judge recalled in more than 80 years in California. Opponents of the recall argued that it undermined judicial independence and would make other judges more prone to impose severe sentences in cases where leniency might be appropriate because, politically, it's always safer for a judge to throw the book at a convicted criminal rather than make allowances for his human frailty. Since nearly 70% of the people in prison in California are Black or Latinx, the people who would suffer most from more punitive judges would not be white boys at frat parties. Black and brown folk would bear the brunt of more zealous punishment. Clearly, Turner's violent crime was odious and despicable. But six months in a cage followed by a lifetime on a sexual offender registry, with its many serious privations and humiliations, was and is real punishment, especially for someone who was a teenager at the time of his wrongdoing, in light of the growing recognition that the brains of youth, and hence their cognitive and volitional capacities, are not fully developed until their mid-20s.

Dauber and I have had a few Twitter tussles over these issues, which hinged on my contention that epistemic humility requires us to favor leniency, whenever appropriate, pitted against her carceral progressivism demanding vengeance for vulnerable victims. Nigga Theory challenges those committed to making deep cuts in mass incarceration to resist the retributive urge when the temptation is strongest to otherize, monsterize, and niggarize a violent wrongdoer who has preyed on vulnerable and marginalized victims—whether he is black or white. It also challenges us not to strike out at wrongdoers who are political enemies in ways that are draconian. Three such wrongdoers who escaped accountability for years and whom I accordingly blasted regularly on social media and in lectures, speeches, talks, and podcasts were R. Kelly, Harvey Weinstein, and Paul Manafort.

◆

R. Kelly has been charged with 11 new counts related to aggravated criminal sex assault, criminal sex assault, and aggravated criminal sex abuse of a victim between the ages of 13 and 16, according to court records. For progressives dedicated to ending racialized mass incarceration, he is a good litmus test. When a powerful victimizer preys on young black girls, some of this nation's most marginalized and vulnerable victims, what is the proper reaction? If as a progressive you preach "decarceration," but violent and morally condemnable wrongdoers so inflame your retributive urge that you can only think about retribution, retaliation, and revenge, then you're a carceral progressive, because many people in prison are such offenders. If we cannot curb our collective retributive urge toward serious, sexual, and violent offenders, we cannot make deep cuts in mass incarceration, because so many people in prison committed serious, sexual, and/or violent offenses. The brand of Critical Race Theory I've called "Nigga Theory" centers on the most reviled criminals—like Stanley "Tookie" Williams, co-founder of the Crips, whom We the People executed in 2005—because they are the hardest to humanize. So even though I've been extremely critical of sexual predators like Bill Cosby and R. Kelly for years, and have always added my voice to the chorus of those demanding that they be held accountable, that accountability should not simply be the most punitive punishment possible. I've said the same thing about racist cops who under color of law killed an unarmed black person. I first and foremost—as with Cosby and R. Kelly—want the cop held accountable. But as a foe of mass incarceration I can't consistently demand the most punitive possible punishment—that kind of demand is what got us mass incarceration. Mass incarceration is a mentality, an ideology, a way of thinking about and responding to serious offenders, accompanied by a politics of retaliation and revenge. So, like many others, I'm rejoicing at the prospect of R. Kelly finally being brought to justice, but we should resist reveling in the retributive urge.

Must R. Kelly be punished? Hell yeah! I don't go as far as those who argue for the abolition of all prisons. To deter him from more assaults, to deter other potential molesters, and to promote his own rehabilitation, he must be removed from society for a significant amount of time. The key question then is, what constitutes a "significant amount of time" for a serious and serial offender like R. Kelly? Demanding life without parole returns us to the same punitive responses and attitudes that ushered in "The New Jim Crow." How much, then? This "how much" question is answered very differently in different countries, and also very differently in the same country over time. Many states meted out much shorter sentences for murder and manslaughter in the 1950s and 1960s than today. The just deserts of serious wrongdoers aren't discoverable facts of nature. Rather they're reflections of social judgments we collectively make about whether to give more weight to retribution, retaliation and revenge or restoration, rehabilitation and redemption in criminal matters.

Disgraced film mogul Harvey Weinstein allegedly sexually assaulted scores of women. When Harvard Law professor Ronald Sullivan, Harvard's first black faculty dean, joined Weinstein's defense team, the university removed him from his position as dean. Students believed that defending Harvey Weinstein made Sullivan unfit to be their dean, and the university agreed. But this undermines a core constitutional principle—that all defendants, even the most indefensible, are entitled to legal counsel. Some argued that students feeling uncomfortable was an adequate reason to remove him, but that can't be the measure of a person's fitness. Lots of people aren't "comfortable" around Muslims, LGBTQ+ folk, and Blacks—but such prejudices should never justify a dismissal. Discomfort rooted in prejudice—or other rank irrationality—should never be the only justification required for removing someone from any position, whether dishwasher or dean.

I have urged students and faculty to show leniency for men on death row guilty of acts every bit as unconscionable as Weinstein. So in that sense I, too, have "represented"—and do "represent"—the moral equivalents of Weinstein, even though it upsets and offends many champions of "victims' rights."

◆

A student who follows me on Twitter said he'd feel frustrated if I represented Harvey Weinstein, but I told him he did not understand much about my racial and social justice work if he would feel frustrated about me representing and trying to humanize the most otherized, "nigga-rized" wrongdoers in America's criminal justice system—murderers, rapists, and other violent offenders. Mass incarceration, as a style of politics and way of looking at the world, includes the idea that people who victimize members of socially marginalized groups (like women or minorities) are scum, and anyone who represents such wrongdoers or their interests are scum. Rather than "Nigga Theory" you could call my brand of Critical Race Theory "Scum Theory," inasmuch as it seeks to curb the retributive urge toward so-called "scum" in the name of due process, restoration, rehabilitation, and redemption. So when you advocate for greater compassion for *all* wrongdoers, as Nigga Theory does, you don't get to pick and choose among wrongdoers. Nigga Theory gives real teeth to the mantra "All of Us or None" in criminal matters—it doesn't allow us to cherry-pick more sympathetic offenders. If a socially marginalized victim suffers harm at the hands of a socially dominant wrongdoer, erstwhile foes of mass incarceration turn into "law and order" retributionists who view any regard for the interests of the accused as proof of callous indifference for victims' interests. As a foe of the carceral state, paying the price of your convictions means respecting the rights and interests of wrongdoers—and not denigrating their advocates—even when wrongdoers are accused of violent, heinous acts against victims from socially marginalized groups.

Many of those supporting Harvard's action against Sullivan today will be preaching against mass incarceration tomorrow, without a trace of cognitive dissonance. But tarring alleged wrongdoers and those who represent with the same brush reflects the kind of mindset that fuels incarceration. It's unfortunate Harvard did not turn this into a teachable moment, opting instead for expediency over principle. The message is clear to those of us who advocate for the most stigmatized, otherized, and condemned among us: Do so at your own professional peril. Still, in my writing and activism I'll keep representing the most loathed and despised wrongdoers among us—the so-called niggas—and welcoming dialogues about why. At the same time, I'll keep fighting like hell for socially marginalized victims. It's possible, and necessary, to do both.[330]

◆

Finally, consider the case of Paul Manafort, former lobbyist, political consultant, and chair of Donald Trump's presidential campaign, serving a prison sentence for federal financial crimes. As news spread that Paul Manafort might be transferred to Rikers Island and held in solitary confinement until trial, I saw many left-leaning people rejoicing and issuing praise for "karma."

Watching people in the criminal justice reform community cheering and celebrating a political enemy going to solitary confinement at Rikers was a sad reminder that no one is immune from the punitive impulse. But we must resist it. We must be so principled in our calls for reform that we want them even for our enemies.

Of course it can feel satisfying to see a person of privilege finally sent to a place that staggering numbers of black folk have been sent to through the years. But Rikers is still unfit for any human to have to suffer. Even Paul Manafort. Rikers Island and Solitary Confinement are both tortures no one should be condemned to.

When we support inhuman treatment and deny the presumption of innocence for one—no matter how much we might loathe them or think they "deserve it"—we further fortify an unjust system for all. Our system of racialized mass incarceration was literally built on anger and fear and hatred for "the other." Every time someone commits a horrific crime or a particularly odious character gets caught, we must not simply repeat history.

If we ever want truly transformative change and deep, lasting cuts in mass incarceration, and more lenient sentences for wrongdoers, we must resist the strong temptation to inflict pain and suffering on others in the name of justice. We must love and protect each other so radically that we don't allow our feelings for a few to legitimize pain and suffering for the many. Supporting solitary confinement—legalized torture chambers—for Paul Manafort means supporting it for everyone.

When someone like Manafort faces jail or prison, we see who really cares about fair sentencing and prison conditions and who doesn't. We can't scream for punitiveness with Manafort, then turn around and plead for leniency with those with whom we sympathize. That's hypocrisy. When we demand draconian treatment for our political enemies, just know that when the laws are passed that support such treatment, they won't be used on people that look like Paul Manafort. Because 89% of those on Rikers are Black and Latinx folk, and most are poor.

◆

This book has made a frontal assault on the apparent moral and legal differences between traditional Jim Crow and the current mass incarceration of Blacks, upending these dichotomies by discrediting the widespread misconceptions about morality, psychology, and law on which such distinctions rest, misconceptions that obstruct a view of the social oppression *in* voluntary self-destruction. If Nigga Theory's assault on these commonsense distinctions has succeeded, readers will be better able to see both traditional Jim Crow and the mass incarceration of Blacks as analogous social injustices.

Nigga Theory weaves together three distinct but interdependent stories aimed at unifying law-abiding Americans and black criminals who bear the brunt of our criminal justice system:

1. a new "law and psychology" story;
2. an absurd but true "law and morality" story; and
3. an edgy "law and language" story about what Toni Morrison calls "the midwifery properties of language" in which the "troublesome" but perfectly apt word "nigga" plays the leading role and from which this book takes its title.

By subverting the moral and legal distinctions between black criminals and non-criminals, the first two stories set the stage for the N-word-laden third. First the "law and psychology" story showed how unconscious bias in judges and jurors makes the legal distinctions between black criminals and non-criminals error-ridden and unreliable. It focuses on how unconscious mental processes undermine the objectivity and neutrality of "the rule of law." It demonstrates how black criminals are forged, not found in the "factfinding" process of a criminal trial, how criminals are created by the bias-ridden cognitive unconscious of judges and jurors. To prove this point, I first created a new model of one of the oldest requirements in Anglo-American criminal law—namely, that of a "criminal intent" or "vicious will" or "guilty mind" or "*mens rea*"—and then used this new model to reveal where bias lives in the criminal law and its processes. This story shows how unconscious bias induces honest, well-meaning, racially liberal judges and jurors to make harsher moral judgments of black wrongdoers than of similarly situated white ones, and thus in a real sense they manufacture, mint, or "socially construct" many black criminals in the jury box.

The book's "law and morality" story took one of the most fertile insights in moral philosophy, the paradox of moral luck, and used it to systematically attack the moral distinction between criminals and non-criminals. The absurd and radically counterintuitive but irresistible finding of moral philosophers that *all* praise and blame and moral responsibility turns on fortuity— it's all a crapshoot—provided a fresh framework and vocabulary for thinking about age-old questions of free will and moral responsibility in criminal matters. A different part of the book's law and morality story was about how much room the law gives judges and jurors to directly judge the wickedness of wrongdoers, how such moral judgments are based on sympathy rather than moral maxims or categorical imperatives, and hence how unconscious mental processes like "ingroup empathy bias" and "attribution bias" cause ordinary decision makers to make systematically harsher moral judgments of black hearts and minds than of similarly situated white ones. By focusing on the role of empathy and attribution in the moral judgments that ordinary people make of others, the book provides a fresh framework for understanding the relationship between moral judgments and unconscious bias.

Despite its assault on conventional morality, this book is moral through and through: it seeks to activate the capacities for sympathy, empathy, and understanding in its reader toward reviled wrongdoers.

By undermining the psychological and moral bases for our tendency to automatically otherize or niggarize violent black offenders, these first two stories paved the way for the third story about "law and language" and the power of creative word work—including transgressive, disreputable, and uncomfortable words and symbols—to create political solidarity, produce social change, and promote racial justice.

Language is something lawyers and law professors like me think about a lot—we live with a constant and forced recognition of its nuances and complexities. I ask my law students to think about four occupations whose bread and butter is word work: Lawyers, Writers, Poets, and Rappers. I encourage them to see links between the poetic and the legal imagination, to see the law—in its hunger to connect the general with the particular, in its metaphorical movements, and in its ceaseless struggle with the limits of language—as a kind of poetry. I encourage them to see gangsta rap as political communication, as an important way we have of living with language and with each other through language.

This book used the N-word to test and prove two core premises of the "law and literature" movement: first, the *mutability of meaning* claim that language is not stable but changing, and second, the *politics of language* claim that language is perpetually remade by its speakers, who are themselves remade, both as individuals and as communities, in what they say. Because the NAACP buried the N-word in Detroit in 2007 precisely on grounds of its indelibly negative meaning, it provided a perfect test of the *mutability of meaning* claim; and because the work of Ice Cube, Tupac

Shakur, Nas, Jay-Z, and other artfully vulgar "gangsta rap" artists clearly has political content as they liberally sprinkle the N-word through their lyrics, the word also provided a perfect test of the *politics of language* claim that all language—even the vilest—is perpetually remade by its speakers, who are themselves remade, both as individuals and as communities, in what they say. Nigga Theory's expanded definition of "language" includes nonlinguistic forms of symbolic communication—including Afros, hoodies, tattoos, music, dance, sculpture, painting, architecture, and marching bands—and most humanities and fine arts. All these objects, performances, and forms of expression can be seen as political communication, revealing the political power of the beautiful and the sublime.

When words lose their meaning, as the detached and calcified language of the academy had for me, the question becomes whether the speaker can make a new language, remake an old one, or radically repurpose old words to serve new ends? I opted to radically repurpose "nigga" and "Nigga" throughout this text to establish a critical, adversarial, oppositional relation with conventional moral and legal language and to reconstitute my cultural resources—my possibilities for establishing and maintaining meaning— to make them adequate to my needs. Specifically, I inverted the N-word's negative moral meaning into a call for solidarity in catchphrases like "Call *me* a Nigga" and "*my* Niggas" to pinpoint unwarranted condemnations of black criminals and to forcefully challenge the legal and moral distinction between criminals and non-criminals, moral guilt and moral innocence, blame and praise, the wicked and the worthy—to strongly contest, in other words, the legal and moral distinction between so-called niggas and the law-abiding rest of us. Put differently, implicit in every inverted, positive use of the word "Nigga" in this book—and even in many of my wry negative deployments of it—was a substantive critique of prevailing moral and legal vocabularies and frameworks. I use the N-word to show how individual and social identities are established and maintained in language and how people use words—sometimes the very same word—to embrace or push away, recognize or deny, others.

A Royal typewriter and the Queen's English was all that stood between my dad and a lifetime in a cage. I hope that in this book's reflections on the midwifery properties of word work, the reader could hear the echoes of his manual keyboard click-clacking from a long-ago captivity. As Toni Morrison put it, "We die. That may be the meaning of life. But we do language. That may be the measure of our lives."

ACKNOWLEDGEMENTS

I presented portions of this exuberantly interdisciplinary book over the course of several years at various workshops, colloquia, faculty seminars, lectures, and discussions at USC Annenberg School of Journalism, the Los Angeles Human Relations Commission, The Row Church, LA Times Festival of Books, American Documentary Film Festival, University of La Verne College of Law, The Office of the Federal Public Defender & The United States Attorney's Office, USC Visions & Voices, Alpha Phi Alpha Fraternity, American Constitution Society, The Veritas Forum, Loyola Law School, UCLA Psychology Department, Zócalo Public Square, Los Angeles Urban League, Soros Open Society Foundation Fellowship Conference, Pan African Film Festival, The Gene Siskel Film Center, First African Methodist Episcopal Church (FAME), California African American Museum, Kirk Douglas Theatre, Pico Union Project, Univ. of San Diego Law School, Renaissance Arts Academy, Los Angeles City Hall, William Morris Endeavor, University of Pennsylvania School of Law, UNLV Law School, Pitzer College, USC Gould School of Law, Muslim Public Affairs Council (MPAC), California State University Los Angeles, California State University Dominguez Hills, UC Irvine Law School, UC Irvine Center on Law, Equality, and Race, The Midnight Mission in L.A.'s Skid Row, Mosk Courthouse (Downtown L.A.), USC School of Dramatic Arts, Public Policy Exchange, The Landmark Theater L.A., The Church in Ocean Park, Crossroads School for Arts and Sciences, USC Keck School of Medicine, California Institute of the Arts School of Theater, Santa Monica Art Studios, Skirball Cultural Center, USC Sol Price School of Public Policy and Center for Social Innovation, Feminist Majority Foundation, The Pasadena Playhouse, American Association of Law Schools (AALS) President's Program on Diversity, San Quentin Prison (No More Tears Program), Tolerance Education Center (Rancho Mirage), The Shakespeare Center of Los Angeles, USC Dworak-Peck School of Social Work, POLITICON (Pasadena Convention Center), Cal State Long Beach, The Center for Healthy Communities (Los Angeles), The Mic Sessions, USC School of Cinematic Arts, UCLA Law School, USC School of Philosophy. I gained much from these presentations, discussions, symposiums, and workshops, and thank all those who participated.

Outside these organized forums, Elyn Saks, Ron Garet, Ed McCaffery, Phreda Devereaux, S. Khin May Lwin, and Jeff Armour read large portions of the manuscript and made many helpful remarks.

I am also grateful to Tom Lutz (LARB editor-in-chief) and Albert Litewka (LARB chairman of the board) for their unflagging support for the intellectually adventurous spirit of this book from the very beginning of its journey to publication. I am also thankful to Stephanie Malak for her editorial contributions, to Nanda Dyssou for her marketing expertise, and to LARB Books, the publishing division of the *Los Angeles Review of Books*.

NOTES

1 J.L. Austin, *How to Do Things with Words* (Oxford University Press, 1962).

2 Tupac Shakur, "Life Goes On," *All Eyez on Me* (Death Row and Interscope Records, 1996).

3 A recent study, "The Impact of Light Skin on Prison Time for Black Female Offenders," by Jill Viglione, Lance Hannon, and Robert DeFina of Villanova University assesses how perceived skin tone is related to the maximum prison sentence and time served for a sample of over 12,158 black women imprisoned in North Carolina between 1995 and 2009. The authors controlled for factors such as prior record, conviction date, prison misconduct, and being thin, as well as whether the woman was convicted of homicide or robbery since these crimes usually carry lengthy prison sentences. With regard to prison sentences, their results indicated that women deemed to have light skin are sentenced to approximately 12% less time behind bars than their darker skinned counterparts. The results also show that having light skin reduces the actual time served by approximately 11%. The authors conclude that it is not sufficient to understand racial discrimination in terms of relative advantages of whites compared to non-whites. Among blacks, characteristics associated with whiteness appear to also have a significant impact on important life outcomes. *The Social Science Journal* 48 (2011): 250-258. Furthermore, researchers have examined whether the likelihood of being sentenced to death is influenced by the degree to which a black defendant is perceived to have a stereotypically black appearance. Controlling for a wide array of factors, they found that in cases involving a White victim, the more stereotypically black a defendant is perceived to be, the more likely that person is to be sentenced to death. Jennifer L. Eberhardt, Paul G. Davies, Valerie J. Purdie-Vaughns, and Sheri Lynn Johnson, "Looking Deathworthy: Perceived Stereotypicality of Black Defendants Predicts Capital-Sentencing Outcomes," *Psychology Science* 17 (2006): 383-386. See also Jennifer L. Eberhardt, Phillip Atiba Goff, Valerie J. Purdue, and Paul G. Davies, "Seeing Black: Race, Crime, and Visual Processing," *Journal of Personality and Psychology* 87 (2004): 876-893, finding that police officers view more stereotypically black faces as more criminal; in other words, police officers imbue physical variation with criminal meaning—the "more black" an individual appears, the more criminal that individual is seen to be.

4 Eric Foner, *Tom Paine and Revolutionary America* (Oxford University Press, 2005), 66.

5 Kimberly Chrisman-Campbell, "When American Suffragists Tried to 'Wear the Pants,'" *The Atlantic*, June 12, 2019.

6 Dalina Castellanos, "Geraldo Rivera: Hoodie Responsible for Trayvon Martin's Death,"

Los Angeles Times, March 23, 2012.

7   Kamala Harris, *The Truths We Hold: An American Journey* (Penguin, 2019).

8   Larsen, a neo-Nazi, was arrested for a crime he did not commit, was poorly represented, and was convicted and given 25 to life under the three strikes law. When the Innocence Project established the facts of the case, Harris worked against his release. Victoria Kim and Weston Phippen, "Man behind Bars Two Years after Judge Orders Release," *Los Angeles Times*, August 21, 2012.

9   Molly Redden, "The Human Costs of Kamala Harris' War on Truancy," *Huffington Post*, March 27, 2019.

10 Casey Tolan, "Campaign Fact Check: Here's How Kamala Harris Really Prosecuted Marijuana Cases," *San Jose Mercury News*, September 11. 2019.

11 Michelle Alexander, *The New Jim Crow: Mass Incarceration in the Age of Colorblindness* (The New Press, 2010), 209, 6, 101, 102. See also page 60: "Convictions for drug offenses are the single most important cause of the explosion in incarceration rates in the United States...Nothing has contributed more to the systematic mass incarceration of people of color in the United States than the War on Drugs."

12 *Id.*, 216, 215, 217

13 *Id.*, 216. One reason the New Jim Crow analogy works so well for low-level nonviolent offenses like drug use, gambling, or non-coercive prostitution is because through conventional moral lenses voluntary transactions between consenting adults raise issues of paternalism and personal choice that make it questionable that they should even constitute criminally culpable conduct at all. What the law viewed as a vice in one era (alcohol, weed, interracial and same-sex intimacy) may be widely acceptable in another. So punishing low-level nonviolent offenders over voluntary transactions between consenting adults increasingly runs contrary to the evolving moral standards of many Americans in criminal matters. But for many, applying those same "evolving" but still conventional moral lenses to violent offenders wreaks havoc with the New Jim Crow analogy. Accordingly, in keeping with prevailing values and moral norms, Alexander draws a deep distinction between violent and nonviolent offenders and attributes racialized mass incarceration to racist crackdowns on the latter.

14 US Department of Justice Bureau of Justice Statistics (December 2016 and April 2019): at year's end 2015, state and federal prisons had jurisdiction over 1,526,792 prisoners, only 196,455 of whom were held in federal prisons; at yearend 2017, the number of prisoners under state and federal jurisdiction dropped to 1,489,363 people, only 183,058 of whom were held in federal prisons.

15 Violent offenses drove 60% of the growth since 1990 in state prisons, where 86% of US prisoners reside. German Lopez, "Want to End Mass Incarceration? This Poll

Should Worry You," *Vox*, September 7, 2016.

16   *New Jim Crow*, 228

17   James Boyd White, *When Words Lose Their Meaning* (University of Chicago Press, 1984), 14–20.

18   *Chaplinsky v. New Hampshire*, 315 US 568 (1942)

19   Alexander, *New Jim Crow*, 255-261.

20   *Id.*, 16.

21   *Id.*, 58: "Once again, in response to a major disruption in the prevailing racial order—this time the civil rights gains of the 1960s—a new system of racialized social control was created by exploiting the [economic] vulnerabilities and racial resentments of poor and working-class whites." In fact, they may not even be motivated by racism at all, from this perspective, but rather by these underlying economic concerns. Yet, rather than racial justice advocates showing compassion and making allowances for their precarious economic circumstances, the "[r]esentment, frustration, and anger expressed by poor and working-class whites was chalked up to racism," she laments (257).

22   Mark Lilla, "There's Been a Slightly Hysterical Tone About Race," *Slate*, August 25, 2017.

23   Kevin D. Williamson, "The Father-Fuhrer," *National Review*, March 28, 2016.

24   "I have people that have been studying [Obama's birth certificate] and they cannot believe what they're finding," he said in 2011. "If he wasn't born in this country, which is a real possibility...then he has pulled one of the great cons in the history of politics."

25   Stop and frisk inflicted years of demonstrably unnecessary suffering on black and Latinx folk, unnecessary because ending it did not lead to an increase in crime. Philip Bump, "The Facts about Stop-and-Frisk in New York City," *Washington Post*, September 26, 2016; see also, Kyle Smith, "We Were Wrong about Stop-and-Frisk," *National Review*, Jan 1, 2018.

26   Alexander, *New Jim Crow*, 256.

27   Chauncey DeVega, "White Fear Elected Trump: Political Scientist Diana Mutz Explains the 'Status Threat' Hypothesis," *Salon*, May 7, 2018.

28   Paul Krugman, "The Ultimate Zombie Idea," *New York Times*, November 3, 2012.

29   "Racial Overtones Evident in Americans' Attitudes About Crime," *Gallup Poll Monthly*, December, 1993, 37–42.

30   Alexander, *New Jim Crow*, 209.

31   *Id.*, 210: "The fact that some black people endorse harsh responses to crime is best understood as a form of complicity with mass incarceration—not support for it." (Emphasis in original.)

32   *Id.*, 174.

33   See link at https://www.youtube.com/watch?v=bfk1A9AVno0.

34 Personal communication.

35 Rawls, John. *Theory of Justice*. Cambridge: Belknap Press of Harvard UP, 1971.

36 Thomas Nagel, *Moral Luck, in Mortal Questions* (Cambridge University Press, 1979), 24; Bernard Williams, "Moral Luck," in *Moral Luck: Philosophical Papers* 1973–1980 (Cambridge University Press, 1981), 20.

37 What follows is a reworking, for the purpose of this book, of an article by the same name. I dedicated that *Ohio State Journal of Criminal Law* article to the Ohio State Law School students who in the late 1960s helped my wrongfully convicted dad find the key to his own jailhouse door in the hornbooks, casebooks, treatises, and reporters that they provided. #PoeticJustice

38 See Richard Rorty, *Contingency, Irony, and Solidarity* (Cambridge University Press, 1989), 28–34, which identifies metaphoric redescription as the source of revolutions in science, morality, and law.

39 See *Model Penal Code and Commentaries*, Comment to §210.2 at 21-22 (1980): "In a prosecution for murder, however, the Code calls for the further judgment whether the actor's conscious disregard of the risk, under the circumstances, manifests extreme indifference to the value of human life. The significance of purpose or knowledge as a standard of culpability is that, cases of provocation or other mitigation apart, purposeful or knowing homicide demonstrates precisely such indifference to the value of human life."

40 See *Commonwealth v. Malone*, 47 A.2d 445, 447 (Pa. 1946) (quoting 4 William Blackstone, *Commentaries* *199). "At common law, the 'grand criterion' which 'distinguished murder from other killing' was malice on the part of the killer and [for unintentional killings] this malice was ... 'the dictate of a wicked, depraved and malignant heart.'"

41 Ice Cube, "The Nigga Ya Love to Hate," on *AmeriKKKa's Most Wanted* (Universal Music Group, 1990). Then USC President Steven B. Sample made this comment in criticism of Ice Cube's performance of "Fuck tha Police" on the stage of Bovard Auditorium as part of Race, Rap, and Redemption.

42 Sanford H. Kadish et al., *Criminal Law and Its Processes*, 9th ed. (Aspen Publishers, 2012), 7; "For an inner-city black male, the lifetime risk of arrest and incarceration may approach 90 percent," citing Jerome G. Miller, *Hobbling a Generation: Young African American Males in the Criminal Justice System of America's Cities: Baltimore, Maryland* (National Center on Institutions and Alternatives, 1992).

43 See White, *When Words Lose Their Meaning*, 284.

44 See generally Randall Kennedy, *Nigger: The Strange Career of a Troublesome Word* (2002), 28

45 H.L.A. Hart, *Punishment and Responsibility: Essays in the Philosophy of Law*, 2nd ed. (Oxford University Press, 2008), 231; Immanuel Kant, *The Philosophy of Law* (W. Hastie trans., Edinburgh, 1887), 228; Herbert Morris, *On Guilt and Innocence* (University of California Press, 1976), 39; Meir Dan-Cohen, "Causation," *Encyclopedia of Crime and Justice* (Macmillan, 1983), 1:165–66.

46 White, *When Words Lose Their Meaning*, 17.

47 Toni Morrison, "Lecture Upon the Award of the Nobel Prize for Literature" (Dec. 7, 1993), available at http://www.nobelprize.org/nobel_prizes/literature/laureates/1993/morrison-lecture.html.

48 Rorty, *Contingency*, 20, 37.

49 See generally Lauren J. Krivo and Ruth D. Peterson, "Extremely Disadvantaged Neighborhoods and Urban Crime," *Social Forces* 75 (1996): 619; Lauren J. Krivo and Ruth D. Peterson, "The Structural Context of Homicide: Accounting for Racial Differences in Process," *American Sociological Review* 65 (2000): 547; Ruth D. Peterson and Lauren J. Krivo, "Macrostructural Analyses of Race, Ethnicity, and Violent Crime: Recent Lessons and New Directions for Research," *Annual Review of Sociology* 3 (2005): 331; Ruth D. Peterson and Lauren J. Krivo, "Race, Residence, and Violent Crime: A Structure of Inequality," *Kansas Law Review* 57 (2009): 903.

50 Brian Mann, "Timeline: Black America's Surprising 40-Year Support for the Drug War," *PrisonTime*, Aug. 12, 2013; Naomi Murakawa, *The First Civil Right: How Liberals Built Prison America* (Oxford University Press, 2014), 124: "13 of 20 voting members of the CBC had voted for the Anti-Drug Abuse Act of 1986."

51 Michael Harrington, *The Other America: Poverty in the United States* (Macmillan, 1964). 15, 17.

52 Daniel Patrick Moynihan, *The Negro Family: The Case For National Action* (Office of Policy Planning and Research, United States Dep't of Labor, 1965) available at http://web.stanford.edu/~mrosenfe/Moynihan's%20The%20Negro%20Family.pdf; Edward C. Banfield, *The Unheavenely City Revisited* (Scott Foresman, 1974), 61–62.

53 "It is when a system of cultural values extols, virtually above all else, certain common success goals for the population at large, while the social structure rigorously restricts or completely closes access to approved modes of reaching these goals for a considerable part of the same population, that deviant behavior ensues on a large scale." Robert K. Merton, *Social Theory And Social Structure* (Free Press, 1968), 200; see also Robert Merton, "Social Structure and Anomie," *American Sociological Review* 3 (1938): 672; Steven Messner and Richard Rosenfeld, *Crime and the American Dream*, 5th ed. (Wasworth, 2013), 9–10.

54 Barbara Ehrenreich, "Rediscovering Poverty: How We Cured 'The Culture of Poverty,' Not Poverty Itself," *TomDispatch*, Mar. 15, 2012. As Barbara Ehrenreich points out, Charles Murray argued in his popular 1984 book *Losing Ground* that "any attempt to help the poor with their material circumstances would only have the unexpected consequence of deepening their depravity."

55 In 1992 Bill Clinton famously campaigned on the promise to "end welfare as we know it." Douglas Besharov, "End Welfare Lite as We Know It," *New York Times* (Aug. 15, 2006). On August 22, 1996, Clinton signed into law the historic welfare legislation the Personal Responsibility and Work Opportunity Reconciliation Act of 1996, Pub. L. No. 104-193, 110 Stat. 2105 (codified as amended at 42 USC. § 1305) [hereinafter "PROWORA]. The PROWORA rewrote six decades of social policy, ending the federal guarantee of cash assistance to the poor and turning welfare programs over to the states. Clinton and Joe Biden also spearheaded the 1994 Omnibus Crime Bill (Violent Crime Control and Law Enforcement Act of 1994). See, e.g., Carrie Johnson, "20 Years Later, Parts of Major Crime Bill Viewed As Terrible Mistake," *NPR*, Sept. 12, 2014.

56 Trevor Coleman: "In the African American community, the very definition of a Morehouse man is someone who is a leader, who is taught to go out and make a difference in his community." Vanessa Williams, "To Critics, Obama's Scolding Tone with Black Audiences is Getting Old," *Washington Post*, May 20, 2013.

57 Obama has been making this point—and stirring controversy—since he was a candidate in 2008. Jesse Jackson Sr. was incensed by what he saw as Obama's "talking down to black people," yet it was Jackson who was criticized. Paerry Bacon, Jr., "Jackson Incident Revives Some Blacks' Concerns About Obama," *Washington Post*, July 11, 2008. Many in the black community believed that Obama's chastisements were necessary to make himself politically palatable to white voters." See also Ben Cohen, "Obama Should Stop Lecturing African Americans," *www.thedailybanter.com*

58 Jody David Armour, *Negrophobia and Reasonable Racism: The Hidden Costs of Being Black in America* (NYU Press, 1997), 13-15. See also Jody D. Armour, "Race Ipsa Loquitur: Of Reasonable Racists, Intelligent Bayesians, and Involuntary Negrophobes," *Stanford Law Review* 46 (1994): 781, 782–83.

59 Saul Kassin, Steven Fein, and Hazel Rose Markus, *Social Psychology*, 7th ed. (Wadsworth, 2007), 185; citing E. Ashby Plant and Michelle Peruche, "The Consequences of Race for Police Officers' Responses to Criminal Subjects," *Psychological Science* 16 (2005): 180, 181–82. That the targets were unarmed makes it clear that we are focusing on mistakes and excuses rather than justifications. What's more, subjects were also quicker to decide to shoot an armed black target than a similarly situated armed white target.

60 Jody D. Armour, "Stereotypes and Prejudice: Helping Legal Decisionmakers Break the Prejudice Habit," *California Law Review* 83 (1995): 733, 738.

61 See *Restatement (Second) of Torts*, § 63 (1965). We could recognize strict liability in tort for reasonable mistakes about the need for deadly defensive force; specifically, we could adopt the logic of *Vincent v. Lake Erie Transp. Co.*, 109 Minn. 456, 459 (1910) and hold

that a deliberate appropriation of another's well-being to promote and protect one's own interests triggers a duty to compensate the injured party even though the injurer acted reasonably and was in no way at fault. Alternatively, perhaps we could think of law enforcement as an ultra-hazardous activity subject to strict liability vis-à-vis innocent blacks in light of demonstrable unconscious bias.

However, unlike strict tort liability, legally vindicating innocent victims of reasonable mistakes through imposing strict criminal liability on their injurers would be impossible without fundamentally violating the culpability principle that is the cornerstone of our criminal jurisprudence. See *Morissette v. United States*, 342 US 246, 250–51 (1952) ("The contention that an injury can amount to a crime only when inflicted by intention is no provincial or transient notion.... A relation between some mental element and punishment for a harmful act is almost as instinctive as the child's familiar exculpatory 'But I didn't mean to.'").

62 See Ellis Cose, *The Rage of a Privileged Class* (HarperCollins, 1994), 95.

63 Lazar Treschan, "Letter to the Editor: Police Stop-and-Frisks," *New York Times*, Dec. 29, 2011.

64 Bill Cosby, Address at the NAACP on the 50th Anniversary of *Brown v. Board of Education*, at Constitution Hall, Washington D.C. (May 17, 2004): available at http://www.americanrhetoric.com/speeches/billcosbypoundcakespeech.htm.

65 Massey and Denton have argued and shown that residential segregation serves to channel the racial inequality in rewards (e.g., high income) and disadvantages (e.g., poverty) evident in a racially stratified society into distinct neighborhood environments. Douglas S. Massey and Nancy A Denton, *American Apartheid: Segregation and the Making of the Underclass* (Harvard University Press, 1993), 122–23.

66 Heather Kelly, "Ghetto Tracker Site Offends, Dies and Returns," *CNN*, Sep. 6, 2013; Lydia O'Connor, "'Ghetto Tracker,' App That Helps Rich Avoid Poor, Is as Bad as It Sounds," *The Huffington Post*, Sept. 5, 2013. Ghetto Tracker's ratings of neighborhoods weren't based on any hard crime data but rather on the impressions (and perhaps biases) of ordinary people. "This website is not about race or income, as some of the PC myrmidons have asserted.... Again, it's about safety."

67 Drawing inferences of bad character traits from the commission of an *actus reus* or prohibited act is, as George Fletcher points out, a standard part of *mens rea* analysis. George P. Fletcher, *Rethinking Criminal Law* (Oxford University Press, 1978), 799–800.

68 This presumption of subjective culpability or *mens rea* may seem at odds with the "presumption of innocence" guaranteed under the Due Process Clause of the Fourteenth Amendment. *In re Winship*, 397 US 358, 364 (1970) Compare *Patterson v. New York*, in which the Supreme Court plainly stated that the Winship mandate of proof beyond a reasonable doubt of every element of a "crime" applies to the *actus reus* requirement

but, as Powell points out in the dissent, the majority in *Patterson* leave open the possibility of a state legislature making the presumption of innocence extends only to the *actus reus* requirement, not necessarily to the *mens rea* part, where the burden of proof on those matters of guilt and innocence may be shifted to the accused. 432 US 197, 225–32 (1977) (Powell, J., dissenting).

69   *Model Penal Code* would allow a duress excuse for someone who ran over another person with a gun at his head, but most courts would not allow the excuse for the intentional taking of human life. See *Model Penal Code and Commentaries* § 2.09(2) cmt. 3 at 375–78 (1985).

70   Fletcher, *Rethinking Criminal Law*, 798–99

71   I know that provocation doctrine can be narrowly limited to a few adequate forms, but I'm following the *Maher* line of cases that allow most claims of provocation to reach the jury subject to the judge playing the role of gatekeeper. See *Maher v. People*, 10 Mich. 212, 222 (1862). Other fully exculpatory excuse claims include criminal negligence and criminal recklessness: Sanford Kadish rightly views negligence and recklessness as "excuses in *mens rea* clothing." Kadish, "Excusing Crime," *California Law Review* 75 (1997) 257, 260–61.

   Jurors excuse or condemn on the basis of this decision rule. Decision rules are addressed to the fact finder and guide their judgments of defendants at trial; conduct rules are addressed to the general public and guide their behavior as citizens outside the courtroom. See Meir Dan-Cohen, "Decision Rules and Conduct Rules: On Acoustic Separation in Criminal Law," *Harvard Law Review* 97 (1984): 625; Paul H Robinson, "Rules of Conduct and Principles of Adjudication," *University of Chicago Law Review* 57 (1990): 729.

72   Mark Kelman, "Reasonable Evidence of Reasonableness," *Critical Inquiry* 17 (1991): 798, 802. As Martin Wasik puts it, in cases of duress "the accused claims that there was no act by him." Martin Wasik, "Duress and Criminal Responsibility," *Criminal Law Review* (1977): 453, 453; see also *State v. Woods*, 357 N.E.2d 1059, 1066 (Ohio 1976), vacated in part, 438 US 910, 910 (1978), and overruled on other grounds by *State v. Downs*, 364 N.E.2d 1140, 1144 (Ohio 1977), vacated in part, 438 US 909 (1978).

73   Which one it is depends on case law, the trial judge, and even the legislature (in self-defense law, for instance, legislatures have required courts to recognize evidence of battered women's syndrome, essentially requiring courts to individualize the reasonable person test in such cases). See, e.g., Va. Code Ann. § 19.2-270.6.

74   See Kadish, *Excusing Crime*, 459 (citing *Model Penal Code and Commentaries*, § 210.3 cmt. at 62–63 [American Law Institute, 1980], emphasis added). The Model Penal Code states this in the setting of the Extreme Emotional Distress defense, but it applies equally to self-defense, duress, recklessness and negligence. *Id.*

75   This victim-centered approach is incident-focused and begins the narrative with the crime. Like critiques of torts and contract law, the critique of this approach is that it ignores background inequalities in the formulation and application of its rules of decision and in the normative assessment of those decision rules; changes in the status quo ante are all that are considered. See also, Victoria Nourse, "Passion's Progress: Modern Law Reform and the Provocation Defense," *Yale Law Journal* 106 (1997): 1331, 1339–40, 1354, 1365–66. Nourse concludes that the Model Penal Code's more expanded formulation of the heat of passion defense (that is, the "extreme emotional disturbance" defense) has aggravated the unfairness to women of the provocation defense by expanding greatly the kinds of frictions in intimate settings that may suffice to reduce a killing from murder to manslaughter.

76   Stephen J. Morse, "Undiminished Confusion in Diminished Capacity," *Journal of Criminal Law and Criminology* 75 (1984): 1, 33–34 (citations omitted).

77   For instance, the commentary to Section 2.09 of the Model Penal Code: *Model Penal Code and Commentaries* § 2.09(2) cmt. 3 at 378 (American Law Institute, 1985). The defendant's blameworthiness is based only on an invariant or so-called "objective" reasonable person test, never an individualized one, and therefore rejects excuses peculiar to someone's social subgroup.

78   Jennifer N. Gutsell and Michael Inzlicht, "Empathy Constrained: Prejudice Predicts Reduced Mental Simulation of Actions During Observation of Outgroups," *Journal of Experimental Social Psychology* (2010): 841, 842; Vani A Mathur et al., "Neural Basis of Extraordinary Empathy and Altruistic Motivation," *NeuroImage* 51 (2010): 1468, 1468.

79   Birt L. Duncan, "Differential Social Perception and Attributes of Intergroup Violence: Testing the Lower Limits of Stereotyping of Blacks," *Journal of Personality and Social Psychology* 34 (1976): 590, 595–97.

80   George S. Bridges and Sara Steen, "Racial Disparities in Official Assessments of Juvenile Offenders: Attributional Stereotypes as Mediating Mechanisms," *American Sociological Review* 63 (1998): 554, 557, 561.

81   Randall Kennedy, *Race, Crime, and the Law* (Pantheon, 1997), 21.

82   John J. Dilulio, Jr., "Prisons Are a Bargain, by Any Measure," *New York Times*, Jan. 16, 1996, A17. According to Dilulio, research shows "it costs society at least twice as much to let a prisoner loose than to lock him up." As proof that "prisons pay big dividends," Dilulio cites Patrick Langan's calculation that "tripling the prison population from 1975 to 1989 may have reduced 'violent crime by 10 to 15% below what it would have been,' thereby preventing [many serious crimes]." So by reducing the prison population, excuses reduce the big dividends prisons pay to black people. Put differently, if more unexcused Black criminals mean more Niggas in prison, then

rejecting excuses and landing more Niggas in prison may be good policy for Black People in that, according to cost-benefit thinking about criminal matters, "prisons are a real bargain." This logic applies even to relatively minor, nonviolent infractions, like broken windows, curfew violations, or nonviolent drug activity. See Kennedy, *Race*, 304.

83 Kennedy, *Race*, 21

84 Jerry G. Watts, "Reflections on the King Verdict," *Reading Rodney King/Reading Urban Uprising*, Robert Gooding-Williams ed. (Routledge, 1993): 244.

85 Kennedy, *Race*, 10

86 *Id.*, 11.

87 David Lyons, *Ethics and the Rule of Law* (Cambridge University Press, 1984), 112.

88 And persons have the capacity to recognize the difference between right and wrong and to act for moral reasons. See generally Peter Arenella, "Convicting the Morally Blameless: Reassessing the Relationship Between Legal and Moral Accountability," *UCLA Law Review* 39 (1992): 1511.

89 Americans share two basic psychological tendencies, namely, "fundamental attribution error" (the general psychological tendency to explain human behavior in terms of personality traits rather than situational factors) and race-based attribution bias (the special tendency of observers to attribute wrongdoing by blacks to personality traits rather than to situational pressures). See Bridges and Steen, "Racial Disparities," 554–57. Thus our racially biased and person-centered social psychology, on the one hand, and the popular person-centered politics of personal responsibility and rugged individualism, on the other, combine to make millions of ordinary Americans skeptical of macro-level social explanations of crime.

90 Emile Durkheim, *Suicide: A Study in Sociology*, George Simpson ed., John A. Spaulding and George Simpson trans. (The Free Press 1897), 297–99, 51.

91 *Id.* at 48–51, 149. Durkheim tests and rejects a variety of possible non-social explanations for these stable and variable rates of suicide, such as heredity, climate, and mental illness, until he whittles down the possibilities to one, namely, the social explanation. By eliminating other explanations, Durkheim claims that these tendencies must depend on social causes and must be collective phenomena.

92 See *Commonwealth v. Root*, 170 A.2d 310, 312 (Pa. 1961), explaining that a drag racing victim's death was caused "by him alone," not his fellow drag racer (emphasis added).

93 Kadish et al., *Criminal Law*, 8th ed., 529.

94 Glanville Williams, "Finis for Novus Actus?" *Cambridge Law Journal* 48 (1989): 391–392. As he goes on to explain: "The legal attitude, in general, rests on what is known to philosophers as the principle of autonomy, which enters deeply into our traditional moral perceptions, reinforced by language.... The autonomy doctrine, expressing itself

through its corollary the doctrine of novus actus interveniens, teaches that the individual's will is the autonomous (self-regulating) prime cause of behaviour."

95   See S. REP. No. 100-165, at 1-14 (1988) [hereinafter Kerry Report]. In addition to the Kerry Committee Report's documentation of links between government agencies like the CIA and groups involved in cocaine distribution, a useful discussion can be found in what historian Arthur Schmidt calls a limited but "important starting point" for understanding links between US policies and cocaine trafficking in the 1980s. See Arthur Schmidt, "An Unhealthy Prescription," *H-NET Reviews* (April 1999), reviewing Jonathan Marshall and Peter Dale Scott, *Cocaine Politics: Drugs, Armies, and the CIA in Central America* (1991)); Peter Kornbluh, "Crack, the Contras, and the CIA: The Storm over 'Dark Alliance,'" *Columbia Journalism Review* (January/February 1997); and Gary Webb, *Dark Alliance: The CIA, the Contras, and the Crack Cocaine Explosion* (1998).

96   591 P.2d 1115, 1120 (Mont. 1979).

97   Kadish et al., *Criminal Law*, 8th ed., 527 n.6.

98   It should be noted that this is a minority position in cases of suicide. This is contrary to the standard common law treatment of assisted suicides; under common law courts refused to find causation on novus actus grounds. See *People v. Campbell*, 335 N.W.2d 27 (Mich. Ct. App. 1983); *People v. Kevorkian*, 527 N.W.2d 714, 739 (Mich. 1994). Although a minority position, Bier shows the willingness of courts to take a flexible approach to causation in cases of voluntary intervening human action.

99   *Herrera v. Quality Pontiac*, 73 P.3d 181, 196 (N.M. 2003).

100   See *Doe v. Gunny's* Ltd. P'ship, 593 N.W.2d 284, 294 (Neb. 1999); *Knoll v. Bd. of Regents*, 601 N.W.2d 757, 764–65 (Neb. 1999); *Sharkey v. Bd. of Regents*, 615 N.W.2d 889, 901–02 (Neb. 2000).

101   *State v. McFadden*, 320 N.W.2d 608, 611–13 (Iowa 1982).

102   *Commonwealth v. Atencio*, 189 N.E.2d 223, 223–25 (Mass. 1963).

103   *People v. Galle*, 573 N.E.2d 569, 570–71 (N.Y. 1991); "Causation: R v. Kennedy," *Criminal Law Review* (1999): 65, 65–67; see generally Mary Kreiner Ramirez, "Homicide Liability for the Furnishing of Dangerous Narcotics," *St. Louis University Public Law Review* 6 (1987): 161 (analyzing numerous cases where the state court held a provider of heroin liable for the death of another party).

104   This analysis assumes that we don't find the conduct of earlier actors and agents extremely wicked and reprehensible (we may even find it innocent). For if the earlier actors stir a strong retributive urge, the same logic may apply to them and there could be a pull toward finding the earlier actors to be the proximate cause of the resulting harm on that basis.

105   Dan-Cohen, *Decision Rules*, 166 (emphasis added).

106 "Posed in connection with the retributive goal of punishment, the question of causation (namely, 'Is there a causal relation between A's conduct and B's death?') amounts to asking whether punishing A is necessary to satisfy the retributive urge aroused by the fact of B's death." *Id.*

107 Kant, *Foundations for the Metaphysics of Morals,* quoted in Nagel, *Mortal Questions* (Cambridge University Press, 1979), 24.

108 Nagel, *Mortal Questions,* 25.

109 Bernard Williams, *Moral Luck*, 21.

110 *Modern Penal Code,* Section 1.13(2).

111 Jeffrie G. Murphy, "Involuntary Acts and Criminal Liability," *Ethics* 51 (1971): 332. A rock lacks moral agency, it lacks control, so it makes no sense to blame or excuse it.

112 Norval Morris, "Somnambulistic Homicide: Ghosts, Siders, and North Koreans," *Res Judicatae* 5 (1951): 29, 29-30.

113 Cf. *People v. Thomas*, 729 P.2d 972 (Colo. 1986), where the defendant was convicted of attempted reckless manslaughter under Colo. Rev. Stat. Section 18-2-101(1), which provides: "A person commits criminal attempt if, acting with the kind of culpability otherwise required for commission of an offense, he engages in conduct constituting a substantial step toward the commission of the offense."

114 Our current moral and legal practice of blaming careless killers more than equally careless non-killers for effects of occurrences subsequent to choice and beyond their control is, as Nagel notes, "akin to strict liability, which may have it legal uses but seems irrational as a moral position." Nagel, "Moral Luck," 61.

115 Durkheim described social currents as collective emotions in a group, which have stronger impact than any individuals own emotions: e.g., "the great movements of enthusiasm, indignation, and pity in a crowd. They come to each one of us from without and can carry us away in spite of ourselves."

116 See William Julius Wilson's description in *The Truly Disadvantaged: The Inner City, The Underclass, and Public Policy* (University of Chicago Press,1993). According to Wilson, after 1970, "As cities were transformed more into centers of financial and other professional services, many young black men who formerly would have taken low-skilled manufacturing jobs have encountered difficulty competing for new jobs that demand more schooling. While many better educated, more advantaged blacks prospered, bolstering a growing black middle class, blacks with less education and skills were left farther behind."

117 Joel Rubin, "Crenshaw Receives a Failing Grade," *Los Angeles Times*, August 19, 2005; "LA High School Loses Accreditation," *UPI*, August 19, 2005.

118 Said of Sydney, in Toni Morrison, *Tar Baby* (Plume, 1981); he and his wife Ondine see themselves as superior to the black "Yardboy" and his "Marys" who come over to do odd chores and laundry.

119   Bob Baker, "View Park," *Los Angeles Times*, August 25th, 1986.

120   Morton Grodzins, *The Metropolitan Area as a Racial Problem* (University of Pittsburgh Press, 1958), the book that coined the term "tipping point" to describe this sociological phenomenon; but see William Easterly, "Empirics of Strategic Interdependence: The Case of the Racial Tipping Point," NBER Working Paper No. 15069 (2009) and "The Tipping Point: Fascinating but Mythological?" *Vox*, 2009, which question empirical support for the phenomenon in data on American neighborhoods from 1970-2000.

121   Wilson, *The Truly Disadvantaged*, 143. But see Massey and Eggers, "The Ecology of Inequality: Minorities and the Concentration of Poverty, 1970-1980," *American Journal of Sociology* 95 (1990): 1153 and Massey and Denton, American Apartheid, who argue that there had been no important increase in economic segregation within the black community during the 1970s—the middle-class migration and underclass isolation in View Park occurred primarily in the 1960s. See also Lincoln Quillian, "Migration Patterns and the Growth of High Poverty Neighborhoods, 1970-1990," *American Journal of Sociology* 1 (1999): 105, whose findings support Wilson.

122   Wilson, *The Truly Disadvantaged*, 144.

123   Yana Kucheva and Richard Sander, "The Misunderstood Consequences of Shelley v. Kraemer," *Social Science Research* 48 (2012): 212–233.

124   In *Losing Ground* (Basic Books, 1984), Charles Murray explicitly stated that welfare generosity was the fundamental cause of the disintegration of black families and joblessness in poor areas. Conservative commentators continue to contend that affirmative action and Great Society programs made things worse for blacks. Wilson's points help refute a more general "culture of poverty" argument—that the poor are not simply lacking resources, but also have a unique value system. The term "subculture of poverty" (later shortened to "culture of poverty") first gained currency in the ethnography *Five Families: Mexican Case Studies in the Culture of Poverty* (Basic Books, 1959) by anthropologist Oscar Lewis. Lewis argued that although the burdens of poverty were systemic and therefore imposed upon these members of society, they led to the formation of an autonomous subculture as children were socialized into behaviors and attitudes that perpetuated their inability to escape the underclass.

125   FBI Uniform Crime Reports. Under UCR offense definitions, "property crimes" consist of burglary, larceny-theft, and motor vehicle theft. In other words, these wrongdoers are guilty of malum in se crimes or crimes of moral turpitude as against what might arguably be malum prohibitum crimes like selling drugs to other consenting adults and other "vice" crimes or so-called victim-less crimes.

126   Witnessed by former Santa Monica police deputy, Eddie Harris, and event planner, Chris Cuben. On these same grounds they've also objected to the parolees and juvenile offenders sentenced to probation that use our home once a week in an intervention program

that I've hosted for years. "Alternative Intervention Methods" and "Leila Steinberg's Microphone Sessions," 2002-2012.

127 By the very same token, South Central Los Angeles is now officially euphemized as "South LA" in the poignant hope of un-linking its name with the LA riots or uprisings of 1992, sparked by an all-white Simi Valley jury's acquittal of four white LAPD police officers caught on videotape beating a black motorist named Rodney King after a high speed car chase; one of the worst in American history, the 1992 riots helped forge associations in the memories of millions between South Central, acute racial tensions, and explosive racial unrest.

128 Jody Armour, "Nigga Theory: Contingency, Irony, and Solidarity in the Substantive Criminal Law," *Ohio State Journal of Criminal Law* 12 (2014): 9, 36-38.

129 For instance, Jerome Michael and Herbert Wechsler (Chief Reporter for the Model Penal Code) explain heat-of-passion excuses as claims that attribute the bad act to situational pressures rather than to the wrongdoer's character flaws: "Provocation...must be estimated by the probability that [the provocative] circumstances would affect most men in like fashion...Other things being equal, the greater the provocation, measured in that way, the more ground there is for attributing the intensity of the actor's passions and his lack of self-control on the homicidal occasion to the extraordinary character of the situation in which he was placed rather than to any extraordinary deficiency in his own character." Jerome Michael and Herbert Wechsler, "A Rationale of the Law of Homicide," *Columbia Law Review* 37 (1937): 1261-1282.

130 Kadish et al., *Criminal Law and Its Processes: Cases and Materials*, 8th ed. (Aspen Publishers, 2007), 742.

131 See Armour, "Race Ipsa Loquitur," 781, and *Negrophobia*. A Negrophobe can actually be "reasonable" both in this individualized sense (a personal history) and in a more general sense (cultural stereotype that drives unconscious responses to Blacks).

132 James A. Henderson, *The Torts Process*, 7th Ed., (Aspen Publishers, 2007), 99.

133 Bob Herbert, "See-No-Evil Mayors," *New York Times*, Jan. 8, 1996, A-11.

134 Justice Holmes recognizes that in the moral arena, or what he calls the "courts of Heaven," a person cannot be blamed for dangerous character traits rooted in bad biological luck, while nevertheless supporting strict civil and criminal liability for the biologically unlucky and therefore morally innocent, so long as blaming the unlucky increases the "general welfare." In Holmes' words,

> [W]hen men live in society, a certain average of conduct, a sacrifice of individual peculiarities going beyond a certain point, is necessary to the general welfare. If, for example, a man is born hasty and awkward, is always having accidents and hurting himself or his neighbors, no doubt his congenital defects will be allowed for in the courts of Heaven,

but his slips are no less troublesome to his neighbors than if they sprang from guilty neglect. His neighbors accordingly require him, at his proper peril, to come up to their standard, and the courts which they establish decline to take his personal equation into account.

Holmes frankly admits that by declining to take congenital defects into account courts are treating morally innocent mistakes as if "they sprang from guilty neglect," but protecting moral innocence is less important to him than maximizing the general welfare.

This confuses moral judgments with policy judgments. Policies focus on states of affairs; good policies increase the general welfare, bad policies decrease it. But moral judgments are of persons, not of the general welfare. Accordingly, while agreeing with Holmes that "[s]ome people are born feckless, clumsy, thoughtless, inattentive, irresponsible, with a bad memory[,] a slow 'reaction time'" and other dangerous character and personality traits, Professor Glanville Williams and others object on justice grounds to blaming and punishing people for the effects of traits beyond their control just because doing so promotes social welfare. Williams, *Criminal Law*, 122-123; Kadish et al., *Criminal Law*, 8th edition, 423.

135   Thomas Nagle, *Moral Luck*.

136   Stephen J. Morse, "Undiminished Confusion in Diminished Capacity," *Journal of Criminal Law and Criminology* 75, (1984) 33-34; Kadish et al., *Criminal Law*, 8th edition, 397.

137   By the same token, acting with care and concern for others on a given occasion may be effortless for someone with ordinary levels of care and concern for others but extremely difficult for someone extraordinarily selfish, cold, and uncaring, yet the extraordinarily selfish and cold person would lack any excuse because legally a "reasonable person" feels ordinary levels of care and concern for others.

138   Kadish et al., *Criminal Law*, 8th edition, 393.

139   The opinion made an exception if "the person whose guilt is in question be shown to have some peculiar weakness or mind or infirmity of temper, not arising from wickedness of heart or cruelty of disposition." This qualification for persons "of peculiar weakness of mind or infirmity of temper" was later rejected in Michigan. *People v, Sullivan*, 231 Mich. App. 510, 520, 586 N.W. 2d 578, 583 n.1 (1998).

140   Catherine A. MacKinnon, "Feminism, Marxism, Method, and the State: Toward a Feminist Jurisprudence," *Signs* 8 (1983): 635, 652-654.

141   The concept of a scientific paradigm developed by Thomas Kuhn in *The Structure of Scientific Revolutions* (University of Chicago Press, 1962) applies as much to the legal as to the scientific arena. "Paradigm" for Kuhn means a model or theory that explains most or all phenomena within its scope. The power of a paradigm lies in its ability to

channel thought, structure perceptions, and define the terms of analyses and debates about a subject; it determines what constitutes "normal science" for an area of inquiry. It achieves this in part by establishing pedagogical priorities that teachers use to inculcate in new students the assumptions and frames of reference widely shared by practitioners. In the legal arena, these trained practitioners then further entrench and disseminate the paradigm by having it inform their work as legislators, advocates, and judges, as well as legal commentators and pundits.

142 George Fletcher, *Rethinking Criminal Law*, 800.

143 I recognize that under the prevailing *mens rea* paradigm, "excuses" are not called *mens rea* requirements; *mens rea* under the prevailing paradigm is limited to the aware mental states and negligence. Even traditional scholars, however, grant *mens rea* status to excuses by saying excuses go to "broad" *mens rea* (see generally Kadish et al., *Criminal Law*, 8th ed.; Fletcher, *Id.* 799.

144 Juilian B. Rotter, "Generalized Expectancies for Internal Versus External Control of Reinforcement," *Psychological Monographs: General and Applied* (1966): 80.

145 Duncan, "Differential Social Perception," 590, 595–97.

146 Bridges and Steen, "Racial Disparities," 563-564 (emphasis in original).

147 *Id.*, 557.

148 Such findings support the anecdotal observation of a California public defender who noted, "If a white person can put together a halfway plausible excuse, people will bend over backward to accommodate that person. It's a feeling 'You've got a nice person screwing up,' as opposed to the feeling that 'this minority person is on track and eventually they're going to end up in state prison.' It's an unfortunate racial stereotype that pervades the system. It's all an unconscious thing." Christopher H. Schmitt, "Plea Bargaining Favors Whites as Blacks, Hispanics Pay Price," *San Jose Mercury News*, December 8, 1991.

149 *United States v. Roston*, 986 F.2d 1287, 1294 (9th Cir. 1993) (Boochever, J., concurring) (citing 9th Cir. Crim. Jury Instr. 8.24C (1992). *Model Penal Code* § 210.3, cmt. at 56 (Am. Law Inst. 1980), citing Glanville Williams, "Provocation and the Reasonable Man," *Criminal Law Review* (1954): 740, 742.

150 Jerome Michael and Herbert Wechsler, "A Rationale of the Law of Homicide II," *Columbia Law Review* 37 (1937): 1261, 1281 (emphases added).

151 Michael and Wechsler (emphasis added). As the court puts it in *Maher v. People*, "In determining whether the provocation is sufficient or reasonable, ordinary human nature, or the average of men recognized as men of fair average mind and disposition, should be taken as the standard." Maher, 221 (emphasis in original).

152 Kelman, 798, 801.

153 For Kelly there are three types of information that people consider when forming an attribution: consensus, distinctiveness, and consistency. Consensus information concerns how different persons react to the same stimulus. Distinctiveness information concerns how the same person reacts to different stimuli. Consistency information concerns the extent to which the behavior between one actor and one stimulus is the same across time and circumstances. Distinctiveness and consistency information generally will not be available to factfinders in that they would involve admitting into evidence historical facts about the defendant and evidence of prior bad acts, and such evidence is generally (but not always) inadmissible. Harold H. Kelley, "The Processes of Causal Attribution," *American Psychologist* 28 (1973): 107.

154   An alternative theory of the kind of information people take into account when making attributions, Edward Jones's and Keith Davis's Correspondent Inference Theory, still finds that social perceivers believe that a person's actions tell us more about him when they depart from the norm than when they are typical or otherwise expected under the circumstances. Edward E. Jones and Keith E. Davis, "From Acts to Dispositions: The Attribution Process in Person Perception," *Advances in Experimental Social Psychology* 2 (1965): 220; see also Elliot Aronson et al., *Social Psychology: The Heart and the Mind* (1994), 176-77.

155   *Model Penal Code* § 210.3 (1962) (emphasis added).

156   *Model Penal Code* § 210.3, cmt. at 62-63 (1980).

157   *Introduction to FMRI*—Nuffield Department of Clinical Neurosciences, Oxford University, online at https://www.ndcn.ox.ac.uk/divisions/fmrib/what-is-fmri/introduction-to-fmri.

158   Mathur et al., *Neural Basis*, 1468.

159   *Id.*, 1472.

160   Gutsell and Inzlicht, *Empathy Constrained*, 841.

161   Mirror neurons were discovered in area F5 of the rhesus monkey premotor cortex and are visuomotor neurons that discharge in response to the execution or observation of similar action. Giacomo Rizzolatti and Laila Craighero, "The Mirror-Neuron System," *Annual Review of Neuroscience* 27 (2004): 169 (citing G. Di Pellegrino et al., "Understanding Motor Events: A Neurophysiological Study," *Experimental Brain Research* 91 (1992):176; V. Gallese et al., "Action Recognition in the Premotor Cortex," *Brain* 119 (1996): 593; Giacomo Rizzolatti et al., "Premotor Cortex and the Recognition of Motor Actions," *Cognitive Brain Research* 3 (1996): 131.

162   "Simulating others' actions and expressions elicits the associated autonomic and somatic responses, thereby increasing social sensitivity." Gutsell and Inzlicht, 841.

163   The idea that observers mirror the actions of ingroup more than outgroup members finds behavioral support in studies showing that people mimic others' expressions, gestures, and body postures with less frequency for outgroup members. *Id.*, 842.

164 Henri J. Gastaut and Jacques Bert, "EEG Changes During Cinematographic Presentation," *Electroencephalography and Clinical Neurophysiology* 6 (1954): 433, 438; Deziree Holly Lewis, "Mu Suppression, Mirror Neuron Activity, and Empathy" (May 2010), unpublished honors thesis, Texas State University, https://digital.library.txstate.edu/bitstream/hndle/10877/3223/fulltext.pdf.

165 Gutsell and Inzlicht, 842.

166 *Id.* at 844.

167 R. A. Duff, "Choice, Character, and Criminal Liability," *Law and Philosophy* 12 (1993): 345, 346.

168 E.g., *Morissette v. United States*, 342 US 246, 250 (1952); Sanford H. Kadish and Stephen J. Schulhofer, *Criminal Law and Its Processes: Cases and Materials*, 7th ed. (Aspen Publishers, 2001), 203; Hart, *Punishment*, 28; Williams, *Criminal Law*, 122; Larry Alexander, "Insufficient Concern: A Unified Conception of Criminal Culpability," *California Law Review* 88 (2000): 931, 949-952

169 Martin R. Gardner, "The *Mens Rea* Enigma: Observations of the Role of Motive in the Criminal Law Past and Present," *Utah Law Review* 1993 (1993): 635, 668. In cases of negligent inadvertence, some commentators do not view this as legitimate forms of *mens rea*, E.g., see Alexander, *New Jim Crow*, 949-952 and Williams, *Criminal Law*, 122. In the words of Williams, "With the best will in the world, we all of us at some times in our lives make negligent mistakes. It is hard to see how justice (as distinct from some utilitarian reason) requires mistakes to be punished."

170 Descriptive standards are legal directives that reduce the grounds for liability to predesignated and dispositive "facts" that fact-finders can determine without making moral judgments. Alan C. Michaels, "'Rationales' of Criminal Law Then and Now: For a Judgmental Descriptivism," *Columbia Law Review* 100 (2000): 54, 62, 75.

171 Kathleen M. Sullivan, "Foreword: The Justices of Rules and Standards," *Harvard Law Review* 106 (1992): 22, 57–58 (footnotes omitted).

172 The worry that more nondescriptive directives may redound to the detriment of socially marginalized groups finds support in recent research on different tests for heat of passion. Professor Nourse found that in jurisdictions employing nondescriptive approaches, a significant number of cases got to juries involving women who were killed for simply rejecting or trying to separate from the killer without any evidence of infidelity or violence. No such cases got to juries in descriptive jurisdictions. Moreover, cases involving so-called "infidelity" after the relationship had ended were far more likely to reach juries in nondescriptive than descriptive jurisdictions. Nourse, "Passion's Progress," 1331.

173 Paul H. Robinson and Jane A. Grall, "Element Analysis in Defining Criminal Liability: The Model Penal Code and Beyond," *Stanford Law Review* 35 (1983): 681, 686 n.21.

174   Kadish et al., *Criminal Law and Its Processes: Cases and Materials*, 10th ed. (Aspen Publishers, 2017), 259.

175   *Model Penal Code* § 2.02(2)(d) (1962).

176   J. L. Austin, "A Plea for Excuses," *Proceedings of the Aristotelian Society* 57 (1956–1957): 1–3.

177   Dan B. Dobbs, *The Law of Torts* (1st ed. 2001), 305–06.

178   Keeton et al., *Prosser and Keeton on Torts* 5th ed. (West Group, 1984), 196 (emphasis added). In the words of one civil court, in an emergency, the actor's choice "may be mistaken and yet prudent."

179   Dobbs, *Torts*, 308 (emphasis added).

180   Keeton et al., *Torts*, 197 n.32 ("doctrine merely emphasizes the 'under the circumstances' portion of general standard of 'reasonable under the circumstances'").

181   Hart, *Punishment*, 154.

182   *Model Penal Code* § 2.02(2)(c) (1962).

183   *Id.*, § 2.02(2)(d) (1962).

184   Kadish et al., *Criminal Law*, 10th ed., 421 (emphasis added).

185   *Model Penal Code* § 2.02(3) (1962): "Culpability Required Unless Otherwise Provided. When the culpability sufficient to establish a material element of an offense is not prescribed by law, such element is established if a person acts purposely, knowingly or recklessly with respect thereto." See, e.g., *R v. Cunningham* [1957] 2 QB 396 (Eng.).

186   See generally Mark Kelman, "Interpretive Construction in the Substantive Criminal Law," *Stanford Law Review* 33 (1981): 591.

187   James A. Henderson, Jr. and Aaron D. Twerski, "Intent and Recklessness in Tort: The Practical Craft of Restating Law," *Vanderbilt Law Review* 54 (2001): 1133, 1141–1142 (internal citations omitted).

188   *Hines v. Morrow*, 236 S.W. 183–187 (Tex. 1921).

189   Clarence Morris, "Proximate Cause in Minnesota," *Minnesota Law Review* 34 (1950): 185, 193.

190   Kadish et al., *Criminal Law*, 10th ed., 278.

191   *Model Penal Code* § 202, cmt. at 237 (1985).

192   Kadish et al., *Criminal Law,* 10th ed., 216.

193   See Larry Alexander, "Insufficient Concern: A Unified Conception of Criminal Culpability," *California Law Review* 88 (2000): 931, 933-935.

194   *Model Penal Code* § 202, cmt. at 237 (1985).

195   Kadish et al., *Criminal Law*, 10th ed., 279

196   *Id.*, (citing Kimberly Kessler Ferzan, "Opaque Recklessness," *Journal of Criminal Law and Criminology* 91 (2001).

197   Kadish et al., *Criminal Law*, 10th ed., 279.

198　*People v. Hall*, 999 P.2d 207, 210 (Colo. 2000).

199　*People v. Hall* at 224.

200　"Colorado Skier Is Convicted in Fatal Collision on Slopes," *New York Times*, Nov. 18, 2000, 9.

201　"The vicious will was the *mens rea*; essentially it refers to the blameworthiness entailed in choosing to commit a criminal wrong. The requirement of *mens rea* reflects the common sense view of justice that blame and punishment are inappropriate and unfair in the absence of choice." Kadish et al., *Criminal Law*, 10th ed., 258.

202　Kadish et al., *Criminal Law*, 9th ed., 431.

203　*Young v. State*, 428 So.2d 155, 158 (Ala. Crim. App. 1982).

204　*State v. Thompson*, 65 P.3d 420, 427 (Ariz. 2003).

205　*Commonwealth v. Carroll*, 194 A.2d 911, 916 (1963).

206　Formally, it is possible to go further than "no time is too short" for the necessary premeditation to occur approach in Carroll by holding, as Pennsylvania decisions after Carroll have, that "the requirement of premeditation and deliberation is met whenever there is a conscious purpose to bring about death.... We can find no reason where there is a conscious intent to bring about death to differentiate between the degree of culpability on the basis of the elaborateness of the design to kill." *Commonwealth v. O'Searo*, 352 A.2d 30, 37–38 (1976).

207　Tom W. Smith, "Ethnic Images," General Social Survey Topical Report No. 19 (National Opinion Research Center, Dec. 1990)

208　*People v. Zackowitz* 172 N.E. 466, 467 (1930).

209　*Id.*, at 469.

210　Zackowitz, 172 N.E. 466.

211　See Fed. R. Evid. 404(b): "Other crimes, wrongs, or acts. Evidence of other crimes, wrongs, or acts is not admissible to prove the character of a person in order to show action in conformity therewith. It may, however, be admissible for other purposes, such as proof of motive, opportunity, intent, preparation, plan, knowledge, identity, or absence of mistake or accident."

212　Edward W. Cleary et al., *McCormick's Handbook of the Law of Evidence*, 2d ed. (West Group, 1972), 447. Bad character is the 800-pound gorilla in the middle of criminal trials of blacks, "but in the setting of jury trial the danger of prejudice outweighs the probative value."

213　Zackowitz, 172 N.E. 468.

214　*Id.*, 467.

215　Kadish et al., *Criminal Law*, 10th ed., 27.

216　For a defense of jury nullification in cases where it would promote rather than subvert racial justice in criminal matters, see generally Paul Butler, "Racially Based Jury Nullification: Black Power in the Criminal Justice System," *Yale Law Journal* 105 (1995): 677.

217   *Krulewitch v. United States*, 336 US 440, 453 (1949) (Jackson, J., concurring).

218   *Dunn v. United States*, 307 F.2d 883, 886 (5th Cir. 1962).

219   See Joel D. Lieberman and Bruce D. Sales, "What Social Science Teaches Us About the Jury Instruction Process," *Psychology, Public Policy and Law* 3 (1997): 589, 601.

220   See Saul M. Kassin and Lawrence S. Wrightsman, "Coerced Confessions, Judicial Instruction and Mock Juror Verdicts," *Journal of Applied Social Psychology* 11 (1981): 489, 503–04.

221   *Spencer v. Texas,* 385 US 554, 565 (1967).

222   *In re Winship* 397 US 358 (1970).

223   Cleary et al., *McCormick's Handbook*, 447. See also *Michelson v. United States*, 335 US 469, 475–476 (1948): "The inquiry is not rejected because character is irrelevant; on the contrary it is said to weigh too much with the jury and to so overpersuade them as to prejudge one with a bad general record and deny him a fair opportunity to defend against a particular charge."

224   Kadish et al., *Criminal Law,* 10th ed., 34–35.

225   See, e.g., Ariela J. Gross, "Litigating Whiteness: Trials of Racial Determination in the Nineteenth-Century South," *Yale Law Journal* 108 (1998): 109.

226   *People v. Zackowitz*, 172 N.E. 466, 469 (1930). As a propensity argument the evidence goes to the increased likelihood that a bad person will premeditate the intent; as a character argument the evidence goes to that he deserves punishment whether or not he premeditated!

227   *People v. Roe*, 542 N.E.2d 610 (1989).

228   The Model Penal Code appears to oppose murder liability for inadvertent risk creation: "The Model Penal Code provision makes clear that inadvertent risk creation, however extravagant and unjustified, cannot be punished as murder...At least it seems clear that negligent homicide should not be assimilated to the most serious forms of criminal homicide catalogued under the offense of murder." *Model Penal Code* § 210.2, cmt. at 27-28 (1980).

Nevertheless, the Model Penal Code provides in Section 2.08(2) that recklessness need not be shown if the defendant lacked awareness of the risk because he was voluntarily intoxicated. Model Penal Code § 2.08(2) (1985). But this approach contradicts the Code's own claim that "inadvertent risk creation" or "negligent homicide"—"however extravagant and unjustified"—"cannot be punished as murder." This approach treats negligence in drinking before driving as sufficient *mens rea* for murder where, for instance, the defendant honestly but stupidly believes that he can safely drive drunk and has a substantial personal history of doing so without incident. See *United States v. Fleming*, 739 F.2d 945 (4th Cir. 1984); *State v. Dufield* 549 A.2d 1205

(N.H. 1988). The illusion of a bright descriptive line (awareness) between murder and manslaughter if not between criminal and civil liability cannot be nursed under these approaches.

229 Kadish et al., *Criminal Law*, 8th ed., 429.

230 *Id.*, 217.

231 *Model Penal Code* § 210.2, cmt. at 21-22 (1980).

232 See Fed. R. Evid. 404(b)(1, 2).

233 Leslie Bender, "A Lawyer's Primer on Feminist Theory and Tort," *Journal of Legal Education* 38 (1988): 3, 31-32.

234 Sharon Guice, "The Controversial Use of the N-word, Will It Ever End?" *The Sojourner's Truth* 13, (Oct. 31,2007), https://www.thetruthtoledo.com/pdf/2007/103107pdf. pdf.

235 George Lakoff, *Women, Fire, and Dangerous Things: What Categories Reveal About the Mind* (University of Chicago Press, 1990), 118, 121-122.

236 William P Alston, *Philosophy of Language* (Prentice-Hall 1964).

237 John Locke, *An Essay Concerning Human Understanding,* ed. A. Pringle-Pattison (Oxford: Clarendon Press, 1924), book 3, chap. 2.

238 David Bloor, *Wittgenstein: A Social Theory of Knowledge* (Columbia University Press, 1983), 7.

239 Bertrand Russell, *The Analysis of Mind* (Allen and Unwin, 1921), 201.

240 Michael Mazza, "One of the Great Intellectual Testaments of the 20th Century," Amazon.com, Dec. 27, 2000. A review of Audre Lorde, *Sister Outsider: Essays and Speeches* (Crossing Press Feminist Series, 2000).

241 Leslie Bender, "A Lawyer's Primer on Feminist Theory and Tort," *Journal of Legal Education* 38 (1988): 16–17.

242 Karl Marx, *On the Jewish Question*, in The Marx-Engels Reader 2nd ed. (W.W. Norton, 1978), 43. Emphasis added.

243 Jeremy Waldron *Nonsense upon Stilts: Bentham, Burke and Marx on the Rights of Man* (Routledge, 2014), 146. He continues: "The freedom in question is that of a man treated as an isolated monad and withdrawn into himself...[T]he right of man to freedom. It is the right to this separation, the rights of the limited individual who is limited to himself."

244 Jeremy Waldron, *Id.*

245 See Richard L. Abel, *Torts,* in David Kairys, ed., *The Politics of Law: A Progressive Critique* 3rd ed. (Basic Books, 1998), 445–470. Part of learning accident and contract and criminal law is learning the general irrelevance to legal liability of gross disparities in wealth and power between the parties to the dispute.

246 Austin, *The Meaning of a Word*, 72.

247 Wittgenstein pointed out that many of our everyday, ordinary conceptual categories, like the familiar category game, are not classical since there are no common properties shared by all games—not all games have competition or winners and losers (e.g., ring-around-the-rosy), not all involve more than one person (e.g., solitaire), not all involve luck (chess), not all involve skill (plugging a slot machine). Instead, what makes game a category, observed Wittgenstein, is the family resemblances among its members—both basketball and ping pong involve competition, skill and athleticism; both basketball and poker involve competition and skill; both poker and solitaire involve cards and entertainment; and so on. Like family members, games are similar to one another in lots of different ways. A little reflection reveals that a great many categories we use in everyday and political communication are not classical but constructed and based on family resemblances, that is, many (like the categories mother and game) are structured around prototypes rather than (like the categories duck and triangle) around common properties. The N-word, too, as we will see, is a constructed category like game and mother rather than a classical one like duck or triangle.

248 Lakoff, *Women, Fire, and Dangerous Things*, 83

249 Another way a word develops different senses is through chaining within a category. In Austin's words ("The Meaning of a Word," 72): "Another case is where I call *B* by the same name as *A*, because it resembles *A*, *C* by the same name because it resembles *B*, *D*...and so on. But ultimately *A* and, say *D* do not resemble each other in any recognizable sense at all. This is a very common case: and the dangers are obvious when we search for something 'identical' in all of them!"

250 Lakoff, *Women, Fire, and Dangerous Things*, 84

251 "Our language can be seen as an ancient city: a maze of little streets and squares, of old and new houses, and of houses with additions from various periods; and this surrounded by a multitude of new boroughs with straight regular streets and uniform houses." Wittgenstein, *Philosophical Investigations*, trans. G.E.M. Anscombe (Macmillan, 1953), 18.

252 *Id.*, 693, 180, 23.

253 Wittgenstein, *Zettel*, ed. G.E.M. Anscombe and G.H. von Wright, trans. G.E.M. Anscombe, (Basil Blackwell, 1967), 31.

254 Wittgenstein, *Philosophical Investigations,* 43. Most simply, we do not express ideas with language, we do things with words—words are social acts with social consequences and understanding words is knowing how to do certain things with them.

255 By the same token, thanks to their common position in relation to a subordinate group, whites have "common interests" in relation to blacks; men have them in relation to women; the rich have them in relation to the poor.

256 *Dred Scott v. Sandford* 60 US 393 (1857).

257   In certain settings the word enhances my capacity to label a particular kind and source of injustice (namely, unwarranted attempts to otherize and morally condemn black criminals), and thereby to isolate a punitive eye-for-an-eye "them" and to mobilize a less punitive and less retributive "us."

258   The Thomas Paine Library, http://libertyonline.hypermall.com/Paine/Default.htm.

259   Foner, *Tom Paine*, xxxi.

260   Through our struggle over the range of application of the word, we can create and maintain a unified and committed "us" of black criminals and compassionate non-criminals capable of resisting an identifiable "them" of eye-for-an-eye retributionists who exalt personal responsibility and individual choice over collective accountability and epistemic humility.

261   Recall the uniforms of the American Revolution's freedom fighters.

262   Clifford Geertz, *Negara: The Theatre State in Nineteenth-Century* Bali (Princeton University Press, 1980), 103.

263   Geertz, 120, 104.

264   My colleague, Ron Garet, was an indispensable producer of the project from the outset; Joanne Morris joined as executive producer once funding was secured.

265   Statement of Decision, Request for Clemency by Stanley Williams, (Dec. 12, 2005) (corrected version) available at http:/perma.cc/K3PZ-QNKK. Sarah Kershaw, "Governor Rejects Clemency for Inmate on Death Row," *New York Times* (Dec. 13, 2005).

266   Geertz, *Negara*, 120, 104.

267   White, *When Words Lose Their Meaning*, 15.

268   *Id.*, 17.

269   Toni Morrison's Nobel Prize Acceptance Speech 1993 (emphasis added).

270   In re Winship, 397 US 358, 363-364 (1970).

271   Jeff Guo, "Stop Blaming Racism for Donald Trump's Rise," *Washington Post*, August 19, 2016.

272   Peter Burns and James Gimpel, "Economic Insecurity, Prejudicial Stereotypes, and Public Opinion on Immigration Policy," *Political Science Quarterly*, 15 February 2013.

273   Guo, *Id.*

274   Dan M. Kahan and Donald Braman, "Cultural Cognition and Public Policy," *Yale Law and Policy Review* 24 (2006): 149.

275   Michael Tesler, "Economic Anxiety Isn't Driving Racial Resentment. Racial Resentment Is Driving Economic Anxiety," *Washington Post*, August 22, 2016.

276   *Id.*

277   Nicholas Carnes and Noam Lupu, "It's Time to Bust the Myth: Most Trump Voters Were Not Working Class," *Washington Post*, June 5, 2017.

278   Brian F. Schaffner, Matthew MacWilliams, and Tatishe Nteta, "Understanding White Polarization in the 2016 Vote for President: The Sobering Role of Racism and Sexism,"

Political Science Quarterly 133 (March 2018): 9–34.

279   Carnes and Noam Lupu, *Id.*

280   Robert Griffin and John Sides, "In the Red: Americans' Economic Woes are Hurting Trump," *Democracy Fund Voter Study Group*, September 2018.

281   Griffin and Sides, *Id.*

282   Schaffner, MacWilliams, and Nteta, *Id.*

283   Michael Tesler, "The Education Gap among Whites This Year Wasn't about Education. It Was about Race," *Washington Post*, November 16, 2016.

284   Nate Cohn, Twitter, Nov 8, 2016 (10:49 PM).

285   Michael Tesler, "Obama Won Lots of Votes from Racially Prejudiced Whites (and Some of Them Supported Trump)," *Washington Post*, December 7, 2016.

286   James Barrett, "Michael Moore Slaps Down Attempts to Smear Trump Voters as 'Racist," *The Daily Wire*, November 12, 2016

287   Diana C. Mutz, "Status Threat, Not Economic Hardship, Explains the 2016 Presidential Vote," *Proceedings of the National Academy of Sciences*, May 8, 2018. As Mutz notes, "Panel data utilizing within-person change over time are ideal for purposes of statistically identifying the relatively small changes that can change the outcome of American elections."

288   Tyler T. Reny, Loren Collingwood, Ali Valenzuela, "Vote Switching in the 2016 Election: How Racial and Immigration Attitudes, Not Economics, Explain Shifts in White Voting," *Public Opinion Quarterly* (May 2019): 91–113.

289   "Racial resentment" is supposed to measure dog-whistle or color-blind forms of racism, but some criticize the concept and questions designed to measure it as unfairly conflating the distinction between conservative beliefs or race-neutral norms and racism. To address those (probably overblown) concerns, researchers created a second measure of racial attitudes—called the "black influence animosity" index—based on questions that more directly examined voters' views on whether the US government favors blacks over whites and how much influence blacks have in US politics.

290   Sean McElwee and Jason McDaniel, "Fear of Diversity Made People More Likely to Vote Trump," *The Nation*, May 8, 2017.

291   Robert Griffin and John Sides, *Id.*.

292   Daniel Cox, Rachel Lienesch, Robert P. Jones, "Beyond Economics: Fears of Cultural Displacement Pushed the White Working Class to Trump," *The Atlantic*, May 9, 2017.

293   Marshall Cohen, "The Social Contract, Explained and Defended," *New York Times Book Review*, July 16, 1972.

294   Murphy, "Involuntary Acts," 332.

295   Tom R. Tyler, *Why People Obey the Law* (Princeton University Press, 1990), 60.

296 Commonwealth's Brief for Respondent July 15, 2019, 22, 33.

297 Cass R. Sunstein and Adrian Vermeule, "Is Capital Punishment Morally Required? Acts, Omissions, and Life-Life Tradeoffs," *Stanford Law Review* 58 (2005): 703, 722-723.

298 *In Re Winship* 397 US 358 (1970); William Blackstone, *Commentaries* 352 (1765), 4.

299 Kadish, et al., *Criminal Law*, 10th ed., 41.

300 James Fitzjames Stephen, *A History of the Criminal Law of England,* Vol. 2 (1883 ed.), 81-82.

301 E.g., Jerome Deise and Raymond Paternoster, "More Than a 'Quick Glimpse of the Life': The Relationship Between Victim Impact Evidence and Death Sentencing," *Hastings Constitutional Law Quarterly* 611 (2013): 40.

302 *People v. Levitt,* 156 Cal. App. 3d 500, 516 (1984)

303 *Payne v. Tennessee,* 501 US 812 (1991).

304 Rough paraphrase of the Grandmother's victim-impact testimony in *Payne v. Tennessee.*

305 Another justification for the death penalty and other punishments concerns what I'll call the expressive function of criminal punishment. The way you express your care and concern for victims from socially marginalized or vulnerable groups—women, blacks, LGBTQ folk, children—is to be as punitive as possible with their victimizers, especially if those victimizers are from socially dominant groups (e.g., straight, white, or male).

306 Immanuel Kant, *The Philosophy of Law* (W. Hastie trans., 1887) (originally published 1797).

307 *Gregg v. Georgia,* 428 US 153 (1976)

308 *Woodson v. North Carolina,* 428 US 280 (1976)

309 *Gregg* required the jury to find one of a list of aggravating factors, one such factor being the offense "was outrageously or wantonly vile, horrible or inhuman in that it involved torture, depravity of mind, or an aggravated battery to the victim." *Gregg v. Georgia* 428 US 153 (1976), n.48.

310 *Woodson v. North Carolina*, 428 US at 302.

311 *Lockett v. Ohio*, 438 US 586, 604 (1978).

312 *Eddings v. Oklahoma*, 455 US 104, at 112.

313 Some contend that because the Court mandates the admission and consideration of so much mitigating evidence, it's only fair to present victim-impact evidence to balance out all the extenuating information. But this is a false equivalence. As we've discussed, victim-impact testimony is logically irrelevant to a defendant's subjective culpability.

314 Hyman Gross, *A Theory of Criminal Justice* (1979) 436.

315 Jeremy Bentham, "An Introduction to the Principles of Morals and Legislation" (1789), in Jeremy Bentham and John Stuart Mill, *The Utilitarians*, (University of California

Press, 1961), 162, 166: "The general object which all laws have, or ought to have, in common, is to augment the total happiness of the community; and therefore, in the first place, to exclude, as far as may be, every thing that tends to subtract from that happiness: in other words, to exclude mischief."

316   *Ewing v. California* 258 US 11 (2003).

317   This "narrow" formulation of the Eighth Amendment's proportionality principle comes from Justice Kennedy's concurrence in *Harmelin* (where the Court upheld a sentence of life without possibility of parole for a first offender found guilty of possessing 672 grams of cocaine); Justice O'Connor stated in her Ewing opinion that "the proportionality principles ... distilled in Justice Kennedy's [*Harmelin*] concurrence guide our application of the Eighth Amendment."

318   *Lockyer v. Andrade*, 538 US 63 (2003): 83.

319   *State v. Berger*, 134 P.3d 378 (Ariz. 2006). The Arizona Supreme Court upheld the sentence.

320   *Rummel v. Estelle*, 445 US 263 (1980). SCOTUS upheld the sentence.

321   Again, Scalia hit the nail squarely when he pointed out that "Proportionality—the notion that the punishment should fit the crime—is inherently a concept tied to the penological goal of retribution."

322   *Kennedy v. Louisiana* 554 US 407 at 439 (2008). In *Kennedy* the Court overturned a statute authorizing capital punishment for the rape of a child under the age of 12.

323   As Scalia points out in his dissent, the *Atkins* majority never really addresses the penological justification of incapacitation.

324   E.g., in *Coker v. Georgia* 433 US 584 (1977), the Court held that the sentence of death for the crime of rape is grossly disproportionate and excessive punishment, and it is therefore forbidden by the Eighth Amendment as cruel and unusual. The objective evidence of present public judgment or evolving standards of decency the Court consulted included the fact that Georgia was then the only State authorizing the death sentence for rape of an adult woman, that it was authorized for rape in only two other states, but only when the victim was a child (later, the Court in *Kennedy v. Louisiana*, 554 US 407 (2008) makes death impermissible even for rape of a child), and that, in the vast majority of rape convictions in Georgia (9 out of 10) since 1973, juries had not imposed the death sentence.

325   *Atkins v. Virginia* 536 US 304 (2002): "As Penry demonstrated, moreover, reliance on mental retardation as a mitigating factor can be a two-edged sword that may enhance the likelihood that the aggravating factor of future dangerousness will be found by the jury."

326   Significantly, the Court in *Roper* considered evidence of societal consensus other than domestic legislation, giving greater attention and weight to international laws and perspectives than it had in *Atkins*. The Court noted that "the United States is the only country in the world that continues to give official sanction to the juvenile death pen-

alty," that international human rights conventions had repudiated capital punishment for juveniles, and that the United Kingdom (the soil of origin for our Anglo-American legal system) had long ago renounced the practice. *Roper v. Simmons*, 543 US 551, 569, 571.

327 Kadish, et al., *Criminal Law*, 10th ed., 1024.

328 *United States v. Brawner*, 471 F.2d 969, 1032 (D.C. Cir. 1972) (Bazelon , C.J., concurring in part and dissenting in part); David L. Bazelon, "The Morality of the Criminal Law," *Southern California Law Review* 49 (1976): 385.

329 Jennifer L. Eberhardt, Paul G. Davies, Valerie J. Purdie-Vaughns, and Sheri Lynn Johnson, "Looking Deathworthy: Perceived Stereotypicality of Black Defendants Predicts Capital-Sentencing Outcomes," *Psychological Science* 17 (2006): 383-386.

330 For folk claiming that Prof. Ronald Sullivan was fired as a Harvard dean because he was generally failing to promote a positive campus climate rather than because he chose to represent Weinstein, please do a little math and exercise a modicum of common sense. Harvard did not initiate a review of Winthrop's "climate" until AFTER Sullivan joined Weinstein's team, AFTER Harvard emailed students that his 'choice' to do so might be a problem, and AFTER weeks of student protests (including vandalism) due to his representation of Weinstein. Clearly the brouhaha set off by Sullivan's decision to represent Weinstein preceded and precipitated the investigation into Winthrop's climate. And students who campaigned for his removal because of his decision celebrated Harvard's action as proof of their agency. Don't be mealy-mouthed. If you think Sullivan could not be a good dean and represent Weinstein at the same time, fine, say so—own it! Don't twist timelines and deny obvious connections to disguise your true concerns. When demagogues on the right do that, we rightly excoriate them. Some left-leaning folk who deny that Sullivan's dismissal was caused—at least in part—by his decision to represent Weinstein, despite the timeline, illustrate the power of motivated reasoning: they want to support the students without trashing vital values, so they say, "Sullivan's dismissal had nothing to do with who he represented, it was other non-objectionable factors—namely, his own personal deficiencies—that explain his plight" as they celebrate the political agency and success of the students protesting him for representing Weinstein. Don't insult the intelligence of anyone who can look at a timeline with fictions about Sullivan's own internal deficiencies causing his dismissal rather than political expediency and the exigencies of the #MeToo movement. But the very valid and too-long-ignored concerns of the #MeToo movement shouldn't render irrelevant the concerns of the anti-carceral movement, which gives great weight to fair process protections—including a presumption of innocence and zealous advocacy—for accused persons.

It's especially hard for some of my friends on the left to remain faithful to fair process protections when victims are from socially marginalized groups (e.g., women, racial minorities) and victimizers are from socially dominant ones (men, whites). It's hard for me, too! It's hard to care about the rights of alleged rapists when we know how many of them roam free and how many rape victims are never believed or vindicated. Sticking to certain principles can be hard, costly, unpopular, and uncomfortable. But down the unprincipled road more massive racialized mass incarceration lies. That's the lesson Harvard should have modeled for its students. Instead it modeled hypocrisy—it showed how an institution can extol the virtues of fair process and academic freedom in theory while undermining both in practice.

INDEX